THE UPSTAIRS WIFE

THE UPSTAIRS WIFE

AN INTIMATE HISTORY OF PAKISTAN

—— RAFIA ZAKARIA ——

BEACON PRESS
BOSTON

BEACON PRESS
Boston, Massachusetts
www.beacon.org

Beacon Press books
are published under the auspices of
the Unitarian Universalist Association of Congregations.

19 18 17 16   8 7 6 5 4 3 2

This book is printed on acid-free paper that meets the uncoated paper
ANSI/NISO specifications for permanence as revised in 1992.

Text design and composition by Kim Arney

Many names and other identifying characteristics of people mentioned
in this work have been changed to protect their identities.

Library of Congress Cataloging-in-Publication Data
Zakaria, Rafia.
The upstairs wife : an intimate history of Pakistan / Rafia Zakaria.
pages cm
ISBN 978-0-8070-8046-7 (paperback : acid-free paper)
ISBN 978-0-8070-0337-4 (ebook)
1. Zakaria, Rafia, 1978—Family. 2. Karachi (Pakistan)—Biography.
3. Aunts—Pakistan—Karachi—Biography. 4. Muslim women—Pakistan—
Karachi—Biography. 5. Polygamy—Social aspects—Pakistan—Karachi.
6. Women—Pakistan—Social conditions. 7. Misogyny—Pakistan.
8. Pakistan—Social conditions. 9. Pakistan—History.
10. Pakistan—Religious life and customs. I. Title.
DS392.2.K3Z26 2015
954.91'830509252—dc23
[B]
2014027339

To the brave women of Pakistan

CONTENTS

PROLOGUE

DECEMBER 27, 2007

It was a mild winter evening whose spring-like bloom had inspired many to leave their barred windows ajar. Through the metal screen, the sounds of children playing, of distant hawkers and car horns and the smells of exhaust fumes and the neighbor's cooking all wafted in. My mother, grandmother, and I kept an uncomfortable vigil in our living room by the telephone. We had spent the afternoon in prayer, because my aunt's husband, Uncle Sohail, had been rushed to the hospital earlier that day after suffering a sudden stroke. Engrossed thus, we had not thought to turn on the television or check the news.

Benazir Bhutto, herself a daughter of Karachi and a fixture on the city's political scene, was the freest woman we knew. A few days earlier she had returned to Pakistan after a six-year exile. All week Pakistan's news channels had been covering news of a rally she was to address that evening in Rawalpindi. It must have been just a little after 6 p.m. when the telephone rang through the stillness of the sitting room. It is almost dusk, I remember thinking; soon we will hear the call to prayer.

And then, as I picked up the receiver to the old, gray phone, the world slowed. My father was on the other end of the line, calling from the hospital. My mother and grandmother stared at me. "Do you know what has happened?" he asked, his voice rising above the voices of a crowd in the background. "No," I replied, my own voice faltering under the gaze of the two women who waited with me. "Is he okay?" I asked into the wail of ambulance sirens on the other end. "Do you know *she* has died?" my father answered with a question. "Is *he* okay?" I asked again. It took him a minute to sort through the collision of questions. My uncle had survived his emergency surgery, he told me. And then, as if it were more important, he added, "Benazir Bhutto has been assassinated in Rawalpindi."

A single moment birthed twin confusions. Uncle Sohail had lived and Benazir Bhutto had died. The complexities of each defied singular emotion; I could not celebrate the continuation of my uncle's life or mourn the cessation of Benazir's. In the moments after I hung up the phone, we said nothing. We had been praying for him to live, for his life to be spared, but were these prayers different from the ones we said decades ago when my grandmother and aunt coined elusive bargains with God to grant my aunt children? Did our sympathy for his present catastrophe erase the memories of his past culpabilities? My mother, grandmother, and I laid out our rugs to say the dusk prayer, as we had done thousands of times before. In the familiar rhythms of our rising and falling prayers, of mouthing verses that had fallen from our lips so many times before, we buried these questions.

Around us the city devolved into riots. It was rush hour when the news broke and angry mobs blocked all the exits of the main highways. Thousands of vehicles caught in traffic were set on fire or simply demolished with crowbars and sticks. My cousins and friends who were caught in the frenzy left their cars and walked to nearby houses for shelter. My father was stranded in the hospital with my aunt while my uncle remained in recovery. Karachi burned for days as news channels played the tape of Benazir's assassination over and over again, a red circle marking her attacker and her last flailing moments. For one odd, brief, and singular moment, the catastrophes of my family and my country had come together, showing me how they were woven together, knotted and inextricable, inside and outside, male and female, no longer separate.

THE UPSTAIRS WIFE

CHAPTER I

The Return

DECEMBER 1986

It is the most ordinary of days that enclose tragedy within their sealed lips: after years of neat, regular morsels, dutifully swallowed, that singular, bitter bite. And so that December morning had been forgettable until Aunt Amina appeared unexpectedly at our breakfast table, her tear-sodden face hung like an incongruous portrait between the toast and the tea.

The day had begun, as always, with crows and cars and clattering cooking pans from the neighbor's kitchen sounding together in the morning chorus. There had been the same hurried washing of face and hands, eyes screwed against the sting of soap; the same squabbles with my brother over this or that; the frantic search for the homework book.

It must have been around seven thirty when we descended into the kitchen, the humming, brimming heart of our house, and there we found the silence. My aunt Amina—puller of cheeks, maker of treats—had been thrust into the middle of our morning like a cold, sharp jab. She sat at the far end of the teak table, her wilted head drooping into a teacup. It was the pale yellow one, ornate and delicate, and a present from my father to my mother, cupped in his hands all the way back to Karachi from a business trip to Thailand. I had never seen anyone else drink from it.

Aunt Amina had been absent from the breakfast table of her father's home, which was also her brother Abdullah's and our father's home for nearly eleven years. A dangler on the edges of adult conversations, I knew, even at ten years old, that married women did not come back to spend the night at their parents' home. A bride's departure from her father's house was the beating heart of every marriage ceremony: the severing of one life and the start of another was commemorated in every wedding song I had ever sung and every nuptial ritual I had ever seen. At the *rukhsati* (leave taking), the bride, laden with gold and garlands, said her final good-bye to each one of her family members. It was a weeping finale to weeks of wedding celebrations, drawing into its cathartic fold all the married women in attendance. At every wedding, they cried with the bride and for the bride and for themselves and the homes and lives they had left behind.

I had seen Aunt Amina's wedding only in pictures, its details shut within the photo album that my grandmother Surrayya kept in the deep shelves of her metal wardrobe. In it sat Aunt Amina and her husband, Uncle Sohail, as bride and bridegroom, arranged next to relatives, aunts and uncles and cousins, all in their wedding finery. The bride had worn a gold and red sari, its fabric so stiff that it angled at every fold, making a tent-like point in the middle of her head. The elderly women who supervised the dressing of brides in those days had taken away the glasses she always wore. In the few pictures in which she did look up at the camera, Aunt Amina looked as she probably felt: a bit blind.

——— ———

On our way to school that morning, stuck in the back of the little brown hatchback in which my mother ferried us, I squirmed with questions. Our daily journey was a long one, threading from the suburban streets of our neighborhood in the southeast of the city to the deeper, denser heart of Karachi's smog-smeared downtown. Well-tended villas standing guard over manicured lawns slowly gave way to grimy apartment buildings teetering over shuttered shops.

The point of demarcation between the familiar Karachi, of home and friends and nearly clean streets, and the darker, grumpier heart of the city was the *mazar* of the Quaid-e-Azam, Pakistan's founder, who died on September 11, 1948, when the country was just a year old. The mausoleum's white dome rose up pristine and commanding from its park of scrubby trees and bushes just as we turned from Shaheed-e-Millat Road onto M. A. Jinnah Road, named after the founder himself. I had been inside just once, for a school trip in the second grade. Under the cavernous atrium of the dome, we stood on the side of the pink marble tomb, thirty girls in a dutiful line. Solemn and serious, I had imagined the man whose staring face was on the rupee lying just under the carved stone: a stern, male Snow White.

After the Mazar, the traffic broke from the hesitant outings of suburban housewives gathering up tomatoes and potatoes and the right cuts of meat to the frenzy of men in pursuit, fueled by the fever of an urban hunt that began every dawn. There were buses with working men hanging from their sides, chauffeurs toting executives, and rickshaws and donkey carts ferrying all the rest. Those who lived here in the old parts of the city lived in tenements, crawling out every morning into the crowded streets, cramped from nights spent squeezed in small, airless rooms. Beyond the Mazar lay the Karachi of crude realities; of heroin addicts who sat crouched under blankets on the medians, of newly arrived farmers who tried to sell live chickens to harried clerks on their way to work, of street urchins that pressed their dirty, snot-crusted faces against car windows, looking into other lives.

As we entered this Karachi the easy, smiling contours of my mother's face pulled tight and then even tighter. She had fought for this, learning to drive just so she could take us to school, to the best schools, insisting that it could be done and that she could do it. For this she had sat awkwardly between my father and my grandfather, arguing her case against their objections. For this she had tolerated our crying chorus, every Monday and Wednesday, when the instructor from the driving school showed up at the door at 9:00 a.m. sharp. For this, she had tolerated the weeks and months of my grandfather Said, insisting that he, who could not himself drive, must nevertheless accompany her on every trip, because a woman, even one with a driver's license, could not be trusted to drive alone. Her battle to be permitted to drive had not been an easy one.

Five years had passed and now she was allowed to drive alone and without my father or grandfather correcting the timing of her turns, the certainty of her navigation. But despite her victory, the descent into this other Karachi, the sweaty, angry, male Karachi, was still my mother's daily test.

Because children never pick the right moment to burst in, I blurted out a question that appeared on the periphery of my mind: "Is Uncle Sohail dead?" My twin brother, Zaid, turned around to glare. I wanted an answer, and so I asked again: "Is Uncle Sohail dead?"

My mother did not respond when the light turned green, or at the next light, or as we descended even deeper into the city, onto roads flagged by beggars and hawkers and aimless men hanging around corners. She was quiet as we drove past the row of cinemas, the Capri, the Nishat, the Regal, the Star, past the bloody face of Sylvester Stallone, the jutting hips of a Punjabi actress stilled in midgyration. We passed the electronics market with its unlit neon signs (Hitachi, Sanyo, Toshiba) exposing their wiry entrails.

It was only as our car pulled up before my brother's school that my mother spoke. "No, Uncle Sohail is not dead," she said in the tiny moment before the gates would shut and leave my brother punished for being tardy. "He is not dead, but it would have been better if he were."

These words, my mild-mannered mother's wishes for a man's death, tumbled out behind us, stumbling into our lunch boxes and schoolbooks. I carried them into my classroom, where I took in a lesson on the Indus River valley, where I completed a test on fractions. I said them to myself in recess as I tried to swap my jam sandwich for a carton of fruit juice: "He is not dead, but it would have been better if he were."

——— ——

Aunt Amina was there when we returned home from school that day and the one after. She stayed as one December day flowed into another and everyone dragged out their shawls and sweaters to bundle up against the barest bit of cold. She was there and not there, a diminished Aunt Amina, an approximation of the witty woman whose jokes and inflected barbs spiked up casual afternoon chats and whose cuddles had infused me with warmth for as long as I could remember. The woman I saw had been wrung out like the washing that hung outside the kitchen window: twisted, drained, and turned to squeeze out every drop of spirit.

Morning and night, she lay curled up on the bed in my grandmother's room, under a blue woolen shawl, toying fringe and fabric and grief between thumb and forefinger. When the calls to prayer unfurled from the minarets, she rose from the bed, following my grandmother in her ablutions as the sounds from the first, the second, and then the third neighborhood mosque rippled through the morning, the afternoon, the tepid dusk, and finally the night. Mother and daughter washed their faces and arms to their elbows, swished the water around their mouths, and rinsed their feet and ankles to purify themselves for prayer. Before the window that faced the mango tree in the backyard, they laid down their prayer mats. Side by side they repeated the rituals that sectioned our daily lives into five portions. And then to bed Aunt Amina returned.

Sometimes she appeared at dinner, sitting on the extra chair brought into the kitchen from the larger table in the formal dining room. She ate little, small morsels of chapati doused in yogurt or rice absently tucked in her mouth, and mechanically swallowed. The conversation was careful, as if the grown-ups had culled it of every controversy before they appeared at the table to act out their parts. The menu almost always included fish, and so my grandfather, who always began the banter, would say something about the fish, its freshness or softness or saltiness, its date of purchase, its breed or its standing before fish of other kinds. If there was no fish, its absence provided a topic in itself. The rest of the cast would then perform their bit roles and walk-ons, adding opinions about the fish, agreements or disagreements or minor digressions. My mother usually contributed some comparisons—how our fish rated next to what her sisters might have served that week at their dinner tables. My father would assist with a comment or two, my grandmother would ask a question about when and how much more fish should be purchased to insure we had plenty. We, the children, were not expected to speak, and so we listened and noted that Aunt Amina never said anything.

Between meals floated the uncertainty that had colonized our house. The smells in the kitchen, the arrangement of bedrooms, the allotment of affections had all been shaken up by the return of a woman who had been honorably given away in marriage to another family. There was no precedent for it, and so my grandfather, newly retired, did the only thing he knew to do, which was to enlist the advice of others—as many others as he could think of. As the days passed, elders from the tiny transplanted community of Bombay Kokanis, who had migrated to Karachi in the decades after Partition, filtered in and out of our house. The men were led through the black gate, past the tall palms that lined the drive, and through the carved front door. Inside they were seated in the formal living room, with its tall windows opening to the garden beyond. Here, resting on cushions verdant with blooming roses and peonies embroidered by Aunt Amina in the days before her marriage, they debated what was right and what must be done, who had erred and who was wronged, who must submit and on what terms. It was a thorny question: What to do about a woman who had left her husband and returned to her father?

One afternoon, as I hung around outside the living room windows, ditched by my brother, who had gone off to play cricket in the streets, where I was not allowed, I saw yet another man being led into the formal dining room. A tall column of white and gray, his bearded form was followed by the bowed, respectful heads of my father and grandfather. I remembered him—I remembered his beard, the sharp white triangle, severe and precise, it formed against the brown skin of his face.

The occasion had been Aunt Amina's *nikah*, the signing of the marriage contract that happens just before the wedding reception. It is a solemn legality left to the men, an exchange between the father of the bride, giving her away, and the groom to whose family she would soon belong. But my memory of the man came from a picture in the yellow photo album: the same column-like body, folded between my grandfather and the groom, the same triangular beard, white even then, nearly brushing the paper that he held up to be signed by father and husband. Aunt Amina was not in the picture: like all brides she had not been present at her nikah. I imagined her busy with the rituals of becoming a bride, with henna on her palms and her bridal finery laid out at her feet, her hair getting tamed and teased for the reception that evening, anxious and excited and never knowing the exact moment when the marriage contract was signed and sealed and she had become a wife.

Now the men sat surrounded by a terse silence. I watched them unnoticed from a side window. When they spoke, they passed between them a long piece of paper, tracing their fingers over one sentence and then another. Again and again they did this: my father, then my grandfather, looking at the paper, reading from the paper, and then looking up at the man with the triangular beard. Their voices were soft and low against serious faces. I could not hear what they said. I did not know, then, that the piece of paper was Aunt Amina's marriage contract. My father and grandfather were asking the man, the imam who had married them, if she could ask Uncle Sohail for a divorce. Aunt Amina was not in the room that day either.

If until then the adults had conspired successfully to keep up some façade of regularity, that resolve crumbled the afternoon of the imam's visit. There was no dinner that day as the grown-ups retreated to my grandparents' bedroom and did what was almost never done in our house: they shut the door. Except for Zaid and me the rest of the house was empty. Dusk settled in, dimming the corners, chilling the empty kitchen, and hanging heavy over its pots and pans.

Zaid and I waited, expecting the receding light, the calls to prayer, the dinner hour to draw them from the room into the world where we had been left behind. We sat at the head of the marble stairs at the center of the house, our knees touching, debating whether we should turn on the lights, go to the kitchen, or knock on the door. We floated our guesses as to what was happening. She was getting divorced, I said. She was dying, he said. We had never really liked Uncle Sohail, we agreed, and now we hated him.

At nine thirty my mother finally came out of the room, her face puffy. We sat on the kitchen table, chastened by the oddity of the moment. Then she retrieved a frying pan from the pantry and some eggs from the refrigerator. With two quick thwacks she cracked the shells on the edge of the marble counter and into the sizzle of the pan. She slid the eggs, sunny-side up, each saddled by a slice of white bread, onto two plates. Then she sat between us at the teak table, and told us why Aunt Amina had returned. Uncle Sohail was getting married again to a new wife, a woman whom he had met at work. According to our Muslim custom, he was supposed to ask Aunt Amina for her permission. He had done so, but she had refused to give it. Uncle Sohail had said he would marry his new fiancée anyway, and so she had left and come back to our house.

DECEMBER 1986

All cities by the sea follow the same gradations of wealth. Those neighborhoods farthest from the ocean are the most replete with yearning: they are the unrequited lovers who know the sea is there but cannot see it, hear it, or smell it in their inland banishment. It was in one of these recesses, settled by need rather than desire, that the trouble started. Traced on a map, and there were few accurate ones of Karachi then, it would be the point where the low arid plains rising from the sea are suddenly accosted by a pair of jagged hills, a final barrier against the desert that lies beyond and appropriately named the Dividing Hills.

In the early hours of the dawn on December 14, 1986, in a slum colony at the foot of those hills, hundreds of armed men slipped from Toyota trucks into the cold, dusty lanes, their faces and heads wrapped in black bandannas, machine guns slung over their shoulders. They crept into the modest houses, squat installations of one or two rooms teeming with sleeping families curled under quilts and covers. Mothers and children and fathers and grandfathers all woke to a storm of strangers and bullets.

The assassins weaved in and out of the houses of factory workers and vegetable sellers, day laborers and stone masons. They were bound in death by their common origins as refugees from India, the trailing wreckage of Partition. The gunmen went from Qasba Colony to Aligarh Colony, named after the university town too deep in India to be given to Pakistan. When they didn't go into homes they went into shops, armed with Kalashnikovs, gifts of the Russians, smuggled across another border. They knew the unmarked paths well and had an ordered plan of mayhem, some invisible checklist that told them who was to be killed and who spared. Their mission lasted for hours, and when they were done it was past midday, a day's work of bloodshed accomplished with diligence, leaving piles of bodies strewn on the streets and across doorways.

According to the newspapers the next day, fifty people had been killed in the massacre in Qasba Colony on that winter day. Written in the sedate, edgeless prose of newspapermen who had now endured nearly seven years of martial law, the story said only that "an unprecedented massacre of innocent civilians took place in Qasba Colony, Aligarh Colony and Orangi sector 1-D." It noted that the marauders had been armed with "Kalashnikovs and 7mm rifles."

The clues to who the men might be and why they had come were in the newspaper the day before. On December 13, 1986, the newspaper had reported the culmination of a large operation in the slum of Sohrab Goth on the other side of the Dividing Hills. Situated on the banks of the Lyari River, and at the edge of Karachi, Sohrab Goth was an island of Pashtuns crammed with Afghan refugees and Pashtun migrants. Its network of hovels and shanty shops were growing a reputation as a transit hub in the international drug trade in heroin.

The operation had been aimed at cleaning out Sohrab Goth of its heroin and its weapons. Despite days of searching and seizing, the newspaper article reported the operation had had little success. All the looking had produced only a single Kalashnikov, sixty-five kilos of heroin, and a tremendous, raging desire for vengeance in the hearts of the Pashtuns who lived there. It was revenge that came to Qasba Colony on December 14, 1986, revenge with its face swathed in black bandannas and revenge armed with the Kalashnikovs the police had been unable to find. The massacre in Qasba Colony, unprecedented in 1986, would be the first in multiepisodic saga of vengeance, of massacres that would pile one atop another until it would be hard to tell them apart.

The men who survived that first massacre of Qasba Colony, who picked up the bodies and bathed them and wrapped them in makeshift shrouds and buried them inside hurriedly dug graves, told many stories of that day. Now lifting a shirt and now rolling up a sleeve they would show the mark of where a bullet had entered, and where it had left. Not all the people had died of bullets, some insisted; some had been poisoned, told to drink glasses of water in which their tormentors had mixed some mysterious and lethal chemical. Many hundreds had died, many more than the fifty the newspapers would admit; the widows and mothers added them up as they recounted the men's tales.

APRIL 1986

Another woman had also returned to her father's house that year under very different circumstances. On April 10, 1986, Benazir Bhutto, the thirty-three-year-old daughter of Zulfikar Ali Bhutto, the prime minister executed in 1979, not long after I was born, had returned to Karachi after seven years of self-imposed exile. In a city and country that had become used to the ordered repression of martial law, of news broadcasts revolving around the daily doings of General Zia ul Haque, her return meant things were about to change.

The young Benazir wanted to return specifically on April 4, 1986, the seventh anniversary of her father's execution by hanging in a dark cell of a Rawalpindi jail. Her original plans had been thwarted by the military government, who believed it would deflate the drama of her return. Undeterred, the clear-eyed and dewy-skinned Benazir arrived instead on April 10, greeted by hordes of her party workers. The jubilant procession that began at the airport passed down Sharea-Faisal, the main artery that ran through the city, all the way to 70 Clifton, her father's stately mansion, which was to be her headquarters. Educated at Harvard and Oxford, the young Benazir arrived in Pakistan still unmarried, wearing a traditional *shalwar kamiz*, her striking features marking no hesitation and no discomfort at the throngs of men pushing and jostling all around her. She did not yet cover her head.

We learned of Benazir's return from the Urdu broadcast of the BBC in London, a new source beyond the reaches of the military government censors. To catch the signal, the weather had to be clear and the radio outside. A westerly wind meant we received the Persian broadcast, and if we were too deep inside the concrete walls of our house, we gathered only static. We did manage to catch

BBC Urdu that night, and gather from it the details of a procession that had been only blocks away from our house. Hundreds of thousands had turned out, the voice from London said, cheering not simply a welcome to their leader but also death to dictatorship, to General Zia. A few days later came an even bigger event, a huge rally held in Lahore at the Minar-e-Pakistan, the tower where the leaders of the Muslim League had signed a resolution committing to the creation of Pakistan. Now their revolutionary legacy was being claimed by a new leader, a woman.

The Pakistan that Benazir returned to had changed particularly in regard to its treatment of women, who had borne the weight of an Islamization campaign intended to legitimize the rule of a military dictator. In the five years that Benazir had been gone, hobnobbing with world leaders and sharpening the oratorical and political skills she would need, General Zia ul Haque had passed law after law designed to cut women out of public life and disable them in private. In the name of *Shariat* (the word used in official Pakistani records), one ordinance reduced them to half of men when testifying in court, another put them at risk of prosecution for adultery or fornication if they did not provide four witnesses when filing a complaint for rape.

But such inconveniences seemed far away from the world Benazir inhabited. Her first days back in Pakistan probably began and ended with her holding court for party advisors and workers at 70 Clifton, the loyalists eager to resurrect her dead father's legacy in her, thus enabling their own return to power. When she was not in Karachi, she went deep into Sindh to her father's ancestral lands in Larkana, hundreds of thousands of acres of cotton and sugarcane and mango orchards that had been in the Bhutto family before Pakistan was a reality. Here she met with the poor, dark sharecroppers who worked the land and worshiped their landlords, and now their landlord's daughter.

The military government of General Zia ul Haque, perhaps too secure in its longevity, perhaps secretly anxious about the crowds

that young Benazir could command, watched and waited, inter-
fering only now and then, denying a license for a rally, spiriting
away a party worker. Perhaps they underestimated the power of
the fragile-looking Benazir, laughed at the bravado she affected
in her speeches, wrote off the turnout at her rallies to curiosity,
the exotic appeal of watching a woman deliver a spirited speech,
an entertaining diversion that would never translate into any real
change, any actual threat to their stranglehold on the country.
Against their calculations, whatever they may have been, were the
chants of Benazir's supporters. "Zia must go!" shouted the crowds
at her rallies. "Zia must go," responded Benazir, smiling and waving and chanting at the people she was certain she could lead.

JANUARY 1987

I had never known that a man could have two wives. I had never
been to a second wedding or met a second wife. In the days after the revelation, the idea swirled in my head, expanding into a
sensational epic of injustice. Every night, under the blue flowered
quilt my grandmother had made just for me, I tried to imagine
what a wedding would be like for a man who already had a wife.
Frustrated by my limited experience, the mysterious "other" wife
erupted dark and powerful and witchlike in my head. Bedecked
in bridal finery and cunning, she cast a spell that sentenced Aunt
Amina to a solitary chamber under a curse of silence. With his
first wife gone, she tricked her new husband into believing that she
was a better wife and that his old wife was dead, or disappeared.

At this point, my imagination stalled. Should the spell be lifted
so that the first wife, the good one, could be restored to her prince?
Or should I wish for a different prince altogether, one who would
rescue the first wife and show the duped husband the consequences of his mistake? It was confusing and it did not seem right,
and I would fall asleep vexed.

When I awoke the questions and the unfinished story were still
there. Aunt Amina's home, where I had been an occasional visitor,

became in my head the setting for these tortures. It was built in the old style, with four or five rooms arranged around a central courtyard beckoning in sea breezes and banishing cooking smells. Over a year ago, Uncle Sohail had begun construction on a set of rooms that would sit atop the original four: a new apartment with a brand new kitchen and a bathroom with a shower, not the bucket and cup we used to pour water over our heads. The bottom floor, where Aunt Amina had moved as a new bride, would be rented out, he said, and they would be moving up to the new wing. As the builders marched in and brick was laid upon brick, a feckless Aunt Amina failed to suspect that the extra hearth was to destroy her own.

The man was a liar, and all of us his victims. The bottom floor was for a new wife, the unknown woman whose shadow had darkened our home and Aunt Amina's life. I imagined Uncle Sohail trussed up to receive his new bride: Would he wear a suit or a *sherwani*? Would there be a henna ceremony, with women singing in circles, playing the *dhol* and tambourine, laughing and teasing the new bride? Would there be a reception, I wondered? Was a second marriage just like the first in mirth and merriment?

I tried to mold my visions into coherence, into a single story and hoped for an ending. I was thwarted by childhood and the awkwardness of knowing what I was not supposed to know, what I had gathered from whispered conversations behind closed doors. With great stores of confused compassion, I circled around Aunt Amina, trying out rehearsed jokes or hugging her effusively or pouring out long monologues about some escapade known to all in the fifth grade: I understood incompletely, but felt fully. The second marriage, I had learned one evening as my mother sat chatting with one of her sisters, had been championed by many of our friends and relatives, their betrayals gouging my grandparents' wounded hearts.

One day a visiting older lady assessed my aunt's dejection and rendered her verdict before us all: Aunt Amina owed her husband gratitude, our guest announced between sips of the rose drink we had served. The children of the new wife would brighten her life, Aunt Amina was told; she had no right to weep and make it out to be such a tragedy. Another afternoon, another neighbor said what may have been on the minds of most of our visitors that winter of 1986: "At least he is not leaving you," she said with her good-byes. "At least you will still be his wife."

These visiting oracles had only bit roles in Aunt Amina's saga of torment. The chief villain's role was played by Aziza Apa, Uncle Sohail's older sister. This was the same tall, domineering woman who had arrived at my grandparents' doorstep a decade ago, singing the praises of her youngest brother, begging my grandparents for Aunt Amina as his bride. She had sat on the fancy sofas in her silky red *shalwar kamiz*, the silver and gold boxes of sweets arranged in a towering pile before her. She had choreographed her conversation to allay every fear my grandparents nursed about marrying off their daughter. Their samosas, she said, were just like they had been in Bombay, not the overfilled Pakistani kind you got in Karachi bakeries. Every few sentences she lapsed into the Kokani dialect my grandparents spoke, nursing their nostalgia, kneading what had been a transient acquaintance in the lanes and alleys of the old neighborhood in Bombay into a full-fledged filial bond. By the end of that afternoon, as Aunt Amina and her sisters listened from the adjoining bedroom, Uncle Sohail, who was expected to be just the first of her would-be suitors, had become the only man her parents ever wanted as a husband for their eldest daughter.

But just as Aziza Apa had been the architect of the marriage, she had also constructed the cracks and crevices that would leave it flailing. In the teatime conversations of earlier years, when Aunt Amina had visited in the dead heat of the afternoon, a transformed Aziza Apa had been revealed. The jolly woman who brought gifts and lavished praise had vanished once the new bride had been installed in her brother's home. The new Aunt Aziza expected complete submission from her youngest brother's wife and daily devotion, which spanned from a morning phone call to ask after her health to a full meal cooked and sent to her home every Friday. On Sundays all the wives of her brothers were expected to pay homage to their matriarch, digest her evaluations of their lives, praise her children, and often even clean her house. No detail was too private: for years Aziza Apa had been inquiring every month, before all gathered, whether Aunt Amina was pregnant.

It was Aziza Apa who had passed the verdict on Uncle Sohail's marriage, pulling all her clan on the side of her darling Sohail, whose wife had denied him not just the son he deserved but any progeny at all. "You are barren," she had reminded Aunt Amina. "You should be thankful that he is a good enough man to still keep you at all." Her words had echoed loud and deep; suddenly everyone in the community saw clearly that Uncle Sohail was the self-denying hero whose good-heartedness led him to keep a wife who could not fulfill her duty. Many had exacting broods of children, whose pressing needs grated on their lives; denouncing the barren woman elevated them, made their sacrifices of lost sleep and interrupted meals and mountains of soiled clothes a gift to be cherished.

In our house, on the sideboard of the formal dining room by the tray holding the car keys, invitations for weddings began to pile up as they did every winter. It was the season. There they lay, proof of the celebrations that continued unabated in the lives of others. Every day brought a few more: fat, festive envelopes promising feasts at hotels, or thin frugal ones threaded with gold lettering begging our respectable presence at smaller venues. Neither made it out of their resting places. Weddings—the days and weeks of rituals preceding them and the parties held after them—are the fairy-lit center of Karachi's social life, events that mark for women points of respite from their otherwise secluded lives of cooking for the in-laws and yelling at children. They are where the prosperity of a cousin's blooming business or the extra pounds on a sister-in-law can be witnessed, old scores settled and new gripes gobbled up between mouthfuls of grease and spice. That December many yearned for us to appear at one celebration or another so that, between compliments for the bride and congratulations for the groom, my mother or grandmother could be asked: "How is Amina . . . ? We heard her husband is marrying again and that she has returned to your house." As they threw out the words, they could watch our faces, gauge in the glint of our eyes and the turn of our heads the extent of our embarrassment. With this measure, they could mark the boundary between their conformity and our scandal, the degree of our banishment, which defined, after all, their own belonging.

———   ———

We did not go to any weddings that year. Instead we prayed: special prayers for hard times that went beyond the customary five apportioned to ordinary times. One Friday morning I came down to see my grandmother washing and wiping the silver tray that was kept in the cabinet with our best china. From the recesses of the same cabinet, she then removed sixteen silver cups, each with its rim pulled out into a point. They were oil lamps, precious cargo that had been wrapped in the family's best clothes, packed in one of the trunks that had brought their Indian lives to Pakistan two decades earlier. They were used in a Sufi ritual carried out for generations by my grandfather and his family, followers of a saint who had lived and preached long ago in Baghdad.

After Asr prayers that day, the furniture in the formal dining room was pushed to the walls and the thick black and burgundy rug laid out on the floor. On top of this, a clean, starched white sheet reserved for just this ritual was laid out. On a low table by the wall in a space usually occupied by a vase there sat a tray of sixteen oil lamps, each with a red silken thread twisted into a peeping wick. These would be lit at dusk to represent the happiness and joy we prayed for.

That afternoon, after an early lunch, the family gathered in a circle on the white sheet. In its middle lay a cotton sack always kept with the Qurans in a special cabinet. To begin, my grandfather emptied a small pile of dried nuts from the bag into the circle. There were exactly one hundred, I knew, used to keep count of the incantations we were to perform in a specific order that afternoon. Smoothed with the cares and questions of earlier supplicants, they were shiny and hard. They passed through our fingers with our murmured prayers, Arabic verses written out on a square piece of parchment brown with age, but referred to only by the children, as all the grownups knew them by heart.

At the start of each round, my grandfather would say aloud, for all to hear and follow, the verse we were to repeat. Zaid and I copied him in our best mimicry of adulthood. Each time we grabbed a handful of nuts, intoning the verse in our heads and letting the nuts fall into the growing pile, which signified the verses already read. As the afternoon wore on, our stores of solemnity dwindled, and we each tried to grab more nuts than the other, teetering on the edge of giddiness.

As evening approached the prayers were nearly complete, our family having gone through each of the twenty-one verses, which had to be repeated one hundred times for health and help and intercession against misfortune, known and unknown. The shadows lengthened and the dusk call to prayers began to echo and stretch in each direction of our neighborhood. The men and my brother left to pray at the mosque. My mother, grandmother, Aunt Amina, and I stayed home and aligned ourselves in the direction of Mecca on the white sheet itself. When we were done, and the sheet and rug gathered up, came the best moment of the evening. With a single match my grandmother lit every one of the sixteen lamps in the tray; their tiny lights sixteen points of hope that the prayers we had completed would be answered.

JANUARY 1987

On the last Saturday of January 1987, I awoke to the thwacking of the fish seller's knife hitting the round slice of tree trunk that he used as a chopping board. He was at the front gate, dividing a fish who must have breathed its last in the early hours of that morning. My brother was already awake and downstairs, there for the show. He loved fish, eating up not only the fish itself but also all that came before: my grandmother's expert pressing of the gills; the haggling over price and freshness; the laying out of the selection from the smelly bamboo bags slung over the back of the fisherman's bicycle. From the time he could walk he had been the guardian of the purchased fish. My grandmother would make the selection, agree on a price, and then retreat indoors. My brother would then take over, standing as sentinel, to insure the fish that was now ours was properly scaled and gutted, with no pieces we had paid for snuck back into the bamboo basket. Karachi was full of cheating fish sellers; his was an important task.

In the unrelenting logic of twinhood, I hated fish with the same fervor with which he loved it. The smell, the slimy wetness that passed from mouth to throat, the feathery bones were for me a collection of revulsions, and the arrival of the fish seller a sure sign of the fish curry that would appear at the table to everyone else's delight and my despair. This was going to be a day of much pretending—of hiding pieces of fish skin under my green beans in the hope that my father, who could not tolerate food aversions, would leave the table before I did, or of feigning a stomachache, which if successful could procure a complete absence from the table.

I knew the last trick would probably not work; I had tried it too many times before. I needed some new deception. Perhaps a deal with my brother—a quick passing of fish to his plate while my father was looking elsewhere, taking a sip of water or staring down at his own plate. I plotted through the morning, avoiding the fishy kitchen altogether. To justify myself, I performed a great many hated chores, pulling sheets straight, smoothing bed covers, dusting the tops of tables and the undersides of books, even ironing our uniforms for school, which would begin a week later: modeling the diligence of a dutiful daughter.

Noon arrived and then one o'clock and the meal laid out on the table held no surprises: two bowls of tomato curry with turmeric-tinged fish bobbing in it and two plates of rice. A small bowl of green beans cooked with tomatoes and onions sat in the middle, my hope against the dominance of fish. Bottles of chilled water stood, as they always did, at each end of the table. My mother plated a last minute salad, circles of cucumber and slices of lemon sprinkled with salt and pepper.

I was ready for the challenge, but no one cared about my ability to consume fish that day. My father, usually at the table within minutes of my mother's call, did not appear until the end of the meal. And there was another absence. Aunt Amina's empty chair had been returned to the formal dining table where it belonged. I ate the rice and the green beans and let the fish go untouched and uneaten in the middle of the plate. When my father shuffled into the kitchen, I was already done, carrying my plate to the sink before washing my hands.

A lucky escapee, I scurried from the kitchen into my grandmother's bedroom as my father sat down to eat. The daybed that had been Aunt Amina's sleeping place, where she had sat and laid and slept and wept for the past two months, had been made up. On the bureau, where her glasses and comb and purse had been, a collection of porcelain knickknacks—a basket of flowers, a cherub-faced doll, and a rosy-lipped porcelain baby with a pink bow that I was not allowed to touch—had reappeared. Aunt Amina was gone, having left as silently and suddenly as she had appeared.

— CHAPTER 2 —

Birth of a Nation

JULY 1947

My eighteen-year-old grandmother Surrayya labored at home, sweltering in an inner room and surrounded by a cluster of women. As she counted down the months to this moment, amid the restive pangs of a British Empire pregnant with Pakistan, she had asked for just one thing: that she be taken to the hospital when her time came. Now that time was here, and the women of her husband's family, his sister and aunts, stood there doing nothing: dabbing their faces with the ends of their cotton saris awaiting a stray bit of breeze. But her agony was only one part of the drama of the crowded house. Toddlers waddled among the adults' legs, hawkers screamed at doors, and women gave birth.

Surrayya knew this, and knew what was to come, before the baby, before the army of busybodies, before the month of fasting set to begin before the week was out. She knew it was Friday, a special day in her father-in-law's house, where such special days outnumbered ordinary ones by two or three every week. Her father-in-law, Zainullah Saifuddin, was an elder, his home a community kitchen where several times a week the doors were thrown open to all those who wished to pray with him and share a simple meal. Men ate in one room at the front of the house, and women and children filled all the others. Marrying into this meant mastering the maneuvers of public service, the cooking of large meals, the offering up of space, a bed, a chair, a room to the unexpected guest or the supplicant stranger.

Days after Surrayya's marriage to Said, she had discovered what this meant. In the room where they slept, a makeshift partition of curtain and trunk separated them from two sleeping aunts. There were no closed doors, there was no space that belonged to a single person. The lock on the chest containing her trousseau was the only thing that announced some separation. On days when there were too many guests, Said slept in the front reception room with the men of the household, she with the many women in one of the inner rooms, rising with them before dawn to prepare tea for twenty or thirty, to help feed the babies, and to make the tiffin lunch Said would take with him to work at the British Telegraph Office. Like a train station moving passengers in and out, the unceasing hum of the household engulfed her from those early hours to deep in the night, when the dishes from the final meal were washed, the babies laid to sleep, and the women reunited with husbands finally returning to the inner rooms of the house.

Her labor was not the first to happen in the house, even in the scant months that she had lived there since her marriage. Not long ago she had seen another ripe daughter-in-law give birth in the very room where she lay now. It had been her fourth child, and like a favorite story whose end is awaited but known, her labor was pulled into the humming vortex of the household. The mother to be, despite the discomforts of her condition, had helped with breakfast, neatly preparing her husband's afternoon tiffin before finally retiring to the business of childbirth. When the final moments came, she was surrounded not by one or two helpful women but by a crowd of aunts, cousins of cousins, and friends of neighbors cracking jokes and chewing fennel seeds, happy to have an impending birth grant them an escape from their own kitchens and courtyards. The baby, a little girl, had arrived sometime in the midst of all this, a small punctuation mark somewhere in the middle of the party.

The public nature of Saira's childbirth cast a fear into Surrayya, her trepidation growing right alongside her belly. Hence her campaign to Said, her husband, to be taken to Jamsetjee JeeJeebhoy (J. J.) Hospital, the imposing sandstone building at the far edge of the world she knew, where her brothers' wives had given birth, where things were quiet and clean, and where the stern nurses imposed some order on the hordes of relatives. There would be no smell of garlic and turmeric and fish woven into the threads of the sheet under her body, no tea-stale breath of well-wishers to cover up with her cologne-doused handkerchief. Her sister could be with her and her own mother, not the gossips that would otherwise wend their way into this house. Said had agreed, promising in his usual good-natured way. He was eager to please her but had a weak resolve that she knew could easily be deflected by the demands of others. She did not know if he would really come, if she would really be taken to the hospital.

———— ————

The tradition of delivering babies at home was not all that kept my grandmother from the hospital. Most of her youth had been spent in a Bombay boiling with riots as Hindus and Muslims succumbed to the fever of claiming their own piece of India. Weddings and funerals and schooldays and workdays were at the mercy of frequent curfews. The best of intentions also were at their mercy. It was the women who knew what to do when the curfews silenced the street. The side doors and back alleys, which were their domain, became the lifelines of communities like the one around the Jama Masjid where my grandparents lived. The excess stores of lentils in one home could be added to the stored sack of rice in another; the old woman who never used the powdered milk allotted on her ration card gave it to the young mother to sate the appetites of her three small children. Male entry into this domain was tentative. It required care, loud announcements of "Koi hay" (Is anyone there?) in exaggerated baritones, to insure that no unrelated, uncovered woman languished in the hallway or stood braiding her hair in a deep inner courtyard that was normally her domain. If mistakes were made, they were not mentioned, necessity loosening just a bit the grip of the tradition of sequestering women.

——— ———

The sun had been baking the courtyard for hours when Said's footsteps finally crossed it. There was no curfew that day, but the messenger boy had missed him at the British Telegraph Office; he had already left for Friday prayer at the mosque. The news came to him in a whisper, delivered by his father-in-law just as the imam was about to begin his sermon. Clad in the ironed gray pants and button-down short-sleeve shirt he had worn to work that morning, Said stood up, the sole standing figure among the hundreds of heads topped with white skullcaps. Weaving in and out through the rows, he threaded his way out of the mosque to his wife, the imam's exhortations to remain stalwart in the fight for Pakistan ringing in his ears.

Emboldened by pain, Surrayya screamed when she saw him, removing for the first time the cologne-doused handkerchief she kept on her nose, her armor against the smells that had left her retching for months. A *tonga*, or horse carriage, was called; a motor taxi wouldn't fit in the narrow alleyway that fronted the house. Surrayya, bundled in her chador, a round blob of black, was deposited in the back, all but her eyes covered. Under the chador, she still clutched her handkerchief against her nose, but now against the smell of the horse and the sweat of its driver in the July heat. A cloth bundle prepared long ago for just this journey was pushed in after her.

The carriage carried the little family-to-be down the street, breaking up the games of schoolkids returning home and attracting the stares of women peeping through alcoves, before it made a turn and could no longer be seen. In its wake, hundreds of men poured out from the mosque, the Jama Masjid, into the streets and alleyways outside my great-grandfather Zainullah Saifuddin's house. It was the last Friday before the beginning of Ramzan, or Ramadan, the Muslim month of fasting. It was to be a historic Ramzan, everyone said, one promising transformation, heralding the birth of a whole new country. That evening men from the mosque and their wives and children poured into the house. Like all other Fridays they gathered there for prayer and a meal, a ritual my great-grandfather insisted had taken place before Pakistan and would continue thereafter.

My father, Abdullah, was born one month before Partition, in a still united India. On July 18, 1947, four days after his birth and while my grandmother was still at J. J. Hospital in Bombay, the British Parliament signed the Indian Independence Act of 1947, which divided India and gave birth to two separate nations. It was the middle of the night in Bombay when the BBC reported the news, the street outside the hospital erupting into a chaos of firecrackers and shouts and slogans. The women inside were a mix of Hindu and Muslim, tended to by Catholic nuns in a hospital that had been built by a Zoroastrian businessman and was still run by the British.

It was a dose of history almost too big to swallow for a teenage mother, not least because everything around her seemed still the same. Inside the maternity ward, the ceiling fans turned the humid air and uniformed nurses and orderlies skimmed in and out of rooms and between beds. Each bed was separated from the others by a white curtain, drawn at night or when the patient requested privacy. It was a happy place, not plagued by the illness and dejection of other wards where patients lay recovering from disease or dangled near death. Nursing her new baby in this hopeful setting, Surrayya thought the birth of a new country could only be a good thing.

But if the maternity ward of J. J. Hospital was a place of general rejoicing, of looking to the future, a mere two floors down the hospital halls echoed with the gasps and wails of death and finality. For three days after my father's birth, the city of Bombay witnessed off its shores the worst maritime disaster in the city's history. At three o'clock on the overcast afternoon of July 17, long after most fishermen who went out to sea from Bombay Harbor had returned, their catch sold and packed for shipment into the country, a few near-drowned souls washed up, sputtering and gasping, on the Sassoon Docks. They bore with them terrible news.

The survivors had been on a passenger ship called *The Ramdas* along with six or seven hundred others, all bound for the port of Rewas north of Bombay. They had boarded the ship around six o'clock that morning. They carried with them their carefully preserved belongings, knotted bundles of cloth, stainless-steel tiffins of food, brown paper packages for relatives, toys for children. The Muslims on the ship were returning to villages in anticipation of the month of Ramzan, which was about to begin. The mood on the crowded ship was festive, families camping out on the deck on square sheets, migrant laborers eager for mother's cooking, a respite from the frenzy of Bombay, its tramcars and smoke and insistent demands.

They had just sailed into the Arabian Sea, the buildings of the harbor disappearing into the horizon, leaving only the clear blue sky and a benevolent ocean breeze. Women loosened their *duppatas* and peered up from behind burkas, unpacking tiffins of breakfast, of crusty bread and spicy ground mutton, of potatoes folded into pastries and hot, sweet tea in carefully wrapped thermoses. Some had fried fish carefully wrapped in banana leaves or packets of rice and lentils. Children laughed and ran around the deck, unfazed by the dips and dives of the ship. Less stalwart others held bags around their mouths, returning to them the half-eaten breakfast consumed port side. On the upper deck a small coterie of wealthy businessmen sat on plush chairs sipping tea.

The wave that swept over the deck surprised everyone, dousing all and knocking over many on the port side of the ship. The remnants of picnics and cherished bundles washed across the deck among the ankles of fleeing passengers. The terror and chaos brought on by the tidal swell sealed the ship's fate. Mothers grabbed babies and men pushed, moving in throngs to the still-dry starboard side of the ship, thinking they were running toward safety. But the frenzy was fatal. The rush of bodies tipped the ship into the sea, swallowing in an instant more than 627 lives, leaving only bits and pieces of wreckage floating where the vessel had been and the bobbing heads of a mere hundred who knew how to swim or who managed to clutch a bit of wreckage. A dead passenger's watch found months later read 8:20 a.m., the time the wave had struck.

The captain of the ship, Sheikh Ahmed Ibrahim, survived. The fact that he was a Muslim was not lost on a country still setting its borders. "Gone are the days when captains stayed with their ship, sinking with the passengers who entrust their lives to them," opined one newspaper. Another speculated that the ship's chief engineer, a Christian from Goa with a decade of maritime experience, could just as well have saved himself but had chosen to go down with the ship that was his charge.

The implications were clear: on the troubled vessel that represented India on the eve of Partition, Muslims jumped ship, saving themselves without regard for others. As the wreckage representing the lives and dreams of so many washed ashore in the days that followed, many wondered whether India, like *The Ramdas*, was itself about to sink under the weight of a great tidal wave, creating, like the terror-stricken passengers on the ship, conditions for its own catastrophe.

——— ———

At the home of Surrayya's father-in-law, *The Ramdas* catastrophe had invaded the rhythm of the household. His small house was just a stone's throw from the mosque, which became the center of mourning for those Muslim families who had suffered losses. Families came up from the villages of Parel and Gurgaon to claim bodies and arrange funerals, sleeping in whatever unoccupied corner they could find. Many others came to Bombay searching for sisters and brothers who had never arrived. As bodies continued to wash ashore, funeral prayers rippled from the mosque through the neighborhood. With the disaster arrived the monsoon, making the digging of graves in Bombay's single Muslim graveyard particularly arduous. The symbolism of the wet, muddy ground of Bombay refusing the remains of those the sea had already claimed was duly noted.

My grandparents' relatives had left their villages and settled around the Jama Masjid in Bombay more than a hundred years prior to that summer of 1947. Many of their neighbors had arrived later, and mourned relatives who had perished in the disaster. Catastrophe and change both hung over the community, whose members had drawn close through decades of pooled tears and shared mirth, of marriages and illnesses. But that July of 1947 the meals of Ramzan, eaten at dusk, were just as they always were: the tables laden with large slices of watermelon and spicy samosas and canisters of chilled milk sweetened with rosewater. As they bit down on the sweet dates with which they always broke their fast, Bombay's Muslims asked themselves the question that echoed all over the subcontinent . . . Should they stay or should they go?

My grandparents chose to stay, bolstered by the assurances of others in their community who balked at the prospect of becoming refugees in a land they had fought for, but that remained unpredictable and even mysterious. Pakistan was a gamble whose success remained uncertain. Holding their cards close to their chests, they must have balked at the headlines that September, as trains spilling over with bloodied bodies crept across the newly made borders, as mobs coursed through Calcutta and Lahore burning Hindu shops and Muslims shops, a cycle of massacres repeated again and again. In less empathetic moments, they may have wondered if the exodus would make their own city, with its millions jammed in tenement houses and apartments, a bit less crowded, a bit more comfortable.

The conundrum of Muslims all over India was the same. Most had lived for centuries, not simply decades, in communities throughout the country. In the feverish years before Partition, the politics of the All India Muslim League and the fervid passion of the campaign for Pakistan had held many in its thrall. Bombay had itself become caught up in rallies and riots and bred many of the leaders that led the movement. Few had considered that some of those Indian Muslims now clamoring for a new country would remain in India after Pakistan was created.

The Kokani community of Bombay, to which my grandparents belonged, was no different. In the registers of the Jama mosque that stood at the center of their community, they could trace their ancestry all the way back to medieval times when Arab traders arrived on the coasts of Goa, not far from Bombay. Pakistan was the dream they had nurtured for the past couple of decades, but the Muslims from the Kokan and Malabar coasts were the oldest Muslim communities in all of India. They had always been Muslim alongside Hindus, Christians, Sikhs, and many others; what would it mean to be Muslim in Pakistan? Everyone had ideas: anecdotes about Pakistan carted back from eager visitors who ventured back and forth over the new border.

It was in this atmosphere of expectation and consternation that my father spent his first years. Said had rented the second floor of a row house in Bombay that had been built by the British to house their growing cadre of Indian civil servants. Like India itself, the row house had been sectioned off into bits and pieces. It did not matter much, as the rooms all housed relatives or relatives of relatives who emerged like nesting dolls from corners and crevices and backrooms and cellars. After a week of convalescence at the hospital, Surrayya had returned to her own father's house, where she was assisted in the care of her first baby by her mother and still unmarried younger sister. In the daily visits the twenty-two-year-old Said made to his teenage wife, over the tea and biscuits served to him with appropriate deference, his mother-in-law cajoled him into considering for himself and her daughter and their newborn son the possibility of a home of their own. It could be just a few rooms, and as a matter of fact she knew of some that were just a stone's throw away from the mosque, close to his father's home but with just a bit more room for the many more sons her daughter would soon bear.

Perhaps Surrayya's plan for independence would have gathered some opposition if there had been another woman wielding her shadow of influence over Said, but such was not the case. Said's own mother, the traditional competitor for a man's affections, had died years ago, leaving him to be raised by an assortment of caring aunts and concerned cousins. A few years before his own marriage to Surrayya, his widowed father had married again, bringing into the family a much younger wife. Now a mother herself, Mehrunissa Begum was too overwhelmed with the care of her own brood to be concerned about a stepdaughter-in-law's machinations to break from the conjoined lives of the main house and set up a home of her own. So for Surrayya, Partition and motherhood brought a sort of emancipation. With everyone in her father-in-law's house haunted by the lingering tears of families severed by far more than a few blocks, there was little scrutiny of the small severance she demanded for her own family. They were, after all, staying in India, in Bombay, in the same neighborhood, and by the same mosque.

A narrow stairwell led to their portion of the row house. They had four rooms in all, none of which were ever allotted purposes definite enough to not be changed in minutes and according to the need of the hour: a makeshift workshop for sewing, a guestroom for visitors overflowing from the main house, an impromptu nursery school for six or seven toddlers, or any other assorted occupation that fell into the household. The front room bore three large windows that looked down into the busy alley into which my grandmother could lower a basket tied to a rope, drawing up tomatoes or onions or fresh fish still reeking of the sea. The other two rooms had pallets that could be laid out for sleep and chairs and two large steel wardrobes that bore the family's belongings. Meals were taken in the front room, where the hot plate was on a table that rose only four or five inches from the ground.

My grandmother always spoke with pride of this first kitchen, which she stocked, as she always reminded us, with "British goods"—Earl Grey tea, shortbread biscuits, Nescafé coffee. In those times of ration cards, Said's job with the British Telegraph Service—which had been renamed the Indian Telegraph Service—still insured that he could shop for provisions at the store for company employees. In a land the British had ruled for more than two hundred years, these acts of export consumption conferred quite a bit of status. Every can of coffee, every tin of biscuits was kept long after the contents had been consumed. They stood at attention, looking down on the family and their guests from the top shelves of cupboards: brightly painted Cadbury candy boxes and red tins of Ovaltine holding rice and lentils and garam masala long after the chocolate was gone.

Perhaps they did not know it, but it was not the chocolate or the cookies or the job that made them most British. The fact that they lived there, husband and wife and child, without a bolstering clan, without a mother- and father-in-law whose age and health dominated the rhythms of the day was the most Western aspect of their lives. The nuclear family was virtually unknown in India then, and even if it had happened partly by accident, it was unusual. Surrayya's memories of her early marriage weren't marred by the lack of privacy; by others' demands dictating whether fish or chicken would be cooked, when tea had to be prepared for breakfast, and if an outing to a park or a visit to the doctor could be accommodated between mealtimes and teatimes and the visits of older relatives. Perhaps my grandmother did not realize it then, but the most British thing about her kitchen was that it was exclusively and uncontestably her domain.

NOVEMBER 1950

With the new set of rooms came freedom and privacy and more children. With the drama of Partition dulled a bit by the realities that followed revolution, and the mystery of childbirth already unraveled, Amina's November birth was almost routine. And because a son had already been born and now toddled happily up and down the steps of the house, there were fewer expectations and demands on the new mother and father by the extended family.

Said had been promoted at work, and he was doing well enough to take his wife to the movies one or two times a month, a luxury and liberty few of his forebears would have been able to afford or even imagine. He greeted the birth of his first daughter with elation. The desire for sons left many fathers sulking and angry outside maternity wards, licking the wounds of their victimization by fate: a daughter was a net loss that would have to be fed and clothed only to add to the bounty of some other household. This daughter and the two that would follow all reminded him of his sister Safia. She had died not as an infant but as a young woman about to be wed, the gold embroidery on her red wedding sari nearly complete. When his own daughter was born almost eight years later he wished to name her after his sister, but Surrayya, afraid of the tragedy this could inflict on her young daughter, persuaded him otherwise. The newborn, dark eyed and high cheekboned like her mother, was named Amina instead.

JUNE 1955–JANUARY 1958

Every other Sunday Surrayya and Said bundled up their children and set out for the movies. Independence and the departure of the last British troops from the subcontinent had unleashed a wild torrent of creativity. Poets, songwriters, actors, and filmmakers milled in and out of Bombay's crowded, steamy streets, dreaming of their own face staring down from the poster in the cinema house, their song blaring from the radio, their words pouring out from the lips of famous stars. Surrayya rejoiced that she was lucky enough to be married to a man who would take her to the movies, something her own mother had never been able to do and that many of the other married women in the building, several her own age, were never allowed to do. Her favorite actress was Nimmi, the seemingly demure actress who had risen to stardom with a movie called *Barsat.*

Surrayya looked just like Nimmi, her friends told her, emphasizing the similar curve of their hairlines, the tilt of their chins, the wistfulness of their dark, liquid eyes. And so in the tedium of ordinary afternoons, as she put the rice to boil, ground the red chilies to a paste, soaked the lentils, and nursed her third daughter, she imagined herself playing a part in a movie, a visitor in her life from some other land with other rules. Perhaps like Soni, Nimmi's character in the blockbuster movie *Uran Khatola* (*Flying Carriage*), she was the princess of a land ruled only by women, where women chose their own husbands and men could do nothing but follow their behest.

While a women-ruled island was indeed a fantasy, the beckoning of other lands was quite real. Even as they prospered, with a growing family and Said an emerging leader in the community, they could not stop thinking of those who had chosen differently. Over the years, more and more families from the Kokani community in Bombay had taken the ship to Karachi, settling in another city by the sea: one just for Muslims.

In the first months after Partition, when ghastly stories filtered in—of carnage, of life in refugee tents in a dusty and desolate Karachi—it was easy enough to insist that staying had been the correct choice. Pakistan at Partition, a bumbling country saddled with the leftovers of the British Empire, could be shifted to the periphery of their focus, its magnetism stanched by the rhythm of the known, by the hooting, hollering sounds of the Bombay they loved, and by the closeness of dear ones lulling them to sleep every night.

Choice can be deceptive, especially when it tarnishes reality with the promise of a magical new world. Maybe a vision of Karachi where houses were bigger and roads were broader and everything was cheaper began to haunt them. Or perhaps it was the consciousness of a receding reality, a way of life that could be replicated but not retained in the same way, with so many disappearing into the new land, so many drawn away. The massive excision of India's Muslims at Partition was by the mid-fifties a trickle, but the cumulative departures left gaps all over the community. The steady flow not only drew from it but returned to it stories of wealth and prosperity and hope, set against the darkness and nagging, knotty suspicion that the emerging India would not love them back.

In the winter of 1958, my great-grandfather, Zainullah Saifuddin, passed away peacefully in his sleep. With his death, a way of life that had seemed etched in stone revealed its fragility. The work to provide the deep silver pots of lentils and rice that had seemed to appear so effortlessly, the open doors that welcomed refugees and guests alike, the ethic that all belonged to all had to be shared by all awaited an embrace by a new generation. What had required the minimal effort of attendance now required the arduous exertion of organization and maintenance.

On a Thursday a few months after his father's death, Said opened up the powder-blue double doors of the men's reception room of his father's house to find four of the most elderly men from the Kokani Muslim community standing outside. It was the time of day between Maghrib and Isha, the prayers of dusk and darkness, and he had just stopped there to check on his stepmother and half brother before he returned to eat with his wife and children. Between their short-trimmed white beards and the crotched white caps on their heads their eyes betrayed a glassy, lingering disbelief of those unsure of the altered world they saw before them.

Khaliluddin, his late father's cousin and the tallest of the four, spoke first, his hesitant words unfurling the frown that had gathered on his head. "We know this is a difficult time for your family," he began, the hoarse words falling from his mouth. His companions, men who had been present when Said had been named and when as a boy of four he had first started accompanying his own father to the mosque. Those had been the concerns of a different age, when future generations of children and grandchildren could be expected to fill the empty ranks and rosters of those who worshiped at the Jama Masjid.

The men who came to see my grandfather that day were the appointed elders of the community—the *mushavirs*, or caretakers, of the Jama Masjid, which dated back to 1778 when it was founded by a Kokani Muslim merchant. For more than one hundred fifty years, as the land around the mosque developed from open fields redolent with coconut palms to a crowded, urban neighborhood in the heart of the city, Kokani Muslims had cared for the mosque, expanding the building as the community grew. On that day they had come to ask Said, then thirty-three, to be a *mushavir* of the mosque, the highest honor the community could confer on one of its own.

I can see their plaintive faces now in the proudly sparse room, their elbows and backs resting on the low, long cushions against the wall, the framed picture of Mecca and the dark square of the Kaaba staring out from the wall above them. They had come to his father' s house to connect him to the legacy they believed was in peril, the history of a community that had germinated and grown and flourished around the mosque built for them so long ago. Perhaps they sensed the symptoms of a man succumbing to the allure of Pakistan. They tried to keep him, to enclose him in the mantle of honor and leadership and duty and responsibility that they wore themselves and that had kept them in India, even after Pakistan was born. Perhaps even then, as the call for Isha prayers rang out in the alleys and into the homes around the mosque, they knew that it might be too late. As he took their leave, clasping their wrinkled hands in his, and lowered his gaze in farewell, my grandfather did not say yes; only, very respectfully and quietly, that he would confer with his wife. It was the first time the honor offered had not been accepted in an instant.

--- CHAPTER 3 ---

The Scent of Other Cities

MAY 1961

The voyage to Pakistan was dotted with hardships. The ship had eighteen bathrooms: six for first-class passengers, another eight for second-class passengers, and the remaining four for the anonymous deck dwellers. This meant, for the deck dwellers, that there was a ratio of a hundred people to a single toilet. By the time the horn sounded announcing the ship's arrival at Karachi Port, Surrayya and her daughters had not been able to use the facilities for nearly twelve hours. They squirmed with discomfort as they carried their belongings, which had been stuffed into bags now near bursting. They clambered up the ship's exit ramps, pushing forward along with the rest of the human cargo, all smelling of distress and eagerness, all convinced that some prize would be bestowed upon those clever enough to set foot on the solid ground ahead of the others.

But the land was uninformed about the momentous nature of these arrivals from India. A May sandstorm descended on Karachi soon after the ship had docked at Keamari Harbor, inserting itself between the immigrants and the city of their dreams. Its winds rose red and sharp and hot from the Iranian deserts to the west and blew sand all over the city they had so longed to see.

But the sand could not mask the smell, and it was the smell that led them to the row of lavatories standing all in a row, the doors painted green and the handles painted white in the colors of Pakistan. It was their first stop in Pakistan, it was their first relief. Just as in Bombay, the toilets were holes in the ground but the pits had been dug deep. The toilets had four walls and no ceilings, and the open sky allowed for the gentle mingling of sea salt, the stench of drying fish, and the suffocating sand from the storm. In this delightful mix of smells, Surrayya, Amina, then each of Amina's sisters took their turns in the toilets. Their relief was the first glory of the homeland, and it was short-lived.

Huddling among their trunks and bags near the entrance to the port, the women peered at Pakistan. It was dusty and brown and lonely, and amid the crowd of people, they could see not one familiar face. No one, it seemed, was there to greet them.

The questions rattled about in Surrayya's head as her children jostled around her. Had her brother not received the last telegram they had sent before boarding the ship? Should they have waited to hear his response before they had set off? Had she remembered to send the details of their arrival in a letter; could it have been misplaced? Was the lateness a bad sign, an omen for the future and of their fortunes in the new country? Should they not have come at all, she finally asked herself, numbed to realize that of all the possibilities, the one she had least considered was the prospect of being forsaken by her own.

It was a long hour before they could leave behind the fear of having been abandoned on arrival. The minutes filled with embarrassed replies to fellow passengers who came to ask "if they were all right" and blushing refusals to invitations to come over to the houses of almost strangers until "things were sorted out." Smiles plastered and hearts aflutter, they stood stolid and staring and waiting for their welcome.

It came finally, spotted by Abdullah, who made out the outline of his uncle pushing through the crowd lined up at the far recesses of the Arrivals building, his bald brown pate rising tall from amid the crowd. Their exclamations were louder than they should have been, the shrieks of delight inflected with relief. The entire family clamored around the barely known uncle, still grasping the plastic bags full of gifts and handmade presents that had been thrust into their hands by the last of the friends and relatives who had seen them off in Bombay. Karachi—their chosen city and new home— spread out before them.

MAY 1961

They had expected to fall in love with Karachi, and so they did. In later years, the intimacy of long association would mean that they would never be able to tell whether they loved with a pure passion, unaffected and unforced by the occasion of migration, or because that was the plan and expectation. Whichever it was, in those early days it did not matter. After a few nights spent in the cavernous and silent suburban bungalow of Surrayya's older brother, who had so unthinkingly played with their delicate emotions in the first hours of their arrival, the family, with their trunks and hopes and fervid new love for a barely known city, found themselves in their first home in Karachi.

They were urban people, and so they chose an apartment deep in the heart of the city. Like much of middle-class India, their adulation of all things British had not been tarnished by the historical fact of Independence. Fourteen years after Partition, obtaining an apartment in a building formerly occupied by the British was still considered good fortune. Having been in the custody of only a handful of inhabitants between the departure of the British and their own arrival in Karachi, my grandparents accepted these dwellings as their personal portion of the spoils of empire.

The Olympic Building on Somerset Street was, like so much else the British had left behind, a vestige of a colonial past that served as a status symbol for the prosperous in the postcolonial present. The apartment itself consisted of four large and airy rooms, with a kitchen and a bathroom at the end of a long hallway. In the decade between the British departure and my grandparents' arrival, the property had been refitted to the standard of middle-class Muslim modesty. The front door, serving the British as entryway for the entire family, had become the men's entrance. The back entrance that had once been relegated to household help became the doorway through which the women of the house could enter, leave, or welcome guests without being seen by everyone on the busy street just outside their front door.

This was not the only aspect of the house that pleased Said and Surrayya. Beyond the obvious delights of the sheer number of rooms, which doubled the square footage of their dwelling in Bombay, the high ceilings of their new abode sported an electric ceiling fan. Four rooms independently fanned from above was the very definition of decadently cooled luxury. Their first night in the house, and then the second and then the third, each one of the children and their parents fell asleep to the wondrous motion of the blades in the air and a breeze created at will, just for them, by the mere touch of a button.

Their new abode sat on Somerset Road, which in turn lay in the downtown Saddar neighborhood, the pulsing heart of young Karachi. Like the building in which they now lived, and the street on which it stood, Saddar had been an idea coined by the British, and for the hundred or so years they remained there, it existed to serve them. Then called Saddar Bazaar, its grid was laid out by town planners imported from Britain. Shops and cafés lined busy thoroughfares punctuated by rows of quiet streets, forming neat rectangles on carefully drawn maps. Saddar Bazaar made good, orderly sense to colonists set to tame all that was circular about India and its mess of unmarked lanes and alleys. At the center of Saddar's commercial district, laid out in clean lines and in square blocks, stood fancy shops selling goods from Britain to harried memsahibs trying to replicate the joys of home while their husbands civilized the natives of the subcontinent. Beyond the commercial area were quieter streets, some with parks and gardens for recreation, others reserved for the commodious bungalows housing the subcontinent's white sahibs.

With the departure of the British, Saddar had been claimed by the best of Pakistan. The country's first government offices had been located there, and the founder himself, Mohammad Ali Jinnah, had lived in the neighborhood. The shops and cafés and bookstores and libraries had thrived and still glittered at night. Saddar was still where everyone wanted to be and everyone wanted to go. It was the playground of the wealthy in Pakistan's largest city; it pulsed with life, with political debate and poetry competitions. It had hustle and bustle, sophistication and civility.

Beyond Saddar was another Karachi. This Karachi had grown furtively from the seed of long-ago fishing villages alongside its younger, heftier twin. On the same tramline that ran all the way from Keamari Port (where their ship had docked) to Saddar was the red line, which had, in colonial times, divided the European quarter of the city from the native quarter. Two dried-up springs marking two forgotten gates to two long-destroyed forts, marked the border between the two quarters, Kharadar and Meethadar.

There were no straight lines in this other quarter, no grids or demarcations indicating where one could sell and where one could live. Instead, curvaceous porches rose suddenly from squat hovels and women sold garlands of roses and chrysanthemums and jasmine from the barred windows of their bedrooms. The clanging bells of Hindu temples rang through the air and the stench of drying fish from the port mixed with the incense lit at the shrine of a Sufi saint.

It made sense that they had chosen to live in Saddar and not where the natives had lived, for the people of Kharadar and Meethadar would not have been able to understand the logic of the migrants. Those who packed up and left India baffled them; they viewed new borders and new countries with the skepticism of those who have lived through many such constructions. Likewise,

my newly arrived grandparents could not possibly relate to the natives, to the city's history before the British; for it was the British,
after all, who brought them together in this strange place that was
now home.

JULY 15, 1961

The trouble had begun in the 1950s, when Mohammad Ali Bogra,
the prime minister of Pakistan, fell in love with his secretary. No
one begrudged the boss, balding and middle aged, his dalliance.
He was, after all, a powerful man, adept at making the right impression. When he spoke, it was with just enough British vowels
pinned to his Bengali consonants to announce his class, and with
just enough stately reserve to proclaim his pedigree. When he put
on his neatly tailored suits he added a carefully chosen tiepin or a
curious boutonniere: the hint of nonconformity that would lend
him an air of (utterly unthreatening) eccentricity.

It could have been predicted—even expected—that such a master of aesthetic arithmetic would wish to sample the best of what
was available beyond amenities like cigars and wine. The secretary
he romanced was the young Aliya Saadi, selected by the discerning
Mr. Bogra while he served as Pakistan's ambassador to the United
States before he became prime minister.

Despite his savvy with suits, accent, and politics, in the matters
of the heart Mohammad Ali Bogra made a miscalculation. In adding up the delights his new companion could offer, and in glibly
remembering that he, as a Muslim and as prime minister of the
Islamic Republic of Pakistan, was allowed four such companions,
he left out an essential digit. Absent in his calculations were the
measures of fury the woman he had already wed would unleash on
him. This woman, Mr. Bogra's first wife, initiated his undoing by
elevating his second wife to the centerpiece of her new campaign
for women's rights in Pakistan.

Hamida Bogra was a formidable woman who, until being spurned, had spent her time making her own calculations of the most privileged sort and had given birth to two healthy sons. She could pass days selecting just the right hue of pink or orange to be worn to the Governor General's Ball held every spring or deciding on the theme for the annual gala of the Ladies Welfare Association. The leather-bound calendar she carried in an ever-changing round of shiny purses was dotted with meetings and fund-raisers and raffles and teas, all for the benefit of rural villagers, hapless refugees, and poor, widowed women. On any given day she rushed from the opening of a health center in the midst of hovels to a prize-awarding ceremony at a school built for the daughters of the poor, to a fund-raiser at the mayor's mansion. It was a busy life, but the one expected of the first lady of a new country who took her responsibilities as the exemplary Pakistani woman very seriously.

Arriving in this milieu of beneficence, news of her husband's second marriage was a terrible blow. It floored her, leaving scores of school openings and clinic commemorations without a guest of honor, photo opportunities, or a flower bouquet recipient. When the details of her husband's philandering and her own demotion emerged, they gouged even more flesh from the deep wound of her public betrayal. That the woman was white, like the imported white wives of Mughal kings past, lent the affair an ever more hoary form of subservience. If Bogra was any example, the other new Muslim rulers of Pakistan, for all their pretensions of sophistication and urbanity, their bowties and boutonnieres, were now exposed as no different from the harem-hoarding rajahs of empires past.

After the pain came the anger that sparked the campaign for women's rights and set in motion the legislation that would redefine the terms of marriage for women all over Pakistan. Mrs. Bogra declared war against Mr. Bogra and all Pakistani men, who now, new arrivals in a Muslim country, believed that they had suddenly been given a license to marry, in accordance with Quranic injunction, one or two or three or even four women.

Fueled by her fury, the spurned Mrs. Bogra became the martial Mrs. Bogra. As the most famous wife in Pakistan, she gathered around her the wives and daughters and sisters of ministers and ambassadors and army generals and industrialists. They met in drawing rooms of distinction, and over tea in delicate cups of bone china, served by the most silent of servants, they developed their battle plans. In the tragedy of Mrs. Bogra their own vulnerabilities were suddenly exposed, their status as grande dames presiding over the drawing rooms of the country had been put in jeopardy by the alarming prospect of their men picking new wives from among the secretaries and shopgirls and air hostesses of the working world. If India threatened their borders, the women agreed, polygamy threatened their marriages. An Islamic Republic could not be allowed to be a Republic of men, men who could secretly wed again and again and yet again.

Despite the pain of her public abandonment, Mrs. Bogra was astute in her selection of allies, a skill that proved crucial to her eventual success. As her second-in-command she chose a woman as indomitable as herself and just as desirous to see the men of Pakistan put in their place. Begum Raana Liaquat Ali Khan was the wife of a slain prime minister, shot brutally at a public rally two years into Pakistan's existence. As a famous widow known for her floor-sweeping skirts, she already commanded the helm of the All Pakistan Women's Association. Flush with idealism and cash and without a husband to thwart her agenda, Raana Liaquat Ali Khan became Mrs. Bogra's most stalwart supporter, and the All Pakistan Women's Association made advocating a ban on polygamy its fervent cause. Her second choice was just as momentous: Nasim Aurangzeb, the daughter of Pakistan's joint chief of army staff, the gruff and stern General Ayub Khan. If Raana Liaquat Ali Khan owed her power to a husband now gone, Nasim owed hers to a father who was just emerging as Pakistan's newest strongman.

The women started with the obvious: a boycott of all state functions at which the new, white first lady was invited. At the dinner parties to welcome foreign diplomats, the opening of a national university, the inauguration of a new wing of the Pakistan Secretariat, the presence of the interloping new Mrs. Bogra would mean the absence of all the other wives and daughters and mothers. They were the hostesses of Pakistan's elite gatherings, and they correctly calculated that without them the men would be left without the oil to grease their rusty conversations and the twittering laughter for their bumbled jokes. They would be forced, the ladies reasoned, to acknowledge Mr. Bogra's wrongdoing, and by extension the evils of polygamy. The social boycott would be the first step in their efforts to ban polygamy.

When Prime Minister Bogra's government fell in 1959, the women in the drawing rooms did not shed any tears for lost Pakistani democracy. The fall of a polygamist, even if it came at the expense of a downed democracy, was, all agreed, paramount. Indeed, thanks to their efforts the issue of polygamy was now being investigated by a specially appointed committee. One by one Mrs. Bogra and her allies worked on its members, cajoling them with cakes and conversation in their tastefully appointed drawing rooms. A first wife should not find out about her husband's marriage through gossip, they said, nodding seriously as they told the sordid tale of just how suddenly their dear friend had learned of her own husband's betrayal. The law must respect the rights of wives, their power to say no to a husband wanting another.

Their audience was not entirely convinced. The permission for polygamy was, after all, provided in the Quran they told the women. A complete ban would not really be possible; it would anger too many Muslim men who had sacrificed so much to be a part of the Muslim state. In response the women argued that the country belonged not simply to Muslim men but also to Muslim women. Muslim women, they asserted, required security in their marriages, safety against interlopers, and a future that guaranteed their children freedom from abandonment by wandering fathers secretly in search of ever-younger wives. And so the conversations went back and forth and around in circles for one whole year and then two.

In 1961, two years after the ex-prime minister had taken his second wife, General Ayub Khan, the father of Nasim Ayub Khan, became governor general of Pakistan. It was through the military man's election that the campaigning women were finally delivered a victory. The report of the Rashid Commission, whose perspectives the women had tried so hard to influence, was wrought into legislation under the title of the Muslim Family Law Ordinance, Pakistan's first law on the procedures of marriage and divorce. Polygamy could not be forbidden—even the commission had not dared recommend that—but a marriage to a second woman would require permission from the first; and divorce, still unilaterally the prerogative of Pakistani men, had to be registered with the government. The Muslim Family Law Ordinance of 1961 was delivered to General Ayub Khan, the president of Pakistan, by a procession of chanting, victorious women. At the head of the crowd of women was the president's daughter Nasim, who handed over the proposed ordinance to her father, who then promptly signed it into law.

AUGUST 1961

Inside the apartment on Somerset Street, as their parents unpacked, the children hid behind trunks and peered behind the shutters searching for more surprises. As they jumped and slid and yelped, adorning themselves with scrapes and bruises, the grown-ups dusted and arranged the possessions of their old life in their new one. Here is where they discovered one of the first surprises of their reborn existence: the objects of their past didn't work in their present. Tables were too small and tablecloths did not fit; jars that sat just right on old shelves gaped discontentedly from their new perches; pictures looked too small on walls and windows too big against the apologetic daintiness of old curtains.

Unsettled, they looked to food to evoke the soothing familiarity of home. Surrayya, who was now mistress of a four-burner stove and a kitchen in an entirely separate room, set off for the venerable market she had heard about back in Bombay with a red plastic basket in hand and this objective in mind.

Teeming with fruit sellers and bird trappers and butchers whose storefronts were strung with bloody carcasses, the Empress Market drew her in with the same magnetic power it once had over the disbelieving wives of the officers of the East India Company. Surrayya's homesick spirits rose as her plastic basket grew heavier. From rugged, bearded Pashtuns she bought paper cones filled with pine nuts and dried apricots. From dark-skinned Baloch Sidis she bought the freshest red chilies to be ground into the fieriest of fish curries. In plastic bags knotted at the top she carted back creamy pounds of yogurt and butter. There was not only plenty to buy, it was also so inexpensive that she calculated she could buy all she could possibly want and spend only half the rupees she would have in Bombay.

Their first meal of fish and rice was a triumph, the flavors of Bombay replicated with a most satisfactory exactness. The smell of saffron rose from the kitchen, flowed through the home, and filled the pores of the floors and the walls they were trying so hard to colonize into familiarity. The clang of pots and pans did a bit more, adding a comforting cacophony to the morning, afternoon, and evening hours. The first few days were busy with such discoveries, and what time was left in each day was filled with the necessary rites of their new Pakistani citizenship: filling out forms to enroll the children in schools, obtaining identity cards, and registering their new and permanent address.

It was only after all this, after the children were once more settled into the familiar cycle of waking and hurrying to school, and her husband given over to the setting up of meetings and purchases for establishing his new workplace, that Surrayya discovered what would become the harshest revelation she would face as a migrant. The hours between her husband's departure for work and her children's return from school were empty. Days that had once seemed too short, crammed as they were with conversations over window ledges and stair landings, lay fallow and featureless. When she heard the woman upstairs yell at her maid as she strung out the laundry, she wondered if she should visit, exchange a friendly cup of tea. When her brothers visited with their wives and children and two chairs were needed, she thought to tell her son to knock at the next-door neighbors and ask for spare ones to borrow. After the thought and before the act, she paused, and did nothing at all. She did not yet know the rules of living among strangers in Karachi, and she did not yet guess that she would be, now and forever, surrounded by them.

SEPTEMBER 6, 1961

Seven hundred miles northwest of Karachi, and just beyond the Khyber Pass into Afghanistan, the women of the Sulemankhel tribe prepared for their seasonal migration from the high steppes, where they spent the summer months, into the Gomal River valley, where they always spent the winter. Around the fire lit in the corner of a group of tents, shielded as always from the gaze of any wandering tribesmen, daughters, sisters, and wives prepared the morning bread. From a leather skein hung on the frame of the tent, goat milk was emptied into cups to be strained into yogurt and boiled into tea. Dates were laid out on a piece of paper to dry in the sun and then stored under rolled-up tents for the coming winter months. The bells in the folds of their clothes jangled as the women talked and worked. As nomads, the women wore everything they owned on their bodies, ready to move at any moment.

They had been waiting for the winter journey for a long time, and the new moon that marked the journey's intended start had come and gone. The youngest among them had never known the signs of a missed migration, feeling for the first time the frigid chill of the mountain air against their cheeks. Seven or eight nights ago they had prepared to move as they always did, in the groups of five or six families, each with a male elder, gathering their herds of goats and sheep and rolling up the skins of their tents, their one or two plastic suitcases holding what was most precious: the family's Quran, the silver bells that brides wore at their weddings, extra ammunition for the rifles the men slung across their shoulders. The mood had been festive then; the women humming songs they always sung as they packed, old rhymes that reached far into the recesses of their history, paeans to a fondness for leaving.

The mood had deflated with the appearance of an elder and his son, their foreheads creased against the sun of a mountain noon. The women receded into the tents and waited. The men gathered outside, their sentences rising and falling then rising again as they parsed the unexpected news.

A few days earlier the Pakistani Army had shut down the borders for the first time, at least insofar as they could remember, and now the Sulemankhel tribe could not migrate to the Gomal River valley that lay on the other side. There was some dispute with the Afghan government, the soldiers told the Sulemankhel men who had ridden out ahead of the tribe. These bearers of bad news stood on hilltops as familiar to the Sulemankhel as the gray sky suspended above. They carried guns, which they pointed to the Afghan side; they said to the tribesmen that the line between the two countries lay between the two mountains and it was their duty to guard it.

On September 6, 1961, the women waited for news they'd been waiting for every day since the border was closed. The elders had a radio, and they had heard from the little boys wandering between the men and the women that on this day the border was expected to be opened as the Afghans and Pakistanis had sorted out their differences. The women prayed as they kneaded the bread, waiting for the order to move. The older boys hung around at the edge of the camp, a sharp, jagged promontory that looked to the road beyond. At midday the men had appeared again, without glad tidings.

The border had not been reopened. Instead there were more soldiers, the Pakistanis in their khaki uniforms and their American guns cocked and ready, the blue-clad Afghans pointing their Soviet rifles across toward Pakistan. After the news came, the women sat in silence, only the eldest among them speaking. They had to decide what needed to be done to survive a winter in the mountains.

SEPTEMBER 1961

Bohri Bazaar had existed before Partition, but Partition had elevated it to something more. It was the kind of place that could be cultivated only in a city of refugees, who were at once haunted by memories and yet convinced out of necessity that they had arrived at the best of all possible destinations. Narrow stores with dimly lit openings gazed out into winding alleys full of shoppers. At the mouth of each sat men whose fortunes rested on filling the unspoken longings of wandering customers. In this sense, the shopkeepers of Bohri Bazaar were magicians, their art the ability to satisfy the desire for the artifacts of lives left behind—a copper vase for the memory of the flowers that grew profusely in some faraway village, a glass bangle in the hue of an old front door. By 1961 they had perfected their skills: Delhi was in the aluminum pans and Agra in the incense sticks; the villages of Uttar Pradesh lay hidden in the folds of fabric and Hyderabad sat in the spices. No matter what part of India had been left behind, it was contained within Bohri Bazaar and available for a few rupees.

Surrayya was their ideal customer, consuming not simply the wares but the contact, relishing the comfort of a polite exchange, which was still lacking in her new home. And so she came again and again, to buy one thing or to return another, and they began to call out to her with the respectful "Begum Sahiba" reserved for a married woman of means. If she stopped even for a second, merchants began to unfurl sari after sari or lay out elaborately crocheted tablecloths, pristine white cotton for my grandfather's shirts, dazzling jewel-colored *dupattas* for Amina and her sisters. From yellowing muslin-wrapped bundles in the inner depths of their stores they produced leather sandals and wooden clogs that my father and grandfather could wear to the mosque every Friday. In the hemming and hawing, the haggling, the disinterest she feigned to shave off some rupees and annas from the price, her stern admonitions to stop a shopkeeper's goading, Surrayya found something to fill the hours. She grew to love the rush of buying something and making it her own.

In the flush of this romance, she filled her home with piles of brown paper wrapped packages. A white enameled steel cupboard was delivered one morning; a shiny wood coffee table on another. The kitchen that had had only a few heavy copper pots and pans was now filled with stainless-steel lidded pots and storage bins and delicate plates of bone china. A new set of glasses appeared one day, and a set of wooden spoons for stirring pots of lentils on another. Before long, the family found itself eating not at the wooden pallet with stools that stood only a few inches from the ground but around a new dining table fuming with furniture polish that rubbed off under their fingertips until a clean sheet of vinyl was cut to size to cover it. In Pakistan everything was new, and nothing like it had ever been before.

AUGUST 1947

Not all the men who came to the new country relished the possibility of many wives. Pakistan's first governor, General Mohammad Ali Jinnah, came fleeing the memory of one who had, for just a few moments, lit his solitary life with laughter.

Ruttie Jinnah, the lost love of Pakistan's creator, was a child of Bombay. Daughter of one of the richest Parsi businessmen in the city, Sir Dinshaw Petit, she met Jinnah, already a middle-aged man, and fell in love with him. To marry him, she defied her family, who thought he was too old, too stern, and too Muslim. He too defied the expectations of many Muslims by not picking a Muslim girl from a Muslim family. For Jinnah, Ruttie left her dilettante free-doms, the whirl of parties and adulation and admirers. She also left the name that her parents had given her, transforming from Ruttie, the ravishing girl rebel of Bombay society, to Maryam, the Muslim wife at the side of the leader of the Muslims. He vowed to change his stern and ascetic life and to accommodate the warmth and laughter of his eighteen-year-old bride, who until then had been called "the flower of Bombay."

They married at the Jama Masjid in Bombay in 1918. All the talk around them was about solidarity, of the need of Hindus and Muslims and Parsis and all those living under the yoke of British colonialism to unite under the vast and shady umbrella of a shared anticolonialism. The solidarity did not shelter them. Ruttie's father refused to speak to his daughter after her marriage. In Jinnah's camp, the secretly disgruntled spread rumors that the leader of the Muslims had not had a Muslim marriage at all, but a civil ceremony in a court where there was no Muslim *kazi* and no Quran.

It was not the censures of others that did them in, but perhaps the difficulty of making a life together in times too tumultuous for the ordinary rituals of intimacy. At first it was just as it should be. She moved in and changed the décor of his dour bachelor quarters. He tried to be home earlier and to indulge her little whims. But before long he was taken by the demands of leadership, by the drama of driving out the British colonialists, by concerns larger than the world of two that she wished to inhabit. The bloom on the new Maryam began to fade and with it the marriage began to wither. The birth of a child could not save it; Pakistan and Ruttie both seemed to want all of Mohammad Ali Jinnah, and perhaps Mohammad Ali Jinnah believed that Ruttie would still be there after he had won Pakistan.

She was not. Her decline, borne of her loss of love, her betrayal at the hands of the man who had chosen the task of making a country over making a marriage was not only a metaphor. Like the flower unthinkingly plucked, loneliness drooped around Mrs.

Jinnah. In private there may have been entreaties and arguments, pleas for help and promises to do better. In public there was only a parting. In September 1922, Ruttie Jinnah packed her bags and her baby and set out for London. She returned to India and to Bombay eventually, but it was the first of many endings to their relationship. By September 1927 the couple lived apart.

Love could not overcome. The death of her marriage became death itself for Ruttie Jinnah. Unable to wrest the only man she wanted from his political commitments, the girl who had all her life been feted and fretted over, coveted and coddled, whose wit and charm and beauty were all legendary, fell ill.

It is said that when the end was close, both men who had abandoned her returned to her bedside. Her father, who had refused to see her when she married Jinnah, forgave his daughter and supported her in her last days as an ailing recluse locked up at the Taj Hotel in Bombay. Her husband, Mohammad Ali Jinnah, wept at her bedside when he saw her life slipping away, when he realized it was too late to save her. In her last letter to him she wrote,

> When one has been as near to the reality of Life (which after all is Death) as I have been dearest, one only remembers the beautiful and tender moments and all the rest becomes a half veiled mist of unrealities. Try and remember me beloved as the flower you plucked and not the flower you tread upon . . . . Darling I love you—I love you—and had I loved you just a little less I might have remained with you—only after one has created a very beautiful blossom one does not drag it through the mire. The higher you set your ideal the lower it falls. I have loved you my darling as it is given to few men to be loved. I only beseech you that the tragedy which commenced in love should also end with it. . . .

Ruttie Jinnah died on February 20, 1929. She was buried in one of Bombay's Muslim cemeteries. It was here that Mohammad Ali Jinnah visited her in August 1947, in the days before he left for Karachi, the last days he would ever spend in Bombay. Here at the grave of the woman he had lost, for the sake of the country he had to create, Mohammad Ali Jinnah, was said to have wept. One year later, he too would lie dying, far away in newborn Pakistan. In September 1948, almost twenty years after the death of Ruttie Jinnah, he too would be gone.

Mohammad Ali Jinnah had gained a country but lost his love. He was buried in the center of Karachi, and over his grave a pristine white mausoleum of marble was built. Its unblemished dome could be seen far and wide. Mohammad Ali Jinnah came to Pakistan to die, and in death, he belonged to Pakistan. The children of Pakistan learned a lot about him, about his education, his political acumen, his strategic prowess; but we never ever learned about his (non-Muslim) wife, about the woman he had loved.

SEPTEMBER 1965

Surrayya, Said, and their children found out about the war from the evening transmission of Radio Pakistan. All three sisters, still wearing their blue and white school uniforms, sat cross-legged on the floor. Each word General Ayub Khan said on the radio echoed three times: once from the neighbor's radio upstairs, another time from the watchman's radio outside, and finally from the radio sitting stolidly before them, its top protectively covered by a dust cloth embroidered with flowers. The echo made the general's words, already clipped and terse, even more ominous; their commanding weight making the sisters' already-frightened faces even more sober. It was hot, but they threw their arms around one another, drawing together against some invisible invasion.

Indian forces had attacked Pakistan early that morning, General Ayub told them, nearly making it into Lahore, the capital of Punjab. "The situation was dire, and the Pakistanis had to unite," he admonished from the radio, as if the girls' squabbles over sharing hairclips and shoes were directly responsible for the Indian advance. By the time he got to the end, exhorting the "forces of faith to rally and defeat the Indian Army," they were reduced and diminished, it seemed, to half their bony size.

The words rattled inside the girls' heads. Outside, the honking tramcars and carts had also paused. Even the busiest of businessmen and hawkers and bus conductors were huddling around sidewalk radios to confirm if the talk of war had been true, if the Indian Army was indeed poised to take back Pakistan, if their world truly stood at the brink of destruction. And then in an instant, the moment of silence was gone and the city erupted once again. The call to prayer, a minute late, rose up as always from the first, the second, and then the third mosque. The hum of traffic resumed, returning the vibration that filtered in from the street to its usual cadences. The children who lived a few floors above them rushed down the stairs shouting "It's war!" with the same enthusiasm they called out for the ice seller, who sometimes also hawked sticks of ice cream.

News of the war had actually been pulsing through the rhythms of the girls' day. That morning the headmistress of Amina's school, a portly lady who wore her glasses on a silver chain and had at all times of the day a balled-up handkerchief in her cleavage, had appeared at the morning assembly with even more than her usual air of pedantic gravity. Placing her dangling glasses on her nose, she had surveyed the sea of white-scarved girls with the solemnity of one whose belief in the inevitability of ruin had been vindicated by disaster. "The country is in crisis, girls," she told the scrubbed faces before her. "The future of the nation is in jeopardy." For the remainder of the announcement, the glasses were removed. The girls heard only the first few words of "the school will be closed" announcement; the rest was lost in the din of the young being swept into an unexpected holiday.

At home, battle had been underway all day. The building on Somerset Street had four tenants. Those in the ground floor apartment were last in line for the water that flowed from the rooftop tank and into the taps. Until that day the arrangement had been unexamined, an acceptance borne of plenty. A night of war talk was enough to gut this neighborly tolerance. The trouble started at the top. On that airy floor lived a mother of six, who, tormented by the helplessness of inactivity before great crisis, decided that she must hoard water for her little ones. It was, she convinced herself, a requirement for survival in wartime.

She started early, gathering every receptacle she could find, filling pots and pans and plastic buckets and ceramic bowls and china teapots. It took a while for the consequences of her plans to trickle down. At around ten o'clock, when my grandmother was getting ready to start a pot of rice, she opened the large faucet in her kitchen sink. It responded with a stony silence. She stood for a while before the dry tap, considering if this was an aberration, a delay, or some kind of air-blocked pipe.

By the time the girls returned from school at noon, the water war had settled into a begrudging truce. Mr. DeSouza, a man old enough to get the angry housewives to listen, even if he was unable to convince them that water would not suddenly stop at the beginning of war, had intervened when the women's squabbling threatened to interrupt the one o'clock news broadcast. The women, each now convinced that storing water for their children was absolutely necessary, insisted on a system. Mr. DeSouza devised it and put it into place.

It was decided that when the tank was full again, one family at a time would be allowed to fill their buckets while the others waited. Because the bottom flat had had no water since the morning, it was first. When Amina walked in after being sent home from school, it was precisely when the tank on the roof had filled again and the taps flowed flush. Within seconds, the girls were drafted into the task of amassing water for war. The first step was to collect every container capable of holding it, buckets and glasses and pitchers and jugs and carafes and bottles. Each sister manned a faucet, and Surrayya stood before the kitchen sink. With her shouted orders the filling began.

By dusk, when the announcement of war was broadcast on Radio Pakistan by General Ayub Khan, buckets, pots, bowls, and trunks full of water were everywhere. They were lined up and down the hallway, the red bucket for washing clothes, the green tubs that had once held potatoes and onions, even the pink bucket that was a bathtub for the family dolls. The counters and shelves lining the other rooms held bowls of water big and small, bottles of all shapes and sizes, all full to the brim and standing ready for the time their last drops would be cherished after the dry days of war.

The tenants followed the arrangement for six days, hoarding water one by one for each day of war, emptying buckets and bowls to wash in the hours when the filling schedules of other apartments made their taps run dry. The schedule they had put in place so skewed the system that there was no way to tell whether the water supply was ever really interrupted—whether after the first announcement of war, after news of air raids, or during rumors of a ceasefire. They stuck to their plan, convinced of its necessity.

On September 12, 1965, another radio broadcast announced that the war was over. A whole twenty-four hours later, on September 13, the lady on the top floor decided that the news of peace was true. She drained the unused buckets and bottles of water she had stored overnight into the sink and decided not to refill them, and the building was restored to the plenty of peacetime.

JULY 8, 1967

Mohammad Ali Jinnah had come to Karachi in 1947 with a woman who would be acceptable to the new nation. His sister, Fatima Jinnah, had at that point kept house for her brother for years; after he was gone, she would become the first to contest elections for the country's highest office. A trained dentist and an educated woman at a time when few Indian Muslim women were, Fatima Jinnah had reveled in the role of "Mother of the Republic," never balking at the contradiction that she had not ever married or borne any children of her own. Perhaps it had not mattered as much then, or perhaps people accepted that her child was really Pakistan, the country her brother had wrought from the British. Her demure presence at the elbow of her brother was acceptable to all, even in the contentious moments that preceded Pakistan's birth: her clothes were modest enough to please the mullahs yet sophisticated enough to reassure those who swore by secularism. It was Fatima Jinnah, in pastel tunics and flared floor-length skirts, who presided over state functions at which her brother and the new country required a hostess. It was Fatima Jinnah who tended to the dying Jinnah when he took to his bed one year after Pakistan was born. It was her face, wan and worn, that flashed on news clips across the world at the founder's death.

Two decades later, in 1967, Fatima Jinnah had been pushed to the margins of the city she had presided over in its first days as Pakistan's capital. No longer the sister of the governor general, she lived all alone at the edge of Karachi in a red stone palace near the sea. From here she would make her last heroic effort, contesting elections against the military general Ayub Khan. This woman who was running for office against men could not, however, command the support of other powerful women. When Hamida Bogra's women had begun their campaign against polygamous husbands, they had deliberately chosen to ignore Fatima Jinnah. The virginal spinster sister of the dead founder was of no use to them. How could she, never having been married, understand the fury of a betrayed wife? That sentiment was one reason for their exclusion; the robust other reasons were political. Fatima Jinnah's rival for the position of governor general of Pakistan was General Ayub Khan, the military man who was the father of Mrs. Bogra's friend Nasim Aurangzeb, one of the chief campaigners against polygamy in the new Pakistan.

So the backs of the women who championed women's rights remained turned to the woman who was Pakistan's first female candidate for governor general. They remained averted after she lost to the general and after he signed into law legislation that required men to receive permission from their existing wives before marrying another. So Fatima Jinnah, alive but forgotten, receded further and further from the political consciousness of the country her brother had founded. No one seemed to know or care when or why she moved to Mohatta Palace and shut herself up alone in its twenty-four rooms.

The palace had its own story. Its eerie pink domes and elaborately carved terraces were a remembrance of Shivrattan Mohatta, the Hindu businessman who had lived there before Partition took it from him. The palace had been his summer home at a time when the Arabian Sea, not yet pushed back by land reclamations, crashed its turbulent waves before the palace's front lawn.

In 1947 Pakistan's Ministry of Foreign Affairs requisitioned Mohatta Palace. When Shivrattan Mohatta had wept, no one had listened. When at a state function for Karachi businessmen, the homeless magnate managed to get a minute next to Jinnah, he used it to intercede for his house. He received no sympathy; the founder had himself given up too much. "It is a matter of state," he simply said before walking off.

Nearly twenty years from the day Jinnah uttered those words, his sister found herself in a similar position of wanting. The Pakistan she had heralded at the side of her brother as an independent, democratic, and progressive republic for the subcontinent's Muslims was ruled by a military dictator and rife with ethnic enmities. The spats with India, in 1948 and again in 1965, fomented an attitude of permanent siege that justified routine suspensions of the law and an unquestioning worship of the military. The generals hated her because she touted democracy, and the mullahs now denounced her because she, once merely the sister of a leader, had had the audacity to try to be one herself.

Made incongruous by the country's new reality that had erupted around her, Fatima Jinnah became a relic and a recluse. By the summer of 1967, the woman who had for decades led the most public of lives, instrumental in the ideological contest against the British and fervent in her political maneuvering and visions of Pakistan's future, shut herself up in the quaint palace hoping perhaps to disappear among its looping porches and porticoes. If anyone in Karachi noticed her absence, they said nothing at all about it. Every night she locked herself in the second-story bedroom she had chosen in Mohatta Palace. Every morning when she awoke, she dropped the key from the balcony upstairs so that her attendant below could retrieve it and bring her morning tea.

On the morning of July 9, 1967, no key dropped from the bedroom balcony. No one minded and no one cared. The gardener let himself in and watered the lawns, not giving the old woman a second thought when he didn't see her. Noon passed and then also the afternoon. It was evening when the washerwoman who did Fatima Jinnah's laundry finally called on a neighbor with her worries about the mistress. It was near dusk by the time a locksmith was called and the door opened. Inside her bedroom, Fatima Jinnah lay cold, having passed away hours before she was found.

She left behind a small poodle, a goat, and a duck. A funeral was held on the grounds of Mohatta Palace the next morning. Hundreds of mourners—dignitaries and bureaucrats and politicians and their wives—came and sighed and waited to be photographed. Karachi in July was brutally hot, so fiery that even the electric fans and the nearby ocean could not alleviate the heat under the tents. By early evening, everyone was gone. At dusk on July 9, 1967, Mohatta Palace was shuttered up and left to the stray gulls and thorny bushes. It would remain that way for decades, with all who wanted it unsure of the strength of their claim, or of its wisdom, and whether it must be bought from the distant descendants of the Jinnahs, the government of Pakistan, or even the descendants of the Mohattas, now scattered somewhere across the border in India. It could have been given to Dina, the daughter of Mohammad Ali Jinnah. But she had stayed in India after the birth of Pakistan, stayed an Indian and then married a non-Muslim against her father's wishes. Under the inheritance calculations of the laws of the Islamic Republic, she was not entitled to what either her father or her aunt left behind.

CHAPTER 4

A Suburban Wedding

NOVEMBER 13, 1970

In the decades after Partition, East Pakistan was dotted with rice paddies and jute fields, its lush fecundity itself a rebellion against the craggy plains of its western twin. The two deltas of the Ganges and Brahmaputra Rivers meet here after having watered India and before emptying into the Bay of Bengal. They made East Pakistan the food bowl that fed the famished of the West in the decades after Partition. West Pakistanis—in Lahore and Karachi and Faisalabad—were happy enough to eat the rice and weave the cotton and jute in their newly built factories. But in their desert-fringed, mountain-topped part of Pakistan, they could not picture with any accuracy the life of the farmer who trudged waist deep in standing water, harvesting the slivers of grain they cooked in their pots. The darker, smaller Bengali was to many an alien. Bengalis spoke a different language: neither the brash Punjabi that echoed through the barracks of Pakistan's growing army nor the pedigreed Urdu, peppered with Persian and Arabic, that was spoken by the bureaucrats and industrialists fattened from the spoils of Partition.

The fishermen of Karachi looked out on a different sea, the Arabian Sea that led westward to Mecca and to the Western world. When the dawn came rolling off the silvery gray waters in the morning chill of November 13, 1970, they set out in their boats as usual, their gazes averted from the unseen, unknown, other half of their country, which they had been told existed across the vast Indian peninsula in the middle. In tattered red and blue sweaters they climbed on the hulls of boats and dinghies hung with nets and trinkets, murmuring the centuries-old prayer and chewing on tobacco that always remained tucked in the pockets of their cheeks. They looked at the movement of the water to decide where the fish would be, deducing their daily earnings. Shouts of exasperation inevitably followed when the drawn-up nets carried less in their folds than they had hoped.

As the sun melted the mist that settled over the sea, the bulbous dome of the shrine of Abdullah Shah Ghazi could be seen from a sandy hill that rose over the ocean. The saint had arrived on an Arab trading ship centuries before there was a city or a country, but every fisherman on the shores of Karachi looked to him for protection. For as long as Abdullah Shah Ghazi's dome cast its shadow on Karachi's shoreline, the city, they believed, would be saved from the anger of the sea.

East Pakistan had no such protection. The water simply licked Bhola Island's shore at the mouth of the Bay of Bengal, taunting sleeping fishermen families with the secret knowledge of coming devastation. They did not wake, so they did not know. That November morning in 1970 Cyclone Bhola hit them hard. Minutes earlier the Pakistan Meteorological Department, its staff stunned by the frantic beeping of instruments nearly always silent, had issued a warning, but for the fishermen sleeping in the reed huts, it was too late.

The giant tidal wave spawned by the storm swept over the fishermen and their families and the rice paddies and the general stores and neighborhood schools and mosques. It carried away beds and fishing boats and brides and brothers. In its first landfall, the cyclone swallowed an entire island. Continuing to the shores of East Pakistan, Cyclone Bhola hit the port of Chittagong, its inhabitants awake but just as unprepared. The living now knowingly waited for their end; mothers clutching babies and helpless fathers clambering onto low rooftops.

Before it receded, Cyclone Bhola swallowed more than half a million people, drawing them into the depths of the sea before it spit them out onto the devastated shores. There was little communication or news about those engulfed. The *Times of India*, the largest newspaper close to the affected region, did not report the disaster until November 15, 1970, a full two days after the cyclone first hit. Its report simply stated that on the night of November 12 a twenty-foot-high storm surge had hit the island of Bhola off the coast of East Pakistan. Two-hundred-mile-per-hour winds had destroyed anything that the storm failed to swallow. Bhola Island, Hatiya Island, and many other small pieces of Pakistan existed no more. The news of the disaster and its hundreds of thousands of casualties was not published in West Pakistan until three whole days and three whole nights after the disaster.

NOVEMBER 1970

The plot of land on which the house would be built was purchased in November 1970. It was a neat, rectangular slice of Karachi gravel, sand, and rock topped by some stray, sulking trees. An outline had been set by a decisive chalk stripe, the four corners of the lot punctuated with little red flags like the kind used to mark open sewers on other city streets. "Make sure you have all the papers," Surrayya would say to Said every time he went to meet with the land broker, for the first or the second or the tenth meeting. There was a meeting to look at the land survey, a meeting to discuss the price, a meeting with the clerk at the recorder's office, a meeting with the city council's representative to discuss the tax liability.

At each meeting, two or three wads of paper would be solemnly entrusted to Said. They detailed the location of the land by its physical markers, the dimensions and descriptions written in Urdu and English and authenticated by seals in various inks. There were also maps printed on carbon paper, filigrees of purple ink with red circles around the names of owners. There were bank statements that showed the transactions by which the surveyor had been paid and receipts for the construction, electrical, and plumbing permits.

A special shelf in the white metal armoire kept in the living room was dedicated to these papers. The piles grew taller, the files grew fatter, and new files were purchased for new papers. On the evening after each meeting, as the bubbles of curry began to rise in the kitchen pots and the headlights of cars began flashing into the living room windows as darkness fell, Said would carefully lay out the papers he had collected that day. A place would be found in the correct file—the bank file, the registration file, the tax file, or the extra file—for the new sheets he had carried home under his arm. Each sheet, new or old, sang its own song of reassurance that the house was more than just an idea. He kept two copies of each document: a copy of the original, and then a copy of the copy. If one paper was lost, there would be another and yet another, and together they would avert the catastrophe of lost houses.

The land was part of a "Co-operative Housing Society" where all the migrants who had made it were headed to build dream homes. Just like the shopkeepers of Bohri Bazaar, who knew to appeal to the homesick hearts of their customers, some enterprising developers in Karachi had devised the idea of selling plots of land to communities of migrants craving togetherness. Karachi's surfeit of undeveloped land was enough to allow each little gaggle of migrants from Delhi or Kathiawar or Gujarat to purchase a piece as a cooperative. The cooperative structure of limiting the purchasers to members of the community insured that only migrants from their own Indian corner would live around them.

Thus the glue that had once held them together as Muslims living in a Hindu land would again keep them together as Gujaratis or Memons living in a Muslim land. It was a winning mix of ownership and exclusivity, the definition of having it all: the promise of migration without the loss of community. The Kokanis from around the Jama Masjid in Bombay and adjoining villages eagerly bought into the project. In the housing society was the possibility of recreating the old ways in the new land, living again without boundaries between homes, where all neighbors were cousins or aunts, and all that was mine was also yours.

When dinner was done and while the girls were putting the dishes away or retreating to their rooms, Said would bring out the papers and show them to his wife. Chewing on the fennel seeds she always kept at her bedside, would look them over again with him, her mouth and mind churning in synchrony. Together they pored over the inky details like children rapt by the designs of a kaleidoscope. Neither had ever owned a house or even lived in one not shared with many others. To give his wife an idea of the numbers, the grand dimensions of the rooms drawn neatly on the plans, Said would add his explanations, multiplying the dimensions of their bedroom or living room, "Two times this" or "Five times that," to help her imagine just how much roomier the future was going to be.

Not used to having choices, they agonized over each one. There were so many: the color of the stucco, the shades of the interior paint, whether to have attached bathrooms for every bedroom or just more bedrooms with common bathrooms. Should there be mosaics on the marble floors or just plain polished marble, one faucet with two handles or two faucets with one handle each? The dilemmas were numerous. Sometimes the answers would be gathered from the memories of past longings—the house Said had passed on the street on his way to work in Bombay or one Surrayya had seen in a movie when she was sixteen. To this they added the imperatives of outdoing or at least matching the grand houses of Surrayya's brothers, with their sweeping staircases, marble porches, and commodious servants' quarters.

Their neighborhood's fall from grace in Said and Surrayya's dazzled eyes began the second the plot for the suburban house was purchased. The din that rose from the streets every morning in their first years in Karachi, so reminiscent of the sounds they had left behind, was now a source of agitation. The crowds had got out of control, they insisted to each other, and the streets reeked of rubbish. No sudden siren, no stench of rotting fruit, no overflowing trash bin escaped their notice. As they prepared to leave Karachi, the couple ladled the burdens of a million failures on Saddar, just as they had taught themselves to loathe Bombay in the months before they left it forever.

DECEMBER 7, 1970

One month of sunrises had failed to dry the sodden earth of East Pakistan, leaving millions crouching in damp, sea-soaked shanties or simply gaping at the sky. On December 7, 1970, one month after Cyclone Bhola killed nearly five hundred thousand, elections were held in East and West Pakistan. Up for election were all the members of Parliament; the leader whose party won the most seats would be the next prime minister of Pakistan. It was also the first time women were voting.

It was not feasible to postpone the election, the fiery foreign minister Zulfikar Ali Bhutto insisted to General Yahya Khan, the military man who had vowed to oversee Pakistan's return to democracy. The date for the election had been set before the cyclone, he reminded him, and nature could not be allowed to thwart the progress of democracy. It was not fair, after all, to deprive people of their chance to choose leaders, especially after they have been rendered so powerless before the vagaries of nature. In the dry comfort of West Pakistan, Bhutto's newly formed Pakistan People's Party was riding the crest of his political ascent, turning out thousands of supporters and covering Karachi in their green, red, and black. The Pakistan People's Party was ready for people to vote, and their leader had the ear of the general who would decide when voting would take place.

The votes cast in East Pakistan may have been soaked with water falling from eyes or rising up from the sea, but they were cast nevertheless. According to estimates, more than three-quarters of the voters were still without shelter, food, or medicine; they were wracked with the cholera and malaria that surged in the wake of the cyclone and unsure of where they would go after they cast their vote. Nevertheless, they had rescued their blurred identification cards and dried them in the sun as they sat on the wreckage of legless tables and broken beds. However bereft, the voters of East Pakistan voted, pressing their ink-stained thumbs onto the ballots. When elections were held on December 7, 1971, thirty-one million East Pakistanis went to the polls to choose 169 members of Pakistan's Parliament.

When the results were tabulated, it was these voters who had won. Nearly everyone in East Pakistan had voted for Sheikh Mujibur Rahman, the Bengali leader who had given voice to their discontent and talked of an identity all their own, one that did not force another language down their throats, another unconcerned leader over their heads. Zulfikar Ali Bhutto had failed to win a single seat in East Pakistan but had managed a majority in the West. Bhutto's victory did not matter, though; with 169 seats, Sheikh Mujib had amassed enough of a mandate from his storm-soaked supporters to form a government and rule over both halves of a split country.

DECEMBER 1970

Amina was the first of her family to attend college. Every day, between eight or nine in the morning, under her mother's watchful eye, Amina walked out the door and stepped onto the bus that carried girls from different parts of Karachi to their classes at Khatoon-e-Pakistan Girls College in a different part of the city.

Surrayya, never having left home alone as a girl, did not know how to say good-bye to an unmarried daughter. Her own formal education had ended when she was deemed too old to attend the neighborhood school reserved for the Muslim girls in the community. After that, Surrayya's learning had centered on preparing to be a good wife. She had practiced cooking complicated curries, was scolded when she burned spices in oil that was too hot or failed to chop onions thinly or thickly enough. On other days she tended the babies of older cousins, learning to wash their bodies and treat their minor ailments with home remedies. If any idle hours remained, they had been spent embroidering tablecloths, darning her brothers' socks, and crocheting purses and handkerchiefs.

So it had been for her mother and her grandmother before her. Even the neighborhood school had been a new experience, borne of the belated Muslim awakening to literacy preached by reformers like Sir Syed Ahmed Khan and others, which happened just in time for Amina to go to school. Surrayya's own mother had not been educated at all, taught simply to write a few words, to count out a dozen tomatoes, or to hand out the right number of coins to the man who washed the bed linen at the laundry ghats outside the city. This wasn't just the case with women. Surrayya's grandfather and father had never been to an actual school, having instead been educated by an *ustad*, or teacher, who taught them Urdu, Persian, and Arabic and how to read Ottoman texts, the Holy Quran, and the exegeses of various Islamic scholars. They had followed in the footsteps of preceding generations, unwilling to let go of the legacy of traditional Muslim scholarship that had flourished for centuries under Mughal rule.

Cupping their hands around the flickering flames of the Mughal Empire's melting candles, Muslims came late to the realization that the market for scribes and calligraphers in Persian and Arabic was coming to the end. It was Surrayya's brothers who first insisted that they needed a Western-style education in a school, and her father realized that his sons were right. Best to teach them the new order from the start, he reasoned, than to rely, as he had, on learning the ways of business and British bureaucracy on the go. The boys would go to a real school, and there was no harm in sending the girls too, at least while they were still little, when the classes were held away from the predatory eyes of boys.

Putting a daughter on a bus felt premature to Surrayya. Each morning brought a new fear to her collection of trepidations, each one more dismal than before. What if the bus driver—the only man on the bus—decided to abscond with all the girls, selling them off to strange men who bought and sold young girls? Or, what if the driver lost control of the bus, scattering its precious virgin cargo in the midst of a world full of men? As the bus drove down streets and lanes she did not know, her visions became darker still. She muttered prayer after prayer and ended each one with an invocation that her daughter Amina be returned pure and untouched.

MARCH 24, 1971—DHAKA UNIVERSITY

In 1971 Dhaka was the capital city of East Pakistan, and Rokeya Hall towered over the flat campus of Dhaka University. It was named after Begum Rokeya Hussain, a woman who had been one of the first Indian women to write a story in English. Her work, "Sultana's Dream," told of a world where men and not women were sequestered. In 1971 the female students of Dhaka University lived in Rokeya Hall still separated from the men, but farther along than Rokeya had been in their quest for an education. Drawn from single-car villages along silt-filled rivers, from almost-cities in the distant north of East Pakistan, these girls with dark braids dangling down their backs marched in and out of Rokeya Hall all day. Some rushed to class, some to mail letters, others to make short, scratchy phone calls home from the main campus office, exchanging details of arrivals and departures with parents far away.

Behind the girls was a long spool of history that explained how they had managed to come so far without slipping into the dark, unmarriageable place that lay beyond respectability. Its central pillar was that young women had been coming to Dhaka University for a very long time. The first had come in the early 1920s. In 1938 university officials decided that boarding facilities were necessary for the girls whose parents were committed enough to higher education to send them to Dhaka University. In these special quarters, they imagined, the girls could stay on campus under the care of female teachers who would be hired based on their ability to properly oversee their female charges and provide reassuring support to worried parents. It took awhile for the idea to catch on, so when it was first set up, Rokeya Hall housed only twelve women. Over the years, as the cause of Muslim women's education gained popularity, its population swelled. Ambitious Bengali families began to send their daughters to Dhaka University, having been assured that the rules and regulations placed a complete ban on male visitors, and that the vigilance of the floor wardens, along with the supportive presence of other girls from respectable families, would maintain the separation.

In the days leading to Sheikh Mujib's victory, Dhaka University had been transformed into the focal point of a nationalist insurgency that sought an independent Bangladesh. Student groups held rallies in dormitories and fiery-faced faculty and Bengali intellectuals gave political speeches in lecture halls that resonated deeply with the angry hearts of the young born after Partition. Like a well-knitted glove, this revolution fit every contour of their discontent, transforming them into rebels with its promises of change and self-realization. Young women discarded the languid, boy-shy veneer they initially brought to campus, replacing it with the martial resolve of warriors. On floors littered with pamphlets they took turns marching in line, and in step, their dark hair tucked away as if dispensing with the luxuries of peacetime. Instead of rifles the girls carried sticks, their cries of "Joy Bangla" ("Long live the Bangla nation") echoing through the open windows of lecture halls and cafeterias. It was a cry for freedom in the native Bengali of East Pakistan.

Almost all were Muslim girls, complete in their devotion to the Mukti Bahini, or the Chattra League, and its freedom cause. Not that there weren't individuals who remained concerned about the respectability of girls marching in streets, of long nights of rallies, of the closeness to the boys with whom they sang songs for independence, and plastered walls and posters and posts. But those weren't the women who came to Rokeya Hall in those years. Rokeya Hall was home to the bravest and most rebellious, and all of them wanted independence and the creation of Bangladesh.

On the night of March 24, 1971, Rokeya Hall was suddenly silent, standing dark and severe against the rise of the smoke that engulfed it. Nearly all the girls had left for safer places as the news of an operation by the Pakistani military reached campus. Ordered to do so by their bosses in West Pakistan, the Pakistani military were out to capture Bengali nationalists they believed were hiding on the Dhaka University campus. Warned of the coming raid, the girls of Rokeya Hall had left as if they would return, trailing smells of the coconut oil that they used to smooth the braids and knots of their hair and the tea they made in the middle of the night.

A sliver or two of light still emanated from rooms deep inside the building. Of the nearly eight hundred girls who filtered in and out of the doors and up and down the corridors of Rokeya Hall, only seven remained, all casualties of unforeseen circumstances or misunderstood plans. They huddled now with the ten or so hostel staff in the little house of their provost Begum Akhtar Imam. The woman who had clasped their parents' hands, telling them she would take care of each and every one like her own, now sheltered the girls in her home just a few steps away from the Hall. At dusk, when the phones of the university went dead, they knew the soldiers would come soon, and as evening descended into night they could hear them, the gruff droning of their jeeps, the clanking of bayonets growing closer and closer to the thin walls behind which they sat.

It was late evening when they finally arrived. The men in khaki from the Pakistan Army had already been to Rokeya Hall, hoping for a bounty of virgin spoils. They had ravished the empty rooms, turning over the beds and stripping the cupboards and roughly pushing the tables and chairs against the walls. When they arrived at the door of the provost, they came with the rage of men denied and duped. They fired through the gate and shattered the frail lock on the front door and the glass on the windows. At the entrance to the house they confronted Begum Akhtar Imam, their guns cocked and ready. The girls hid in the back rooms of the house and heard the men say, "Where are the girls?" once, twice, and then a third time. "The girls are gone," Begum Akhtar replied, "the girls are all gone." They left without coming inside.

It was not over. A few hours later another storm of khaki prowling the dark campus appeared at the house of the provost. This second time she could not keep them from flooding the house with their guns and gazes. They went through the kitchen, the drawing room, and the bedrooms, lining up against the wall the women they found. They asked for guns they could not find, for the rifles and mortars and bayonets they had been told would be hidden there, under beds and behind crying women. When they found none, they grew angrier, breaking the leg of a chair here, smashing the surface of a tea table there. The soles of their boots crunched on the porcelain splinters of fallen teacups and kicked shards of plywood. "Where are the women," they asked again, "the hundreds of women of Rokeya Hall?" No one answered them, and they continued to smash and break. Again and again they did this, until finally some beneficent order from their superior, or perhaps a vague premonition of dawn in the silent sky, took them away. All the women survived that night, and as soon as they could, the seven girls from Rokeya Hall were sent back to their families.

APRIL 1971

The dangers invoked by her mother settled before Amina's eyes like a glass lens between her and the city. As the bus wove through Karachi streets she saw the men waiting for the girls. These were the crude village men, in gray or white or black tunics of the villages to the north, their eyes drinking up the girls' fresh faces, unable to stop themselves from rolling out their tongues. She could see them swarming the bus, trying to get inside.

It was not only rough-hewn peasants and migrant workers who longed for the bus full of college girls as a respite from their woman-deprived existence on city sidewalks and dusty construction sites. Some of the better-equipped hunters, who poured out from tidy houses or glared from the windows of cars along the route, employed more evolved strategies. Wearing crisp shirts ironed by the women in their family, they craned their necks to catch a girl's glance and blow an unwanted kiss. These predators looked just like the brothers and fathers and cousins the girls knew, some with fashionably shaggy hair, wide collars, and flared pant bottoms; others with only urgent desire; all of them wanting what was inside.

It took several months of bus trips between home and college before Amina figured out that not all these encounters were accidental. After a while she saw that the man who waited on Monday and Wednesday outside the Paras Medical Store always carried in his pocket a yellow envelope. She saw it again, in the lap of the girl who sat three rows behind her, its mouth torn open. The blue Toyota that appeared after they passed by the intersection of Zebunissa Street was always driven by the same man and watched for by the same girl, their eyes singling each other out in the crowds. Evil, she decided then, was this hunger the men carried, and the pretensions of the girls who relished their power to sate it.

MAY 1971

The road leading up to 70 Clifton Road in Karachi had, even in 1971, some of the oldest trees to be found in the city. They provided a wide umbrella of shade to the avenue through which many notables, from Mohammad Ali Jinnah to British officers of old, had passed. In 1971, the end of Clifton Road marked the edge of Karachi, bordered by a wide promenade called the Jehangir Kothari Parade, built and gifted to the city decades ago by a Parsi trader who was in love with the salty freshness of the nearby ocean. This was the city dweller's sea, glimpsed through arches and colonnades, a respectable distance from the uncertain tides and eager ocean winds. On Sundays, families thronged the gazebos and overlooks, the screams of delighted children and territorial gulls mixing with the smoke rising from carts selling roasted corn.

The Bhuttos lived by the ocean, in a large mansion with strong walls that fortified them against the vagaries of a city that was home by necessity. Zulfikar Ali Bhutto was the ambitious scion of a feudal Sindhi family whose thousands of rolling acres in interior Sindh stretched over mango orchards, sugarcane fields, and anything else that could be grown in Pakistan. His wife was the daughter of a Persian émigré who had left Iran for Bombay. Nusrat Bhutto was pretty and fair skinned, with a tittering laugh and a charming mien that enabled her to land a husband on the rise. With his grandiose hospitality and her flitting grace, they moved with ease among princes and politicians from around the world, charming anyone they needed to. In Karachi, they presided over a vast house whose many rooms held, at any given time, bunches of aunts and cousins visiting from the villages or from schools in London or America or Switzerland. They were attended to by retinues of servants, uniformed men with curled moustaches who appeared soundlessly the moment a drink needed to be replenished, before the need had actually crossed the minds of their masters.

A year earlier the Bhuttos had sent their daughter Benazir away to Radcliffe College in Cambridge, Massachusetts. In the summer of 1971 they welcomed her back to spend the summer with the family. Unlike other landed Pakistanis who never summered in Karachi—its heat and dust too exacting for those who could afford Alpine chalets and Mediterranean retreats—the Bhuttos stayed on through the sweltering months. As their friends were whisked away on Swissair flights to Zurich and London and Lausanne, the Bhuttos remained at 70 Clifton, held at home by the dictates of a unique political necessity.

Benazir stayed with the whole family at the grand house by the sea that could not keep the heat of Karachi at bay. That summer, as the unmoving warm air weighed on the imported silk drapery and the smoke-filled study where Bhutto held court with his advisors, Benazir could have watched her father at work. It had been almost six months since the December elections, six months since Sheikh Mujib and his party had won the majority of seats in Pakistan's Parliament. According to Pakistani law, this meant that then president General Yahya Khan could invite Sheikh Mujib to form a majority government in Islamabad. His party members would then be able to elect him as leader of Parliament, making him the first prime minister to hail from East Pakistan. Six months had passed, and the invitation from the president had not come.

If Mujibur Rahman did not become prime minister, Benazir's father would ascend instead. Zulfikar Ali Bhutto's most persuasive victory had come earlier that year. It was rumored that in March it was he who had convinced General Yahya Khan, the overseer of Pakistan's transition to democracy, to order military operations against the Bangla secessionists. This latter option, he had argued, was better than to ask Sheikh Mujib to form a coalition to create a united Pakistan's democratic government. It was allegedly at Bhutto's home that General Yahya Khan had given the orders to initiate the operation.

Within hours, the Pakistani military had poured into the streets and villages of East Pakistan, rounding up insurgents and anyone who looked threatening—and many others who didn't. There was war in East Pakistan, and that summer its intensity had reached a frenetic pitch. But only bits and pieces of it reached the faraway public of West Pakistan. Thousands had already been killed by that summer, their bodies bayoneted and filled with bullets and dumped in mass graves by Pakistani soldiers egged on by their superiors. Pakistan had been won for Muslims, but it had now splintered in two. To motivate the soldiers, the generals told them that those fighting for independence were forsaking Pakistan, the Muslim country for which they had fought so ardently only decades earlier. If they didn't stand their ground against the insurgents, they simply were not Muslim.

On June 21, 1971, Benazir Bhutto turned twenty-one, a coming-of-age in the impending storm that was her father's anointment. A few months later, when the summer had released its hold on Karachi and the coiffed wives and tanned sons of Pakistan's elite had returned from the retreats where they had escaped the tumult of summertime secession, Benazir flew back to the United States to continue her education at Harvard University. When she returned to Pakistan for the winter break, she found her country reduced by half, with her father presiding as prime minister over what remained.

SEPTEMBER 1971

The house had not been completed, but its concrete shell testified to its eventual heft, promising to loom securely over the neighbors' bungalows, offering vantage points into their walled gardens and driveways. The lawn was still a seeded patch of dirt with only aspirations of lushness, the driveway a cement spine between two rows of newly planted palms. There was not yet a front door, only marble steps, newly cut and polished. Inside, the walls had been completed, sectioning off square blocks of the floor into various functions that its owners had deemed crucial to their new lives. For the housewarming they did what they'd seen others of their ilk do on such occasions: they held a reading of the Holy Quran and invited a hundred of their relatives and friends.

The reading took place on the Friday just before Ramzan was to begin. It was a day whose ferocious heat portended the thirst and hunger of the fast in the days to come. By noon the sun was glaring, and a fine, dry layer of dirt covered everything: settling on the uncovered braids of women scurrying through markets, rising from the spinning wheels of cars and then descending again as a thin film on the fly-encrusted mangoes waiting to be sold. Late afternoon approached, and the sun still refused to blink. Some took cover under the sparse trees, their bodies wrung out like lines of sagging laundry.

The time for the gathering had been set between the late afternoon Asr prayers and dusk. Two tents had been erected on either side of the future lawn, one for the men and another for the women. When Said inspected the tents at noon, they were tidy and spacious, with carpets covering the earth and white sheets covering the carpets, pulled taut and pristine like a freshly made bed.

When Surrayya arrived, freshly powdered in a puffy pink sari, she worried about the heat. Would people come? she fretted as she scanned the tents to see if the rugs had been laid properly. To stanch the growing consternation, she took action, ordering ten thick, sturdy blocks of ice and pedestal fans to whirr over them, guaranteeing some semblance of a cool breeze.

By the time the call for Asr prayers was heard from the mosque, the virgin hosts' concerns about an unattended event had dissipated. Cars began pulling up to the house, laden with people sopping their foreheads with bunched handkerchiefs and rolled-up shirtsleeves. Into the tents they filtered in long lines, wizened old women in somber saris on the arms of girls in shiny *shalwar kamiz*, complaining about the uneven ground and the long walk to the tent, expertly scanning all the while the dimensions of the house they had come to see. Soon the tents were swollen, the fans blowing their fabric walls outward like potbellies slung over belts. In the women's tent, the fans also circulated smells: the sandalwood oil and rosewater dabbed onto sweaty skin, the thin swirls of smoke that rose from the incense sticks planted in the corners, and the freshly fried samosas in the distant corner allotted to the caterers.

Some of the women read the Quran, holding one of the thin, leather-bound chapters close to their faces, their mouths moving soundlessly as their eyes scanned the lines. Five or six of these serious women attended every Quran reading, whether it was on the occasion of a funeral, a wedding, an illness, or a housewarming. Their gaze never rose from the pages before them, except to pointedly meet the gaze of some other woman who was laughing too loudly for a gathering dedicated to a divine purpose. They sat nearest to the round, wooden table that held the towering volumes of the Holy Quran. When one woman finished a volume she would clear her throat and replace the book on the table, quickly taking the next one, as if in silent competition with the others.

Farthest from the table with the Qurans were the women who only feigned interest in the task. They tittered, kissed, and embraced, then gingerly took a single volume from the pile and retreated to their vantage points on the edges of the tents, where all arrivals and exits could be viewed and recorded for the later prediction of impending marriages, fresh pregnancies, and other newsworthy tidbits. These guardians of virtues and gatherers of gossip opened their volumes between greetings and brief exchanges that could be used to snub or slight. At any Quran reading, these women were never observed completing a chapter, but they promised that they would as soon as they reached home that night.

Most of the women belonged neither to the inner core of the truly devoted nor to the gossips that lingered on the margins. Those in the middle wished to do a bit of both, dutifully reading a chapter but sparing a moment or two for gossip and a quick scan of the room for eligible young women newly launched on the marriage circuit sometime following a sixteenth or seventeenth birthday. Those with sons approached this latter task with the same religious devotion that others applied to reading the Quran, taking mental notes that could translate into proposals and then marriages and babies. Often they were flanked by helpers, married daughters or daughters-in-law advocating young women who would further their own husbands' businesses or help with the education of their own sons. The fates of all women were attached to those of other women.

Aziza Apa sat in the middle watching family and friends flit by, holding the plan she had arrived with close to her heart. She was almost unknown to Said and Surrayya's family then, but that would change with the plan's execution. If her location that day had been mapped by a cartographer, it may have been the precise midpoint between the table bearing the Qurans at the center and the fluttering exit to the tent. Hers was an unusual position. Still plump from her fourth pregnancy, she was far too young to belong in the circle of bride-scanning mothers-in-law. These were the ladies who seemed to know the instant a girl turned eighteen and who could recite, over a single cup of tea, her particulars, family history, general disposition, number of siblings, and genealogy.

But as the only older sister to three motherless, bachelor brothers, Aziza Apa belonged in the ranks of the selectors rather than the selectees by coincidence of her mother's early death. Indeed, what she may have lacked in years, she made up for in the scrutinizing accuracy with which she could delineate the possibilities and problems of a potential match. She too had come that day to select a bride, for her brother Sohail, her favorite and most loved. She parked herself next to the cabal of future mothers-in-law, and as she scanned a page of the Quran, she listened to them mutter, gathering details about the girls walking by with glasses of water. Aziza Apa was not thirsty, but she motioned to one for a glass. That girl was their hosts' daughter, Amina.

NOVEMBER 14, 1971

The PNS Ghazi had come from America. She was a submarine built decades earlier by steelworkers under the gray, misty skies of the naval shipyard in Kittery, Maine. Back then, in her other life guarding other shores, she had been called something else. But in West Pakistan she was reborn. Her new name, Ghazi, was the Arabic word for "commander," and she was the first submarine to be commissioned to any South Asian navy, a new Pakistan's pride and joy, a real bit of the military prowess the new nation believed was crucial for its existence. As a submarine she was not only powerful but also secret, and secret weapons, everyone knows, are the most powerful.

By November 1971 the battle that had started between the two halves of Pakistan over the election of a prime minister had become a war between Pakistan and India, which viewed Pakistan as provinces lost from its own pre-British wholeness. In Pakistan's telling it, the Indians were the ones who had sheltered Sheikh Mujib and his supporters and had poured guns and bombs on the passion of jilted East Pakistanis, eventually transforming a political disagreement between two halves of a country into a battle for an independent Bangladesh. As a year full of bad news threatened to deliver yet more, the *PNS Ghazi* was given a crucial mission. It was to snake into the depths of the Bay of Bengal to do reconnaissance on the Indian naval ship *Vikrant*. The ultimate mission was to thwart the Indian effort to hack off a chunk of Pakistan.

The captain of the *PNS Ghazi* was a fresh-faced commander by the name of Zafar Mohammad Khan, part of the hopeful, young cadre of Pakistani patriots who had risen quickly to the top of the military leadership. He left the familiar lights of Karachi Harbor on November 14, 1971. On the Muslim calendar, it was the twenty-seventh of Ramzan, an especially holy day that falls during the last fasts of the month when the Holy Quran was believed to have been revealed to the Prophet Muhammad.

Around Karachi the mosques were lit up and crowded with men deep into the night, their white, gray, and blue backs swaying with the rhythm of Quranic verses read aloud. It was time for Taraweeh prayers, an extra set offered only during Ramzan after the compulsory Isha prayers, and often stretching deep into the night as the faithful took stock of the year, asking for forgiveness for the sins accumulated over its course. If the imams standing on pulpits did not know the details of the fighting, they had been assured of the villainy of the secessionists; they didn't need to be convinced of the meddlesome malice of India. From loudspeakers that bellowed out over hundreds of hunched men, from marble-floored mosques in newly sprung suburbs to the bamboo-matted floors of the one on Manora Island far out to sea, they asked Pakistanis to

pray for the victory of their troops against India, against the traitors who wished to divide and destroy Pakistan.

So secret was Captain Khan's mission, and so pressing the
threat of interception, that he had been instructed not to open the
orders until the submarine was well on its way toward the Bay of
Bengal. The *Ghazi* had only recently been equipped by the Turkish
Navy to lay mines deep under the surface of the peaceful sea. The
first days of the mission went well, the ninety-three crew members
following the rigid rhythms they had learned in training, waking
and sleeping and praying while Captain Khan charted the coordinates with the precision he was famous for. On November 16,
1971, two days and nights after it had descended into the ocean,
the *PNS Ghazi* was reported to be four hundred miles off the coast
of Bombay. Later that day it reported coordinates off the coast of
Sri Lanka, very close to its destination. Finally, on November 20,
1971, it entered the silent waters of the Bay of Bengal.

The envelope detailing their mission to plant mines throughout the bay had by then been opened. With the bay teeming with
explosive mines, the Indian Navy Ship *Vikrant* would not stand
a chance. Once India was weakened, the Bengalis wishing for secession from Pakistan would have no allies, thus preserving the
territorial integrity of Pakistan. This, at least, was the tale told to
the crew.

But the crew of the *PNS Ghazi* knew only half the story. While
they silently scoured the ocean looking for Indian warships, the Indians were planning their own attack on Karachi. By December 4,
1971, Indian ships waited, just out of radar range but close enough
to see through their scopes the unassuming tumult of a day in Karachi Harbor, the fishing trawlers emptying their catch, cargo containers being lifted on and off the berths of merchant ships, the call
to prayer booming across the harbor and over the sea.

The Indians had planned to attack Karachi at night while the
city slept and the military entrusted with guarding them could not
respond as effectively. A night attack would stun everyone, from

the fishermen and the businessmen to the politicians and the pilots. The Pakistani Air Force would not be able to immediately arm their planes and bombard Indian cities in retaliation.

At 11:30 p.m., the Indian naval ships eyeing the shores of Karachi finally launched their missiles, aiming them at the city's Keamari Harbor and warships stationed off the coast of Pakistani naval bases. The explosions could be heard deep inside the city, waking groggy men and bleary-eyed children. Only a few could see the fires that erupted from the oil tankers and warships that had been hit, spewing clouds of black smoke that dissipated into the night sky. Servicemen from the navy ship *Khyber*, having been pummeled by the missile, plunged into the sea to their deaths. Karachi was under attack.

At nearly the same time on the other side of the Indian Peninsula, the wearied crew of the *PNS Ghazi*, now nearly two weeks into their sojourn in the cramped, metal capsule, still searched for its target knowing nothing of the attack on Karachi. Theirs had been a long silence, tense and all-encompassing. They had looked so long and wanted so badly to accost their target that they began to believe what they may have otherwise questioned. The short bursts of commands filtering over the static of their radio controls must be coming from the elusive *Vikrant*. They must be close, they began to think. They had to be close, they argued. But suddenly amid this confusion came an explosion. Investigators would not be able to detect the origin of the explosion until its scraps floated to the surface several hours later. One such piece bore the crucial clue, the fading words "*USS Diablo*," a name from the past life of the destroyed submarine. It was the *PNS Ghazi*.

DECEMBER 10, 1971

The marriage proposal for Amina came just a few days after Eid ul Fitr, a muted celebration that year because it fell in the middle of a war. It was her first marriage proposal and was bestowed with the requisite aplomb, which was met in turn by girlish giddiness. Her head filled with clouds, and her arms and legs seeming to float as if disconnected from her torso. She bumped into doors and stubbed her toes on table legs. As she stood in the window of her new room or peeled potatoes in the kitchen, dreams swirled in her head. Visions of life with Sohail, the man who wanted her to be his bride, who had chosen her over all other girls, unspooled like reels of film. He would be the one to rescue her from what now seemed an unbearably long childhood.

Amina had seen him only once, on the day he had come with his sister and a sister-in-law, a lanky man flanked by two shorter women. Surrayya had offered only perfunctory explanations about why Amina, the eldest daughter, who was always shielded from the eyes of unrelated men, would suddenly be allowed to appear before one. They were not necessary, for like all young girls growing up in Pakistan at the time, she knew exactly why. Knowing all this, Amina stepped into the spotlight of the drawing room at the front of the house. The choreography was too well rehearsed in her fantasies and too often discussed in giggly conversations with engaged college friends for her not to know what to expect. Even so, she pretended, eager to spare her mother, who in one moment started to fawn and fuss, to suggest this outfit over that one, and then lapsed just as suddenly into nonchalance, the possibility of embarrassment ahead. It was as if she had to restrain herself in case things went nowhere, in case her daughter was rejected. Then everyone would want to believe that the episode had not happened, or had been nothing special after all.

The conundrum of doing enough while also behaving as though nothing was unusual hung over all the preparations for the visit. It was not that Surrayya, as a sister and a once would-be bride herself, was a stranger to the suspense of selection that had to be endured. But that had been in Bombay, where intertwined alleys and jammed-together apartments left few opportunities for strangers. Everyone was a relation of some kind, and it was the sisters and mothers who delivered proposals for girls whom suitors and future mothers-in-law had watched as they walked to school or stood next to their mothers buying lemons and tomatoes from the vegetable carts. In that arrangement there was less mystery and little risk. A familiar cast of characters played predictable roles of intermediaries and eggers-on, eager to jump in and arrange the scenes that would lead to a wedding.

In Karachi it was all up to Surrayya. As the mistress of the house and the mother of daughters she had to set the stage, write the script, and execute the finale that would insure a proposal. Every sofa and table and chair had to be a part of the tableau; the novelty of wealth and allegiance to old tastes evoked the promise of Karachi and paid homage to a shared past of Kokanis from Bombay. There were a hundred decisions to make. The milk sherbet with nuts and raisins that they had served to the aunts and cousins who filtered in and out to exchange Eid greetings did not seem special enough for the occasion. A cream cake was ordered from the bakery, but when it arrived it appeared too grand, its flounced top suggesting a celebration, or worse, a sense of desperation. At three o'clock Surrayya made the final call on a plain pound cake and vegetable samosas, a combination quietly signaling both sophistication and hospitality.

From her bedroom window, Amina saw Sohail arrive. She could see little more than the top of his head, reassuringly dark and with no indication of baldness, which some of her other friends had to endure in their husbands. She exhaled with relief as the procession passed by the garden and disappeared inside the house. He was not old, and he was not fat, she observed with a measure of relief. In this, two of her most pressing requirements in a husband had already been met. Satisfied, she took off her glasses and applied makeup on the bridge of her nose. She did not want him to know she was nearsighted; a wife with glasses was not what most men wished for in a bride.

It was over fast, achingly fast. When Amina entered, she was given the task of pouring tea into the delicate cups arranged on the table. It was Surrayya who handed the cup to Sohail; being permitted to see a young woman before he agreed to marry her was one thing, an accidental touch in handing over a teacup was out of the question. Amina would not remember much of the conversation. She could not bear to look up at him, and so she satisfied herself with a careful examination of his hands. By the time the visit was over, she had decided they were exquisite, with long, brown tapered fingers.

The waiting began the second they left. The uncertainty was as difficult to bear as the visit itself had been to orchestrate. On Wednesday, the day after their visit, there was no word, but all agreed that a hasty response would indicate a lack of adequate seriousness about the matter under consideration. On Thursday, the expectation was that the answer would come on Friday, auspicious and holy. But Friday came, and the morning was silent. The men went together to the congregational prayer, and the usual meal of fish curry and rice and vegetables followed, but the absence of casual conversation signaled the beginnings of doubt. On Saturday morning a new rationalization emerged that the visit was not all that momentous. The day was young, but it was not too soon to start saying that the family had never been good enough for their daughter in the first place.

On Saturday evening, an hour before dusk, the telephone rang. Aziza Apa's voice chimed out clear and excited from the receiver. She wished to come again and formally bring the marriage proposal for Amina. They had been charmed by her quiet beauty; their late mother would have been delighted to have such a bride for her son, and they were sure she would light up his house and fill it with a brood of sons. They had searched and searched, Aziza Apa insisted, as Sohail was very particular in his tastes, but once he had seen Amina, there was no doubt. The second they sat in the car, she told Surrayya that Saturday, Sohail had said, "I have found my bride."

DECEMBER 14, 1971

It was above all an act of military theater, the first and only public surrender in modern military history. The official ceremony in which Pakistan gave up East Pakistan was held at Ramna Racecourse in Dhaka, and every detail of its orchestration was meant to humiliate. From the crowds of Indian soldiers, who stood leering behind the Pakistani general signing the document to the single, rickety table placed in the middle of the racecourse ground, all the visuals arranged to insure that the defeated indeed looked as vanquished as they were. The Pakistani general who had been given the task of representing a conquered Pakistan seemed eager to end the ordeal, while the neatly turbaned Indian general seated beside him was deliberately unhurried. Even the land participated in the jeers; the racecourse was where Bangladeshis had celebrated the birth of Pakistan twenty-four years ago, certain then that a single homeland for all the subcontinent's Muslims was possible. On that same ground Sheikh Mujib had announced the end of that dream and the beginning of the quest for Bangladesh. Now the surrender had to happen on this land that had been three different countries in fewer than three decades.

The Pakistanis' roles were parts in a play, allowing no deviation from a ceremony that summarized defeat in a single photograph and a single signature. General Abdullah Khan Niazi, the face of Pakistan's national loss, seemed uninterested in posing for the camera, his tiny eyes focused elsewhere. In the photograph for which the moment was arranged, Indian generals in white, green, and khaki stood shoulder to shoulder behind the table, perhaps unsure that the Pakistani would indeed sign his name, as if his refusal could turn back the course of a war that was already lost. The head of Pakistan's Eastern Military Command bore no such uncertainties his name on a paper was a formality for a reality he could not deny. The language of surrender was simple: "The Pakistani Eastern command agree to surrender all Pakistani armed forces in Bangladesh to Lieutenant General Jagjit Singh Aurora, General Officer Commanding in Chief of the Indian and Bangladesh forces in the Eastern Theatre. This surrender includes all Pakistan land, air and naval forces."

A few days later, another surrender ceremony was held, as if the victors could not sate themselves with this new form of theater that made their victory tangible. This one involved even more Pakistani soldiers, not just the one sitting at a rickety table. This time they were lined up, all still in uniform, in a long queue whose length hinted at the entirety of their twenty-four-thousand-man presence in East Pakistan. On cue, the Indian forces arranging the show told them they must put down their weapons and jog backward, moving backward to convince their foes that they were indeed going home.

Not only the soldiers turned their heels to Karachi that December. In the shadow of defeat were also hundreds of thousands of Bihari Muslims, who had never fought but had doggedly supported the Pakistani dream their fellow citizens had abandoned for Bangladesh. In the drama of Pakistan's defeat and Bangladesh's independence, they did not fit, their story too messy to include in the black and white of winning and losing, jogging backward and forward.

These living casualties of war, who had already propelled themselves from one home in the Indian province of Bihar to the independent East Pakistan, now staggered to Karachi. There, in the craggy northwestern edge of another strange city, far from the ocean they had heard it bordered, and in lanes already puddled with refuse, they founded Orangi Town, a slum that would in the following decades become one of the largest in the world. In its unpaved lanes and open sewers, the people who had been discarded by two countries set up shanties and pinned them with nostalgic names—Usmanabad and Ghaziabad and Hanifabad—harkening back to India or East Pakistan or Bangladesh, a first, a second, or a third migration. They kept coming, with bedrolls and broken trunks filled with carefully wrapped copies of the Holy Quran and bridal gowns and deeds to land they would never see again. They kept coming, until Zulfikar Ali Bhutto, the new prime minister of Pakistan who lived by the sea, said they could come no more, that Karachi was full and had no more room for the migrants of defeat.

CHAPTER 5

Half a Wife

APRIL 1987

The window of the upstairs bedroom from which Amina first saw Sohail became mine. I shared the room with my brother, but the window was mine alone, as only one of us felt compelled to look outside. Not permitted to roam the streets like my brother, the window was my avenue to the world beyond our house. The bedroom was on the second story where we lived with my mother and father, in a house divided between the upstairs and the downstairs, the young and the old, the past and the present. The question of whether they were really two houses in one or a single house shared by two was complicated, and the verdict depended entirely on whom you asked.

If you wished to say that we were one, a single family dispersed across two floors, you could point to the fact that there was no separate entrance and no separate kitchen. These were the hubs of any Pakistani household's existence, and sharing them implied that the important decisions about who came and went, and what was eaten when and who prepared it, were decided collaboratively by amiable consultation between the upper and lower worlds. Those who believed in the one household theory insisted that neither upstairs nor downstairs was a separate realm; it was simply a matter of space. One should not, after all, assume that boundaries between one realm and the other meant a lack of domestic harmony.

Those who believed we were separate had a more circumstantial case. Its crux was a single fact: my grandmother, Surrayya, no matter how urgent the matter, how fast she needed to know if my father would be coming home for dinner, or how eagerly she wished to tell him that his cousin had called from India, or how insistently she needed my mother to come down and attend to something in the kitchen, never ever went upstairs. There was a landing on the staircase between the two floors, and here, as if held back by some invisible but ever-present border, she would stop. Her last outpost was a square space of marble, measuring not more than three square feet; for everyone else a place to pause on an ascent or a descent, but for her a destination. My mother had decorated it with a floor vase, a blue and white creation my father had carried back from a business trip. At first the vase was filled with dried up brown reeds bought in a hurry from one of the hawkers who stood in a line by Clifton Beach. Later, it held a flamboyant sheaf of peacock feathers, obtained after much effort, from a friend who frequently traveled abroad.

I was raised, therefore, with the rules of separation, boundaries and half lives; my grandmother's refusal to ascend and my mother's descent into the shared space of the kitchen, all of which entailed a web of complicated obligations. There were things, my mother instructed me, that could be said upstairs but were not to be repeated downstairs; while my grandmother served snacks that she insisted must be eaten downstairs and not mentioned upstairs. Even the gardens were sliced into halves. The portion at the front of the house was verdant, with a lawn watered painstakingly by an ancient gardener and flowers that blossomed and perfumed with the time of day, gardenias in the morning and jasmine at night. These were the objects guests saw upon entering the black gate of the compound. At the back was my mother's "kitchen garden," which consisted of the tamarind tree, the still-baby coconut palms, the mango tree, and the lemon trees. If the front represented all that the family had wanted before their arrival in Pakistan, the back was an attempt to coax from Karachi's sandy soil the remembered flavors and fruits that had been left behind. Once the coconut palms grew tall, once the buds on the mango trees blossomed into fruit, once the lemon trees began to flower, the best of both worlds, the cherished and the accomplished, would be realized.

I had become an expert in divisions, having witnessed the slicing up of Aunt Amina's marriage so determinedly into what was intended to be equal parts. Since her silent departure into the unusually cold Karachi winter, Aunt Amina herself seemed suddenly reduced by half. Some of it was evident in the ordinary details of her visits, some of which featured Uncle Sohail and others did not. Instead of every Saturday, she came every other Saturday. Instead of every Tuesday she came every other Tuesday. Her visits grew shorter, lapsing into good-byes shortly after hellos, cups of tea gulped instead of sipped. She appeared distracted, always watching not those she had come to see but passing objects like the report card I brought to show off or the new creases on my grandmother's forehead. Sometimes, she spoke at great length about trivial affairs—her recovery from a cold a week ago or the latest soap opera to preoccupy the women of Karachi on Mondays. At other times she would catch herself midsentence answering a question that she clearly misheard.

On the occasions when he accompanied her, Aunt Amina's full attention was bestowed only on her husband, his every expression and comment. In the silences when questions were dropped or forgotten, she looked at her watch, as if recording time and measuring it against some other standard whose details we did not know. She had never worn a watch before, but she did now: the task of measurement was suddenly central to her life. If before, conversation had meandered, covering concerns and foibles and gossip, now it was simply allowed to lapse, my grandparents' embarrassment colliding with their daughter's distracted sadness. I did not know then the metrics of blame and responsibility and suffering that preoccupied the orchestrators and beneficiaries of arranged marriage. During those first days Uncle Sohail remained silent, his small teeth grinning under the moustache he had grown. He had taken to emitting ebullient "heh, heh, hehs" or jaunty "ahems" to punctuate an awkward pause.

The visits were only one portion of Aunt Amina's divided life. The arrangement when one man had to be shared by two women was methodical, inspired by the Quranic prescription that asked every man taking more than one woman to do so only if he could do "perfect justice" between them. In the case of Aunt Amina and Uncle Sohail it meant his time was divided into blocks of single weeks, which belonged to one and then to the other wife. On one Saturday afternoon, he accompanied Aunt Amina to visit her parents, on the following Saturday afternoon he accompanied his new wife to her parents. And so it went, every Eid and every deed, every birthday and every breath was thus divided to accomplish the perfect justice recommended by the Holy Quran.

Aunt Amina, newly deposed, had to insure she was getting her due, and during her visits my grandparents and her other allies watched for clues and gathered evidence. Was he being fair, dutiful, just? Was he the same man? He wore the same clothes, carried the newspaper under his armpit in just the same way and asked every now and then for an extra teaspoon of sugar in his tea. But was he the same man who had so earnestly promised my grandparents that he would treat their daughter like a queen? What was once ritual and even pleasurable was now an obligation, the poison of paranoia gushing through every comment and every gesture, accompanied by the unspoken question on everyone's mind: Is this how it worked with his other wife, his other family? This possibility of replication poisoned everything.

JULY 1987

Sometime in May, after the school year had ended but before schoolboys became brave back-alley cricketers and girls were conscripted into chopping in steaming kitchens, every schoolchild in Karachi would be handed a sheet of paper. These terse circulars contained the nuts and bolts of what we would need to know for our return to school in August. Among the items would be information on fee increases, teacher and classroom assignments, textbooks and exercise books designated for each course, and the place where new school uniforms could be purchased to accommodate our elongating bodies.

Our uniforms had to be purchased at one place to insure that all students' outfits would look identical as opposed to merely similar. Liberty Uniforms was the only authorized uniform shop for students of the Mama Parsi Girls Secondary School and the BVS Parsi Boys School. Only they could sell the A-line, belted white dress I wore to school and the white *shalwars* the older girls wore underneath the dresses to cover their legs. They also carried the correct style of Mary Janes that all the girls aged five to sixteen wore day in and day out and the tight-laced boots with which the boys kicked up the dust in their all-boys courtyard. Only at Liberty could my brother find pants exactly the right shade of khaki, and all these selections were monitored by the prefects who stood every morning at the school entrance, inspecting the white-collared shirt with the colored badge of light blue on the breast pocket for authenticity.

Liberty Uniforms was located in Bohri Bazaar, the outdoor market whose winding alleys had looped their arms so protectively around my lost grandmother when she arrived in Karachi decades before. The bazaar had grown with the city, its lanes becoming ever more crowded and its depths nearly impenetrable by the increasing number of shops crammed into the same space. People jostled against each other in a way alien to us; the almost accidental brushes of strange hands and bodies never happened in our expansive suburb. We could not understand our grand-mother's excitement at being greeted by name by some small, wiz-ened man sitting on a low stool outside a tube-like store lined with aluminum plates and cups and pots and pans. Everything here, except the uniforms, you could buy elsewhere, my mother com-plained, in bigger, better stores near our house. In these new stores that smelled of fresh plastic and had wide entrances flanked by whirring fans you didn't have to socialize with the shopkeeper be-fore you counted out your rupees: you could get what you needed, fast, and then be on your way. Bohri Bazaar emitted a memorable stench of rotting fruit, open sewers, frying oil, and manure from the horse carts that still plied the narrow alleys around it. Walking in it required extreme vigilance; a slight distraction could mean a sandal-footed dip into fetid water, a plunge into the fresh purging of some tired horse or donkey, or a stumble over a jutting stone.

As July sidled into its second week that year of Aunt Amina's return, we were once again readying ourselves for the ritual of pur-chasing uniforms for the new school year. The ladies of the upstairs and the downstairs set the date and time of the outing. That year they conferred about it in the afternoon, after lunch, in the mid-dle ground of the kitchen they shared. My mother was in a hurry as it was a Thursday and the day she visited her own mother and sisters, who lived just a few blocks from our house. They would be waiting for her—her own mother presiding over the tea tray and her younger sisters and their children. Full of anticipation, my mother rushed as she dished out the portions of leftovers al-lotted to the woman who did the dishes and laundry. She snapped at me to put away the condiments—the mango pickle and yogurt bowls—telling me to hurry if I wanted to see my cousins.

My grandmother shuffled in, her slow steps a rejection of our own purposeful tempo. As she settled into the chair where she had eaten a nearly silent lunch a half hour before, my mother's wide, smiling mouth gathered into an uncertain tightness, as if pulled by a drawstring.

On this afternoon, when we were supposed to visit our other grandmother, she sat down to begin a conversation. "The children's uniforms have to be bought," my grandmother began, using the needs of her grandchildren to segue into the discussion she hoped to begin with my mother. Standing at my mother's side I could see her shoulders rise and fall as she calculated the cost of this conversation—the delay in our departure and the disappointment of her own mother who was waiting for her. Hot, hurried, and stalled, we listened. "July is almost in its second week, and we should go soon," she exhorted, as if my mother had plainly forgotten the task herself. "We should set a date now," she concluded, glancing at the calendar hanging over the tea trolley that stood in the corner. It had a picture of the Holy Mosque in Mecca, the same picture for every month.

Having been her daughter-in-law for a decade, my mother knew that this conversation was merely a formality for a decision already made. She knew better than to suggest a date, which would have been perceived as bossy and disrespectful. She was also aware of the implicit facts of the matter: that it was *she* who would drive, and that it was *her* children whose uniforms were being purchased. But resolution could not be rushed, and there were more steps and turns to the dance between the women. "You should tell me when you would like to go," my mother said, having weighed all these considerations in the minutes that had passed. "No, no," my grandmother responded. "Why should *I* select a date? . . . I am just saying, for the children . . . if we are late they will not have any left . . . it is nothing to me when we go . . . I am just an old woman," she sighed. "Of course, if we go I would like to get one or two things . . . but I am not important. You are so busy. You tell me and I will be ready."

My mother knew her mother-in-law's words were at best a test; so, having been seasoned at the game, she replied, "See, here is the calendar. Just tell me in the next week when you would like to go and we will go." Surrayya slowly walked up to the calendar in the corner, making a great show at poring over the dates. "How about next Thursday?" she suggested deftly. My mother, confident a mere second ago, was now stumped and bowled, like an end line batsman in cricket who has not been expecting the ball to come so fast or spinning so uncontrollably. I watched her make assessments: whether to state the reason she would rather not go on Thursday, whether to mention her weekly visit to her own mother, which my grandmother always viewed as a betrayal, a too-close bond with a family not anymore her own, or whether to say nothing. As she paused before responding, the kitchen door banged as the maid left for the day, shouting, "Mistresses, I am leaving. Good-bye." Her steps receded out toward the gate. By the time it clanged shut my mother had a response: "You are right, it is already too late in the summer for ordering the uniforms. But we will go next Tuesday. . . . It is in the middle of the week, and there will be less traffic."

She had almost won. By the time the conference was adjourned and we had piled into the car for the five minute drive to our other grandmother's house, it was half past three, a whole hour later than our usual departure. We would have only an hour to visit and play before leaving at five o'clock amid the chorus of remonstrations to stay just a bit longer. Not that we would ever give in; that lesson, too, had been learned years ago when my father arrived home promptly at five thirty and found that his wife was not there waiting for him.

JULY 1987

She was everywhere, but I did not know her name. By some unwritten rule, no one in our house was permitted to say aloud the name of Uncle Sohail's new wife. Despite this omission her nameless presence was woven into our lives in those early days, from the pause that would follow if aimless conversation accidentally veered close to some detail that required a mention of her, to the task of deflecting questions from all those who knew the details but wished to hear them from the mouths of those nearest the

drama. We all developed strategies for survival, forming stoic re-
sponses for all occasions, terse nods and blank-faced smiles that
could cover up anything.

To satisfy my own curiosity, I became adept at excavating details
of the latest slight from insinuations of Uncle Sohail's recurring
unfairness. When we paid our customary visit to Aunt Amina's
house on the first or second day of Eid, when, according to the
division of days, Uncle Sohail was Aunt Amina's husband, I conducted swift investigations of the site of ruin. While Aunt Amina
chatted with my parents and served the glasses of chilled orange
soda and shami kebabs she always reserved for us on Eid, I roamed
through the apartment, looking for clues that would reveal the details of her life as half a wife, crumbs of evidence that busted the
myth that not much had changed.

Aunt Amina's house smelled of sugar and butter, and the
smell was strongest near the kitchen. This had not changed;
the smell was still there, a bit fainter perhaps but unmistakable
over the pots and pans arranged carefully on the marble shelves,
on the towels that hung beside the washbasin. There I would stand
by the mop bucket and peer through the windows into the courtyard below, into the world of the other wife. I would stand and listen for an echo of some spoken sentence or accidental glimpse into
the world of this unnamed, unseen other woman. The courtyard
looked just as it did when Aunt Amina lived there, before she had
moved upstairs. The edges of its terracotta tiles were a bit more
weathered, or there may have been more potted plants concealing
the cracks along the wall. The clothesline was still there, sad and
sagging as if weighted down by clothes for one person too many,
groaning to bear more than it could possibly hold. This was the
only tangible evidence of the second wife, the tunics and pants and
scarves that had no right to be there, but remained nevertheless.

Every time I saw these pieces of clothing, I judged her with a secret ferocity that may have been too small to annihilate the woman
herself but still burned within me with piercing indignation. If the

tunic was red, I imagined the woman aglow with raging flames, tempting Uncle Sohail into new transgressions against my sweet and unassuming aunt. If it was purple, I imagined it as the darkness inspired by Satan, who had tempted her to invade another woman's home and take for herself a man who was already a husband. The lurid colors affirmed for me our family's superiority over this interloping woman, our muted palette of pastels and neutrals standing in stark contrast to the crude and aggressive shades of the other wife's clothes hanging on the line. In my child's mind, bright colors became persistently coarse and unapologetic, evidence that the woman's heart was surely made of stone, ever reveling in her victory over my aunt, who preferred the quiet beige or the unassuming ivory.

As the months passed, Aunt Amina's tight-lipped distraction yielded and a slow trickle of complaints began to flow in her daily phone calls to my grandmother or in unexpected lone visits on weekday afternoons. She always came during weeks when he was gone, the portion of the rotation that belonged to the other wife. In those fallow weeks Aunt Amina had no reason to wake in the morning, no breakfast to prepare or shirt buttons to sew. With a bitterness that accompanied her anguished voice like an aftertaste, she talked about the confused moments of waking up alone for the first time in a life spent surrounded by people.

Another time she spoke of preparing a curry, chopping the onions and heating the oil and realizing just as she was putting in the teaspoons of cumin and coriander and turmeric that there was no reason to make dinner that day, just like there was no reason to leave the bed in the morning, or to wash her face, or to change the clothes she had worn to sleep. The front room where the television was kept needed no straightening up and would remain cold and empty the rest of the day. At the end of these stories she laughed a laugh that was also new, a hollow, mirthless cackle that gave me the chills whether it came through a phone line or the partially closed door of my grandparents' bedroom.

We heard almost nothing from her on the days he was there. These were, at least in the beginning, the days when old rhythms were restored and past meanings affirmed. She had a reason to wake and a face to gaze on, an arm to squeeze. There were reasons to bathe and occasions to touch, share a thought, or air a complaint. His presence was a reprieve from silence. No longer was she at the mercy of the television and its ramblings over the budget or the floods, empty words that invaded the grief-stricken, empty house around her.

His appearance represented the return of life, the force and fervor that fuels its persistence. On the days he returned waiting had a meaning. Three o'clock meant she should have dinner planned and be heading off to bathe and change out of the clothes she had cooked in. By four she should have pulled the laundry off the clothesline, ironed his clothes for the next day. By five, it was almost time for him to return, when the tea should be poured into the thermos, awaiting his step on the stairs. She was free from the familiar, worn outpourings of her own mind.

But even when she had him, she felt that she had him less than the other woman. After the nights he spent in her bed and ate at her table, the world that lay beyond the house and where he would return in the morning was one he shared only with his new wife. Then he would go to work, where they had met and, it was assumed, had fallen in love. The most wondrous of mornings following the most affectionate of breakfasts could be spoiled with this remembrance that came just before the sharp sting of his departure. With his receding steps came the vision of them settling in to their seats in the car, his glance at the other wife, perhaps the apology he offered every morning for having spent the night with another woman, the woman who was his duty but perhaps never his love.

JULY 13, 1987

They said the bomb had been hidden in a leather briefcase and left on the first landing of a crowded stairway in an even more crowded building. No one knew for sure; the charred hull left behind refused to give up that secret, silent and resolute in its burned-out desolation. It stood dark and skeletal, like an unclothed corpse staring unbelievingly at the life that continued after its own death: the cars that still honked and the people that gaped and the shops that reopened.

On July 14, 1987, on my father's fortieth birthday and one month before Pakistan commemorated the same anniversary, two bombs rocked Bohri Bazaar, the merchant relic from the city's early days as a magnet for migrants. The blasts tore through the winding bazaar's busy central artery and killed more than thirty people in an instant of conflagration. Hundreds more were injured as shards of brick and wood and glass propelled through the market.

After the blasts came the fire. Within minutes it coursed through one, then two, and then three buildings, hungry flames melting flesh and bringing down structures with impossible speed and ferocity. One building housed a restaurant, where minutes earlier women and children had been enjoying chilled sodas and plates of hot samosas. Within seconds they were all consumed by fire, along with dozens of vendors and their wooden carts of fragrant mangoes. Their sweetness, which on ordinary days could cover up so many varieties of unpleasant odors, failed to cover the stench of death.

My father brought the news home from work. He had heard the sound of the blasts miles away as he was preparing to leave for the day. The windows in his fifth-floor office on the outskirts of Saddar had shaken and threatened to shatter. Dozens of his colleagues, bored in the late-afternoon lassitude of the office, had started screaming and rushing for the dank stairwells where others stood smoking and chatting, oblivious. Everyone had rushed out, each with his own reasons for urgency. Some murmured about an aerial attack from India, others yelled that it was an earthquake, others less inventive or dramatic blamed a blown-up transformer on the roof of the building. Once outside, everyone milled about, bursting with the tense energy of an uncertain moment.

Within minutes Abdullah Haroon Road, the busy street that lay in front of the office building, was crammed with cars, each with five or six or even seven men squeezed inside, expectant but unmoving, their drivers honking and cursing out their windows. They still did not know where the sounds had come from. They wanted to be home at once. It took four hours for my father to make the usual half-hour journey home that night, and he arrived in time for the nine o'clock news. It did not mention the blasts at all, only that the president, General Zia ul Haque, would be visiting Karachi the next day.

The morning paper reported the details of the Bohri Bazaar blasts, the first of their kind in Karachi, now a city of eight million. One shop destroyed in the fires after the explosion was Liberty Uniforms. We read the news sitting around the same kitchen table where a few days ago my grandmother and mother had settled on a date for uniform shopping. It was Tuesday, the day we had planned to go.

AUGUST 1987

Of all the schemes hatched in post-Partition Pakistan, the plans for the Housing Societies proved to be one of the most ingenious. Their imprint would stay on the city long after the financiers and bureaucrats who thought it up were dead and gone. The scheme capitalized on a basic fear that germinated and flowered in every migrant heart in the city. Everyone who could afford the dream of building a house worried about who would build the one next to it, where they would come from, and whether they would be adequately respectable. Having come from villages deep inside India or dense urban communities in Delhi or Bombay where the Kokanis of Jama Masjid had lived for centuries, the immigrants to Pakistan had never endured proximity to strangers. The idea of slicing up suburban Karachi into craggy squares to be populated by the newly moneyed émigrés, who wished to stick together rather than be lost among strangers, was bound to make money, and it did. Previously scattered throughout the city, Gujaratis from Kathiawar, Kokanis from Bombay, and Memons from Cutch reconvened in the Housing Societies, with new money allowing them to gobble up the allotted plots or half plots and building on them the haphazard dream houses that had nested in their heads since they began their journey to Pakistan.

They reveled in the joys of living close to their kin once again, making their first Karachi experience of living among strangers seem like a passing penalty. The loud Punjabis from the north and the Sindhis who did not understand Urdu brought on bouts of fear and unease that could now be a thing of the past. Newly reunited, they felt safe, and even if they only barely knew the aunt's cousin who now lived upstairs or they never spoke to the brother-in-law's mother who lived next door, they could at last feel the familiarity they so longed for. Enabled by the Housing Society, they were once again in a position to peer into the lives of others. Determined to return to the old norms, they enacted time-tested rituals, pretexts like sending children for a cup of sugar to squirrel out the identity of guests glimpsed slipping in next door, or appearing uninvited at a kitchen door the morning after a night of overheard arguments.

What was best for community, however, was not always best for capital. The rotund, little land broker guiding an at-once eager and hesitant Said pronounced the land in Kokan Society to be a less than ideal investment. Instead, he suggested another Housing Society, not much farther away but more centrally located along the newly constructed main highways of the city. It was a migrant's compromise between location and relation. Our house would not be in Kokan Society, but near enough for it to be watched and visited and located in the dense circuits through which news and gossip traversed. At the same time, being closer to the airport, to main streets and burgeoning commercial areas, it suggested a faster doubling, even tripling, in value.

When Aunt Amina married, she moved into the heart of Ko-kan Society, Karachi, where a mishmash of near and far relations from Bombay now resided. Hers was a house among narrow houses along a short lane, the inhabitants of each one staring at the house immediately opposite with the same mix of appraisal and affection. Her house was a single story, but those up and down the lane varied in height, giving the little lane the awkwardness of a group of mismatched cousins pushed together in a hurried family portrait.

When Aunt Amina arrived as a bride, she was heartened by the entwined lives of the people in her neighborhood. In the tentative first days of marriage, it was a constant reminder of all she had to be thankful for. When she nodded sympathetically to the complaints of the second cousin who lived next door, listened to the travails of sharing a kitchen with three other sisters-in-law and their five children, she felt an even greater love for her own tidy kitchen, untouched as it was by the manipulation of pushy mothers- and sisters-in-law. When a plate of still sizzling samosas arrived at her front door in the hands of some cousin's ten-year-old boy, she was quick to return the gesture with a plate of kebabs sent back on the same plate a few days later. In those early days, the weekday silence of her own little house felt like a refuge, the calls and visits of neighbors a garnish on the lovely delicacy that was her own home.

The blush and bloom of those first honeymoon months had faded long before there was a new wife. The rhythm of life for the women who lived next door and down the street was dictated by the predictable phases of being: from daughter to wife to mother. Within a few months of her marriage, Shabana, the complaining cousin next door, sported a ripening belly that strained at the seams of the fitted tunics in her dowry. Six months passed and Amina's own belly remained the same; her period arrived every month like a red flag of failure. Her mother counseled patience and prayer. The birth of Shabana's baby, a son, was feted by boxes of sweets distributed to every family in the neighborhood. A year passed and Surrayya gave her a bottle of herbs to take every morning on an empty stomach with a glass of warm water. She took them for a month until they were gone, swallowing them fast to escape their bitterness. Still, her period arrived on time, and there was no baby.

In those later years, when Shabana or any of the neighborhood women visited her, they came to console themselves. The silence of Aunt Amina's house, the pictures of smiling children cut from calendars and pasted on the walls, the toyless tidiness of the drawing room sofas, which had been a rebuke to their own haphazard lives of nursing and pregnancy, now empowered them, reminders to all that their own offspring were a blessing and bounty; their flabby bellies and bloated bodies were battle scars of the truly blessed. Under their scrutiny Aunt Amina receded deeper into her house, collecting their slights even as she directed her own desperation into visits to doctors and healers and holy men. When she was in the middle of a cure there was hope, and when there was hope she said hello—to Shabana, her mother, or any woman in the neighborhood. When hope faltered, she receded, refusing to answer doorbells, averting her eyes in the short steps between car and doorway so as not to face another pitying gaze.

With the arrival of the second wife the eyes of neighbors focused with rejuvenated fervor on Aunt Amina's newly enlarged house. In the evening, the women watched the lights turning on upstairs or downstairs; the men watched the comings and goings of Uncle Sohail, whether he ascended or descended the stairs between his two women, propounding at length about his dutiful virility. The oddity of the household, the only one on the lane where two women shared one man, provided a safe conversation topic at their own dinner tables, a reprieve from nagging concerns about jobs and money and traffic and schools. "Is Sohail upstairs or downstairs tonight?" always managed to draw a laugh from the most harried of housewives, the most overworked of husbands. Thus the newly recreated neighborhood of stragglers from Bombay, reunited on one short lane of houses in Karachi, had found a juicy drama that was reliable fodder for casual gossip.

SEPTEMBER 1987

The inhabitants of the suburban neighborhood in which we lived had built their mansions with the utmost care. Every detail, from the shade of marble floor to the type of flowers in their gardens to the hues of their bedroom curtains had been agonized over and considered at length. Each detail was important. The mansions were, after all, the realizations of dreams, and the transformation of what was wished for into what existed would determine the contentment of years to come.

Despite the painstaking care in the construction and decoration of the houses, there had been one instance of collective neglect; one crucial issue had been forgotten. None of them, not a single one, had considered how the consequences of large living would be discarded. None of the houses had a means for disposing of the trash that collected in their many waste bins and in reeking piles outside their kitchens.

This omission would not have been of particular note to us had it not been for our proximity to what was ultimately deemed to be the solution. Next to our house was a small square of empty land, one that had remained unoccupied even as houses sprang up all along the lane. Empty and unclaimed, it was this plot of land that became, for our neighbors, the answer to the problem of garbage, and for us a taunting nemesis.

The mountains of trash, testaments to just how well everyone was doing and how much they were eating, would grow. Fetid and fuming, the stench would rise, reeking far beyond the retaining walls around the square plot of land. Then, just as quietly as they came to dump their rubbish, these neighbors would light the trash on fire. The smoke from the burning trash would settle over our garden, wilt the brightly colored leaves of plants that my mother tended daily, and eclipse the otherwise heady scents of jasmine and gardenia. The acrid smoke of burning rubber and plastic and paper and fruit stung our eyes and seeped into our throats and put everyone in a terrible mood.

No one knew who owned this empty plot of land; inquiries had yielded only bits and pieces of a story—several owners, a court case, bureaucratic holdups and such, but no explanation of the mystery of how, in such a crowded city, this choice corner of land that faced a busy and increasingly important street could remain so resolutely vacant. Then one night, in the darkness of the ebbing summer when no one was paying attention, someone came with a scythe and cut down all the thorny bushes that had taken over the enclosed plot. A few of the bushes remained, the more compliant and shorter ones that hung about the edges, and in the middle two date palms laden with the ripe golden fruit that grows only in the desert.

There was much speculation the morning after this nocturnal beautification; perhaps all the complicated issues of the property dispute had been sorted out, my father and mother guessed, perhaps the plot finally was to be claimed by its rightful owners. Maybe now the owners would begin to fend off the piles of trash, and we could avoid the spires of chemical smoke that descended directly into our house following every garbage bonfire.

A fortnight later, when the Afghan men first arrived, everyone thought they were builders, laborers hired to erect whatever house the suddenly engaged owners of the empty plot had in mind. It was not unusual for construction workers, many of them migrants from Afghanistan, to live on the site while they were digging foundations and aligning concrete bricks. We saw them everywhere in Karachi, building banks and hospitals and houses, adding new floors and repairing crumbling ones, the dark browns and grays and blacks of their tunics the same colors as their cold country to the north, which had been at war for nearly as long as I had been alive. They were refugees, but the city tolerated them as long as they had a purpose, which usually involved building or selling something.

When they first came, they brought very little, a few dusty bedrolls tied up with rope and carried on their backs with thin, mangy pillows stuffed between. I watched them from an upstairs window that looked over the plot. There were four of them, one old and leathery faced, exuding weariness with each slow movement. Two others were middle-aged, with dark, unruly beards that curved down their chins; they looked always vigilant, their heads continually turning to look over their shoulders, their eyes darting here and then there in quick, expert scans. The fourth was just a little boy of six or eight. He was one of the ruddy-faced, sharp-featured children who plied Karachi's trash heaps with giant parchment bags to fill with bottles and paper.

Behind the windows, I was as good as veiled, the height of the higher floor and the layers of glass and concrete and metal allowing me to indulge my curiosity and comfortably inspect their lives, faces, and intentions. After the bedrolls on the first day came tarps and posts. The morning after that there was a shelter, sprouting out of the darkness as if it had been there all along, its tarp roof neatly stretched over the posts, its two sides the perimeter walls of the empty plot. Inside they had put their bedrolls and a beat-up aluminum trunk. Outside, the old man had set up a kitchen, a blackened pot on a pyramid of firewood, its handle holding a single chipped light-blue cup.

In two or three days, the encampment had become a settlement, with its own rhythm and movements. It seemed untouched by the roar of traffic or the disapproving gazes coming from the big houses all around it. Sometimes I watched the three older men as they sat talking in the morning, shoulders hunched and legs crossed on a pallet they had woven from the leaves of the date palms. I could not hear them, and even if I had, I wouldn't have been able to decipher the Pashto they spoke. During the day the little boy was gone, filling his tarp bag with bottles and cans like all the other Afghan boys wandering over the border and then down to Karachi. I wondered if one of the three men was his father or maybe his brother. The old man either stayed in the shelter or came outside to tinker with pieces of wood or stare vacantly into visions only he could see. At dusk, he lit the fire, stoking the sticks until a small orange glow appeared under the pot and a thin snake of smoke rose into the sky.

The days passed and the men stayed. Others in the neighborhood had noticed their idle presence. The Punjabi family that lived across the street with young daughters about the same age as me became uncomfortable. Day after day the ground stood unbroken, construction implements were nowhere in sight, and neither was a foreman. One Saturday the father of the Punjabi girls showed up at our house to speak to my father. It was the first time the men had spoken of anything other than who dumped trash and who lit the fires. In those hostile chats my father had insisted he take responsibility, pointing out again and again that the crates of mangoes, the old tires, and the empty boxes were all things we had seen his family use. The neighbor refused every time, walking off in an enraged huff.

This conversation was different, the low voices and hushed tones an invitation to collusion. Clearly it was a matter of far greater import than the production and conflagration of trash. The Punjabi man was concerned about the men who overnight had deposited themselves in our midst. He had spoken to neighbor after neighbor, knocked on this door and that, and nobody had an answer. To get to the bottom of it, he had gone to the office of Karachi Municipal Corporation, where he had a friend in high places. Through his friend he had learned that there was no building project and no new resolution over whatever property squabble ailed the empty plot. The men were simply squatters, taking advantage of the quiet neighborhood to occupy a piece of land that had never belonged to them. With his hands in pockets of his green safari suit, the Punjabi neighbor pursed his lips into a thin line and delivered his conclusion. "We are all respectable people. We cannot allow this to happen . . . Our women are here alone during the day. Who knows about these men and what they might do?"

By the afternoon of the following day, the men were gone. I never discovered the details of their eviction, whether terse words were spoken or a few hundred rupees pressed into their palms, whether there had been any threats of calling the police or simply a polite request that they make their exit. They had taken everything they brought—the tarp, the poles, the bedrolls, and the trunk. The pot with its battered cup was there no longer. A small circular spot of soot marked where they had made their fire, the lone remnant of their stay.

For a few days the plot remained silent and empty and clean. In the middle of the second week, a pile of rubbish was flung over the wall and into the plot. In the days that followed, the trash returned, piles of cardboard cartons, dead plants, broken toys heaping to greater and greater heights. Almost one month later, it was set on fire and the smoke, noxious and dark, billowed up into our house. We held our breath for as long as we could and said nothing at all.

NOVEMBER 1987

Aunt Amina had never mentioned celebrating her wedding anniversary. Perhaps as the first and second years of marriage sidled past into unmomentous anniversaries, and as the years became chastisements for the progeny that refused to appear, failing to transform them from a couple into a family, she gave up celebrating the day. It may have been too much work to remind Uncle Sohail to summon the ebullience the day seemed to require. So in recent years she had skipped it over, choosing as the day dawned and died to treat it like any ordinary day.

Now the anniversary mattered, because it fell during a week that belonged to the other wife. The day was hers, Aunt Amina fumed, and ignoring it now would signal an acceptance of the injustice that had become her life, a license to the two of them to deny her even more of what was rightfully hers. This prospect fueled her for many days, through the listless mornings and the silent evenings when she stood at her kitchen window, killing herself slowly with the sounds of their voices from the courtyard below. She imagined that at one time they might have considered her feelings, maybe forgoing an opportunity to mock her. But as the months passed they talked freely, laughed freely, teased freely, oblivious of the woman upstairs. The sounds may have been nothing or something or anything, but wafting into the silence upstairs they were always intimate and always conspiratorial; every squeal was one of delight, every groan proof of pleasure, every creak of the bed a reminder of their contentment.

Tormented as she was by the sea of passion she felt surging downstairs, retaking even a single day represented a victory, a salve for her wounds. She thought for long hours into the night when she should tell him that the date, December 31, was a few weeks away, preceded by a week that belonged to her, then occurring during one that didn't, and then followed by another that did. Was it better to wait until the last minute, when they had made plans for the last day of the year? Would a sudden revelation that would leave her enemy alone on a day that she had looked forward to be more gratifying? Or should she simply tell him now, explain the reason with a stoic calm she was aching to perfect, one that immediately indicted and reminded him that he had forgotten the date, forgotten her, failed miserably in his duty to be perfectly just.

In the end victory was far more delectable than she had imagined. The next week when Uncle Sohail returned to her, he came with a request. She could see it in the awkward bend of his elbows as he rested them on the dinner table; she could see it settle like a film on his eyes. Uncle Sohail ladled curry over his rice, settled a chicken leg over it all, and started to speak. "You hate to travel, Amina," he reminded her, slyly beginning with a past recrimination, a long-ago trip to Lahore that Aunt Amina had turned down because it conflicted with an appointment with a renowned fertility specialist. Then he cleared his throat and dived in: the bank where he worked wanted him and another employee to make a trip to Islamabad. Of course, with all his responsibilities at home, he did not want to go, but his bosses were insisting. In the smallest of voices he added, "You know *she* has never been to Islamabad, and the trip comes in her week." Emboldened by having blurted it out, he went on and on: they would be gone only two days, from December 30 until January 1, and only if it was all right with Amina, and perhaps she could spend the days in her parents' home?

When his mouth fell still, Aunt Amina crumpled. She screamed, she wept, she writhed. She fell from her chair and lay on the floor, she cursed him this torture and begged him for death. In her hysteria he lifted her up and took her to the bed. Amid the tears she spit accusations collected in her silent weeks. If he did not care for the marriage that came first, the wife he had claimed first, he should kill her now. Somewhere in the wetness of her unraveling she told him that he had forgotten the date of their marriage, the day he had brought her to this godforsaken house where she was a prisoner, waiting and watching as he lavished his love on someone else. She could not bear it anymore. If he wished to leave her alone on that day for his new bride, he might as well kill her.

Through the fog of her collapse, Aunt Amina heard him say no, say he was sorry, say that there would be no trip to Islamabad, that she would not have to endure the agony of an anniversary spent abandoned. He had made a mistake, she was right, the day was theirs and theirs alone, he would spend it with her and they would be together. When her sobs subsided and she began to lapse into sleep, he asked for permission to go downstairs and explain the situation, and Aunt Amina, lulled by exhaustion, granted it to him.

NOVEMBER 1987

The purpose of a marriage was a child. The purpose of bearing children was to eventually bear a male child. The purpose of a male child was to be an heir. According to Islamic doctrine, a child was only yours if it was related by blood, borne of your body or nursed at your breast. Boys born to a family were forbidden to marry girls born of the same mother or nursed by the same mother. Girls who were born to a family could appear unveiled before their fathers and before the boys born of the same mother or nursed by their mother. When there could not be a blood relation, there had to be a nursing relation. A child not yours by blood or by nursing, could never really be yours and could not inherit from his father. You could not, per the strictest interpretation of Islamic doctrine, appear before him unveiled. There was nothing forbidding an adoptive mother from marrying her son or an adoptive father from marrying his daughter. What was not forbidden was possible, and to prevent such deviant occurrences in the land of the pure, there were few adoptions.

There were many destitute children. They poured into Karachi every day. Some came with the droves of migrant families, clutching the hands of mothers who would be domestics, sweeping the floors and washing the clothes in wealthy or even modest homes. Others trailed behind fathers who would be stone masons or vegetable sellers or rickshaw drivers. The parents hoped they could convince an old village friend or a relation who had migrated years ago to give them a loan. Their children would work with them, becoming the boys who bagged vegetables for the customer, the girls who took care of the babies while their mothers wrung out the laundry. They came from villages all over Pakistan, their parents fleeing debts or disputes over bits of land too divided between siblings and generations to yield a living.

Some of these children ended up in a set of buildings at the edge of Karachi, where the city ended and the factories began. The buildings belonged to Madrassa Jamia Binoria, a huge complex stretching over more than twelve acres. The madrassa had been established in the late 1970s, and a decade had passed since the money from Arab sheikhs and wealthy benefactors, who expiated their commercial sins by sponsoring religious education for the children of the poor, had started to pour in. Other donors gave less frequently, but there were enough of them to sustain thousands of boys, ages five to eighteen, in the madrassa.

In a city where survival was tenuous, Madrassa Jamia Binoria presented the certainty of being fed and clothed and educated in the faith. It also presented the opportunity to remake your identity. In a city where ethnicities stuck together, whether in slums or housing societies, where one's last name and dialect set up a customized set of obstacles, Jamia Binoria refused to discriminate and took in everyone. If Muhajirs and Pashtuns were fighting over who controlled the transportation system of Karachi, or if Punjabis used their dominance over the police force of the city to boss around everyone else, the purveyors of Jamia Binoria largely ignored these disputes. The boy sent over from Bahawalpur sat next to the orphan from Peshawar, their direction always aligned toward Mecca, and the ethnic mess of the city around them far from their instruction.

Madrassa Binoria was also into politics at a grander, more global scale. In the decade since it had been founded, it had, through a propitious collusion of politics and geography, entered the midst of a conflict that would be a global focal point into the next century. It was to Jamia Binoria that Afghani visitors from Kandahar and Kabul came in the late 1980s, and they did not come for tours through its shining halls or photo opportunities with children rocking back and forth as they memorized the Quran. They came for recruits. Ten years after the Soviet invasion of Afghanistan, it was Pakistani madrassas like Jamia Binoria, swelling with boys raised on piety and eager to defend Islam, that began to supply the insurgency fighting off the Soviet Army.

The best boys from Binoria, young men raised on a strict daily schedule that began and ended with prayer, whose breaks provided opportunities for instruction in Arabic, whose role models were the Holy Prophet and his companions in Medina, all aspired to be selected for jihad. Then, led by veterans of jihad who came to recruit them, they would head north to the Khyber Pass. There, on the vast, unmarked border between the two countries, they slipped into Afghanistan and to a camp that was expecting them. At Camp

Yawar, in the craggy, steep hills filled with caves, they learned everything a guerilla needed to know: basic wiring to hook up explosives, the transformation of glass bottles into grenades, and the common chemical components of fertilizers and bombs. The training was hands-on, and progress through the course meant entry into an actual battlefield. To graduate was to enter the fight and aim a rocket at an outpost chock full of Soviet soldiers.

By 1988 the Afghan mujahideen would prevail, having been fueled in part by the boys sent from Karachi, from places of refuge and reinvention just like Madrassa Jamia Binoria. The Soviet Army, so far superior in arms and armor, in numbers and structures, would fully retreat from Afghanistan over the next year. The supply chain that sent the jihadis, however, remained intact. The destitute boys were raised on piety and produced for war. With the ending of one war, their turbaned teachers guessed, another would begin, and so the constant stream of pious fighters kept making their way from the southern city of Karachi to the battlefield of the day.

DECEMBER 18, 1987

One year after Uncle Sohail took a second wife, another strange wedding took place in Karachi. Like so many others, the marriage was arranged. Like so many others, it brought together a pretty bride with an unsmiling groom. But unlike so many others, this one was watched on television by all of Pakistan, a nation captivated by the bride, who, as the daughter of an executed prime minister, attracted a special kind of attention.

In the week of December 18, 1987, Benazir Bhutto wed Asif Ali Zardari before a crowd of hundreds of thousands of people. Every corner of the city echoed with the sounds of the celebrations. Gunshots were fired into the air by bands of Pakistan People's Party supporters, riding in open truck beds, shooting their guns into the air, and yelling, "Long live Bhutto!" at every intersection. They were young, wiry Baloch men from the slums around the Lyari River wearing tight T-shirts and stonewashed jeans, and even darker men from the interior of Sindh, heads topped with mirrored caps, one shoulder slung with burgundy and black patterns of their *ajrak* scarves and the other with a rifle. Not that the guns were scary—we saw plenty of those on the shoulders of the military men who had ruled us for the past decade (even our Pakistan Studies textbooks included helpful lists of the different sorts of guns). It was something about the men themselves, their cheers bearing something primal, something wild suddenly set loose in the city. We were used to the artificial order and the façade of contentment. Benazir's supporters, these voices of democracy, sounded to us like the voices of anarchy.

In the middle of all this was the bride, one unlike any I had ever seen before. She was not young, she was not coy, she was not shy, and she was not demure. She was not dressed in the heavy finery of a bride, in brocade thick with gold and silver or flanked on either side by the women who would help her walk, eyes downcast, into the guardianship of her husband. Around her neck and on her fingers were only a few jewels, not the scores of necklaces and bangles and rings with which families showed the largesse of what they were giving and what they were taking. Benazir looked like only a bare shadow of a bride. Her neck bore only a single necklace, many of her fingers were bare, and her wrists were festooned not in gold but in glass, the red, green, and black of the Pakistan People's Party. Her head was covered, but she sat up straight, looking not down at her hennaed hands, a prescription given to most in that role, but ahead, at something distant and impalpable. Every now and then she would turn to look at her groom, who sat nearly a foot apart on his own straight-backed chair. Partly festooned and partly simple, acquiescing but rebellious, happy but hesitant, she was something between bride and warrior, and to the eleven-year-old me, it was simply confusing.

Her groom seemed as much a mismatch as her mien. If Benazir looked like a woman enduring a part, the man she was marrying looked like a scion of tradition reveling in his role. The most notable thing about him was his turban, a multistoried creation of cream-colored cloth that towered above his head, announcing his firm grip on all sorts of hereditary claims. He was a landlord from interior Sindh, and like Benazir, the scion of a feudal family, which came complete with serfs and vassals and hundreds and hundreds of acres of Pakistan. Above his lip curled a moustache that showed no courtesy to Western fashion or clean-shaven sophistication. He looked like many Pakistani men ached to look, like a man who had never made a cup of tea or had ever bowed to another man.

The wedding carried on for days, as was expected in Pakistan. There were public and private celebrations. One of the public ones took place in Lyari, amid the tanneries and smoky factories where the inhabitants of the slum went to work. The wedding of their leader was to be a celebration for them, and by all accounts it was. Trucks laden with giant metal pots of *biryani*, the festive rice and mutton served at all weddings, parked behind the tent, doling out as much as any attendee could carry in the plastic bags and on the plates they brought with them. Inside the tent loudspeakers blared songs of praise for Benazir and Asif, and folksingers from Sindh clambered up and down the stage set in the middle, singing and cheering and dancing into the night, as the couple calmly watched over the proceedings.

But if one Karachi slum celebrated, another mourned the return of the woman whose father they blamed for dividing their country, their villages, and even their families in half. In Orangi, the large, teeming slum on the other side of Karachi, life for hundreds of thousands of refugees was still as brutal and precarious as it had been when they arrived sixteen years earlier on the heels of the creation of Bangladesh. Benazir's father's pronouncement that no more of those who had stayed loyal to a united Pakistan could be taken into Karachi still echoed in their ears. With those words, their neighbors and relatives had been labeled traitors to the new Bangladesh and doomed to live in camps where they awaited their repatriation. Amid the gunshots and sounds of revelry, the people of Orangi remained cowering and quiet in their tin-roofed hovels, the smells of the open sewers and the smoke of the cooking fires hanging uncertainly all around them.

What I did not know then and what stoked the skepticism of the adults around me, exhausted by the disruptions that had overtaken the city, was that all these celebrations were really election rallies. Benazir's public wedding was a display of power. If she wore glass bangles, it was to convince the hordes of poor Lyari factory workers and landless peasants that she was like them, not rich but wronged, her father hanged by a general, her youth spent in jails. If she sat on her wedding dais stolid and decidedly unabashed, it was to demonstrate a point not to the man next to her but to the ones watching from afar. In her manner was a message to General Zia ul Haque, the man who still ruled Pakistan, that she was a woman undeterred and unafraid. That even after watching her father being taken to the gallows and witnessing his killer anointed as an absolute ruler, she remained courageous. If she did not look like a typical bride, it was because a powerful bride who wished to lead a country had never before been seen in Pakistan. The only thing that could not be explained then was the man she had chosen as her groom.

DECEMBER 31, 1987

So many years ago, on the first anniversary of Aunt Amina and Uncle Sohail's marriage, my grandparents had thrown a big party for them. The house seemed full of weddings and festivities in those days. My second aunt was newly engaged and my grandparents were in search of a suitable wife for their only son, my father. A large party had made sense; the in-laws of two of the daughters could be wowed and entertained, and new ones solicited for the yet unmarried son. The cool December air carrying the scent of the flower garden would make its way into the hearts of would-be mothers-in-law.

Aziza Apa had been a prominent guest at that first anniversary, taking on the role of the mother and father that Uncle Sohail did not have. It was she who fed the couple their first bites of cake, standing between them, the roles of mother-in-law and father-in-law coalescing into her single person. The moment was memorialized in a photograph, displayed for years in our sitting room.

On the day of his thirteenth anniversary, Uncle Sohail came upstairs for breakfast with Aunt Amina. It had been agreed that the entire day and the next morning would belong to her, carved out of the week that otherwise belonged to the other wife. There had been some complications in coming up with the arrangement, as Aunt Amina had insisted that she wake up with him on the day of their anniversary. He reminded her that they had not woken up together on their wedding day, so spending the one night together would more accurately recall the memory of that day. She had agreed, if reluctantly, and now she awaited him, listening to the slightest rustle of his step. He arrived adequately groggy eyed, his stale breath testifying that he had stayed true to his word and ascended the stairs as soon as he had risen. She heard his noises in the bathroom as she waited for the tea to come to a boil and fidgeted with the omelet she had prepared. Should she have squeezed out a few oranges, she wondered, as she heard the toilet flush and the water in the sink start to run? No, orange juice would seem apologetic, and she wanted to keep the balance of power as it was. He owed her this day; it was her right.

He seemed happy as he ate breakfast, and she decided to be content. They had not yet decided what they would do that evening. She had so focused on winning that day, on relishing his presence upstairs and the delicious thought of the loneliness downstairs that she had not given much thought to the details of celebration. He spoke first and with a firmness that she remembered from before her demotion. "We will be going to Aziza Apa's tonight," he announced, puncturing her hopefulness. "Be ready by six o'clock. I will sound the horn from downstairs."

The day passed in swells of turbulent emotions. As Sohail and the new wife left for the day, she felt only despair. By lunchtime, a meal she usually didn't eat, she felt a bit better, and better still when her mother called to ask after her. Surrayya, by now expertly delicate in her inquiries, did not mention the anniversary. Amina told her mother that she was to go to her in-laws' that evening, and Surrayya helpfully counseled her that it was a mark of importance that Aziza Apa had invited her. To everyone else in the family—Sohail's brothers and their nosy wives—it would show that Amina was still important, that their marriage was deserving of commemoration, that she was still equal as one wife of two, a permanent part of their family.

Aunt Amina stretched that meager dose of reassurance, but by five o'clock its solace had dwindled, replaced by new sorrows and uncertainties. The recriminations that had angered her that morning, the feeling of being cheated, returned with full force as she put on a blue silk *shalwar kamiz*. Her doubts lingered as she sprayed her neck with perfume and slid on the eight gold bangles her mother had given her for her wedding thirteen years ago. By the time she stood by the window a whole fifteen minutes earlier than necessary, she felt that the fate of spending the evening with Aziza Apa, the woman who had played such a crucial role in her devastation, was as terrible as having to spend it alone.

When she sat down next to him in the car, she could feel the seat's warmth underneath her clothes. From the upstairs window she had watched him wait to press the horn until the second wife got out of the car, and the woman had dawdled, saying words Aunt Amina could not hear upstairs. After she heard the first-floor door slammed resolutely shut, she had dawdled herself, to prove she had not waited. When she turned her face to his, he seemed happy, but her nagging doubts prevented her from smiling as well. Was he happy to be with her, or because of those recent moments with the other woman, whom he really loved? She just couldn't know for sure, so she decided to simply reply to his questions; she was fine, she had a good day, happy anniversary.

The traffic thickened as they flowed into the main artery that connected the eastern part of Karachi to the dense suburb of Gulshan-e-Iqbal to the north, as bankers, electricians, plumbers, and shop clerks all tried to make it home to their high rises and little bungalows for the night. Aziza Apa had only recently moved there, the bounty of her husband's employment in Dubai having finally yielded enough to move her and her four children from a fifth floor walk-up and land them in a house of their own. With her own parents-in-law dead and gone, and with her husband laboring on an oil rig in the Persian Gulf for most of the year, Aziza Apa spent her time there organizing the lives of her brothers and their wives.

Cars and motorcycles jostled closer and closer to their little car as they passed Hassan Square, expertly shirking off the beggars who pressed their grimy hands against the glass, begging as they had been taught by the men who ruled the gangs to which they belonged. Uncle Sohail yelled at one of them, a ten-year-old urchin wiping a dirty cloth over their already clean windshield. "Bastard," he hissed, breaking the silence they had chosen. Past Hassan Square the traffic thinned as they entered a part of Karachi that was far enough away to be still uncrowded. They passed the little park that she remembered as being just five minutes from Aziza Apa's new house. It was empty except for a few men crouched in a corner, under a blanket. Addicted to heroin smuggled from Afghanistan, they were part of the landscape, like the slide and swing set that seemed forever untouched by children.

Then they arrived at the house that Gulf money had built; it was painted brown, with "Mashallah" (Praise be to God) written in large, silver script across the upstairs balcony. The red and blue balloons tied to the gate confused her, as did the presence of the cotton-candy man standing just outside the gate. One brother-in-law was walking in as their car pulled up, carrying a large gift-wrapped box. Seeing him, Aunt Amina felt a small, unwanted pang of delight; could it be for them? Could it be that Aziza Apa had recanted, realized how much she had hurt her, decided to have a party that would make her feel welcome and restore her to dignity within the family?

They left the car and went through the gate, past the tiny garden crammed with terracotta planters and a dry fountain. Aziza Apa's face appeared at the door, children's shouts and squeals behind her. Her face was a shade lighter, caked with "foreign" makeup her husband had brought her. Her large mouth, painted plum, spread into her hostess smile. "How lovely of you to come for my Shahid's birthday," she said, looking Aunt Amina up and down. They had not seen one another since Uncle Sohail had married again. As they stood at the door, Aziza Apa, on her tiptoes, looked through the space between their heads. "Where is she . . . Sohail?" she exclaimed. "Why did you not bring her as well?"

——— CHAPTER 6 ———

The Woman in Charge

APRIL 10, 1988

The Stinger missiles first arrived in Karachi from the United States, cushioned in their crates like sleeping babies. On arrival they were cradled in the muscled arms of the Pakistan Navy, promising victory in a war that had haunted the region for a decade. At the Naval Station Mehran in Karachi, where they were unloaded, the Stinger missiles were placed in special containers and flanked by security convoys that would escort them the length of the country and across the border into war-torn Afghanistan.

The lightness of the Stinger missiles made them well suited for transport over the rock-strewn, uncertain terrain. Once at their destination, they would fit easily atop the shoulders of fighters situated on the ground or wedged in the nooks of mountain passes and behind bushes. The Stingers were the magic bullet the boy soldiers scattered along the border were praying for, their heaven-sent help against the Soviet invaders. With these missiles the mujahid could finally take shots at the green tanks crawling like crabs through the crater-filled territory and at the black, low-flying helicopters that patrolled it from the sky. All they had to do was take the shakiest of aims and fire, and the heat-seeking Stinger missile would roar straight into the heart of the enemy's steel carapace.

On their way to these boys, the Stinger missiles stopped to rest in the city of Rawalpindi, just south of the small capital city of

Islamabad, and set deep inside Pakistan in a cozy circle of green-topped hills. None of the ordinary citizens who lived in Rawalpindi knew then that the Stingers were stopping there, and those who did decided not to tell anyone. Rawalpindi served as general head-quarters of the Pakistani military, from whose manicured lawns General Zia ul Haque, the president of Pakistan, ruled the country.

At 10:00 a.m. on April 10, 1988, when the local housewives were just beginning to fry the onions for their daily curries and the schoolchildren had started to squirm in their seats in anticipation of recess, the blasts began. They came from a place known as Ojhri Camp, a depository for military weapons in the middle of Rawal-pindi. Ojhri means innards, the discarded entrails of slaughtered animals, and now Ojhri Camp was on fire.

Once the explosions began, they were everywhere. Bombs crammed with nails and gunpowder blasted into the sky; smooth, mango-sized grenades small enough to fit in a soldier's pocket ex-ploded in a bloody shower. The booms of dynamite added to the chorus in a wild cacophony of destruction that could only signal war. The Stingers too erupted, rising from the gray, unmarked warehouse. The missiles flew high in the morning sun of that feck-less Rawalpindi morning, their furious ascent unfazed by the cur-tains of humidity that always settled on the city at that hour. When they had reached a point high enough to almost disappear, they began to crash down on houses and schools and mosques full of people. Some whizzed horizontally, flying low and hurling them-selves indiscriminately at flesh and cars and buildings.

The people surrounded by the blood and wreckage thought this was the Day of Judgment, the reckoning promised in the Holy Quran. No one knew who selected the targets that day, but the missiles erupted anyway, beckoned by the dense heat of vegetable sellers, paper peddlers, schoolchildren and housewives, the rich, the poor, everyone who happened to be nearby.

Far away in Karachi, the city that had first welcomed the Stinger missiles into Pakistan's arms, the news came through the state-run media. Inter Service Public Relations, the public relations arm of the military, had issued a communiqué announcing that thirty people had died and the situation was under control. It did not mention the thousands of critically injured people who still waited for medical attention, the fires that still burned, and the splintered homes that gaped up at a dusk that would not come.

The communiqué also did not say who had set the fire, how it had lapsed beyond control, or why an arms depot sat among millions of unsuspecting civilians. In the days that followed, more stories and even more bodies were extracted from beneath the shattered glass and twisted pieces of metal, bits of flesh still stuck to them. Tales of the dead were smuggled to newspaper offices, where editors published them in bits and pieces. One official body count was one hundred. The body count based on these unofficial accounts was estimated to be anywhere between one thousand and four thousand people, felled by weapons intended for another place altogether.

The Ojhri Camp massacre showed ordinary Pakistanis just how little they knew about the deals their military rulers reached with the United States. The country that had been wrested from the British as a homeland for the subcontinent's Muslims was now a convoy for funneling arms to the Afghan mujahideen, so they could fight the Soviet Union for the United States. The people in the middle, Pakistanis, were an afterthought it seemed to all involved. In the aftermath of that tragedy, few knew what had really happened at Ojhri Camp. In the years to come, that dénouement—of tragedy always unexplained, never mediated by the facts or by the truth—would become familiar, even routine.

AUGUST 14–17, 1988

We always woke early on Independence Day to the sound of the flag flapping proudly against the post we had attached to the upstairs balcony a solid month before the day itself. At seven o'clock sharp the sound of a twenty-one-gun salute could be heard booming from the grounds of the Mehran naval base, which stood not far from our house. We then watched the parade, telecast live from Islamabad every Independence Day morning. On our screens appeared the thousands of khaki-clad soldiers, undulating seas of brown, marching and murmuring in formation, and entrancing us with their portrait of orderliness and manly acquiescence.

The military world was a vision of Pakistani perfection that existed side by side and inexplicably against the tumult of the world inhabited by the rest of us. Sometimes, its very existence seemed like a rebuke to the disorderliness surrounding the compound. We got a glimpse of it only every now and then—on a school field trip to an air force base on Defense Day, at a birthday party of a family friend who lived inside the cantonment villas reserved for senior military officers. Military bases were magical places where children, even girls, could ride their bikes to the cantonment store alone. Little reminders of its specialness were everywhere: on the tree trunks outfitted in painted uniforms of green and white stripes and in every bush and flower standing at attention. There, you would never be confronted by boil-covered beggars pressing their palms into your face or glimpse Afghan refugee children picking through the trash heaps.

In fact, no trash heaps at all were to be found inside the military bases, the rubbish having been carted away magically to some faraway place, where neither smell nor offensive sight could assault the senses of Pakistan's warriors. On a school field trip to the air force base, terse-faced soldiers presented each sweaty and cowed child with an ice cold soda, for which we parted with not a single paisa. Dazzled and sated we all gulped obediently, without spilling a drop on the glimmering green lawn, where the grass was exactly an inch tall. The military in our minds would always be associated with perfection and free soft drinks.

In school our adoration of the military was cultivated. We learned the names of the army heroes who had been awarded the Nishan-e-Haider, the highest medal of bravery, all of the honorees having sacrificed their lives for their homeland. They were heroes from the wars of 1948, 1965, and 1971, all fought against India, its menacing presence next door underscored by the stories of the soldiers. Our teachers quizzed us on the circumstances of the death of Captain Sarwar Shaheed, who had outflanked the Indian troops in Kashmir, or that of the boyish Rashid Minhas Shaheed, who had prevented a traitorous pilot from hijacking their plane to India in 1971. They prodded us to see if we had memorized with adequate zeal the details of dogfights with fighter planes and understood the endless trickery of the Indians who stood at our borders and threatened to take back the Pakistan they thought should never have existed in the first place. At recess, we showed off the stickers of missiles and medals we had scored at birthday parties or at the stationery store. We affixed the stickers prominently to our pencil cases and our schoolbooks. F-16s, Mirage planes, and sharp-nosed, red-topped rockets stared back at us as we lumbered through quadratic equations and conjugated complex Urdu verbs.

Born and bred on the lore of fighters, we were shocked when we heard the news of the president's death in a plane on August 17, 1988. Our house had stood suspended in the limbo that reigned just before everyone got up for afternoon tea when the phone rang. It was my father. The president of Pakistan, General Mohammad Zia ul Haque, had been killed when his C-130 plane was downed in the skies over southern Punjab. The man who had ruled Pakistan for eleven years was dead, and with this we began to cry.

Afternoon passed with the altered pace of a day suddenly and unwillingly lifted into the uncertain realm of the extraordinary. Ghulam Ishaq Khan, the interim president, appeared on screen sitting morosely between a Pakistani flag and the grim face of Mohammad Ali Jinnah in a picture frame hanging from the wall. Khan's face was funereal as he intoned the details of the death, speaking in a mechanical drone that would become renowned. The crash had occurred at 4:30 p.m., when General Zia was en route to Rawalpindi from Bahawalpur. Everything was going according to plan, until of course it wasn't. An explosion in the sky destroyed the plane long before the pieces hit the ground.

The next day was proclaimed a holiday, with the funeral scheduled to take place before dusk. Like millions of other dumbstruck Pakistanis, we sat at home watching the crowds gather. It was the first funeral we had watched on television, it was the first we had seen at all, its macabre tones heightened by the tearful voices of the television anchors. The Pakistan Television Corporation showed every minute of General Zia's last public appearance, from the flag-wrapped coffin trailed by a military convoy of sorrow-stricken soldiers to the hundreds of thousands of mourners reduced to dots by the panoramic sweep of some high-perched camera.

We learned about his humble childhood in a lush but ordinary village in Punjab, his set of sons, his tremendous rise, and most important of all, his undying love for the country we also loved. We glimpsed the freshly dug grave, the raw and pungent earth ready to receive him.

There were things that we were not told. For example, we did not learn that the wreckage from the plane had been scattered over miles of open farmland in the plains of Bahawalpur. We never knew that the coffin, handled so reverently by the gloved soldiers, contained just a few bits of the general's remains. There was scant mention of the thirty-one other men who had also died that day. One of them was General Akhtar Abdul Rehman, the general of Ojhri Camp and the chief caretaker of the Stingers that had killed so many others a few months earlier, but no one commented aloud on the coincidence. There was also silence about the two Americans on board. What could be found of the bodies of the American ambassador to Pakistan and the American in charge of military aid to Pakistan were surrendered to the soft-spoken aides who came to take their remains back home to their stunned families.

But the men on television repeatedly announced that the general's copy of the Holy Quran, the well-read one that he carried with him on every single journey, had been discovered in the wreckage unharmed. Crowds of hundreds of thousands were captured in the broad sweep of the camera, chanting Zia's own slogan: "*Pakistan ka mutlab kya? La Iilaha illalah.*" ("What is the meaning of Pakistan? There is only one God.") It was half in Urdu and half in Arabic, half Pakistani and half Quranic, and together it rhymed.

SEPTEMBER 1988

Despite the general's death, the wedding season of 1988 began early, months before the weather cooled. Two years after Aunt Amina's disgrace, we had stepped forth with the tentativeness of the recently wronged into the frigid waters of social life. We didn't start with weddings but with funerals, whose less frequent occurrence and solemnity allayed the possibility of social rejection. To share a tear, everyone agreed, was nobler than partaking in the joyous frivolity of a wedding party and hence a more acceptable platform of reentry for the ostracized. Parked in a corner of the home of the recently departed, my grandmother could offer her sincere sorrow, her charitable presence a rebuke to those who should have stood up for Aunt Amina but chose not to. One-upmanship in the dispensation of spiritual and personal duties was victory.

Weddings were trickier. One couldn't rely on a corpse to lull the gossips or to make up for the absence of the Quran table, whose radius of reverence offered shelter to the sheepish. On the contrary, weddings provided a natural space to vent old grievances, pose sharp questions in front of a captive audience, and inflict calculated public slights and snubs. But ironically, the two years between the implosion of Aunt Amina's marriage and our reemergence had turned the churning wheels of gossip to our advantage. A girl who had run off with a poor taxi driver hit the double whammy of shame—not only did she run off, she had run off with a poor man! That scandal was then displaced by the sinister matter of the forty-year-old mother of two who became possessed *bya djinn*. At henna parties and Quran readings, her neighbors told tales of nocturnal routs and her bellowing musings in Balochi, a language she had never known. These bits of other unraveled lives granted Aunt Amina a much-needed reprieve. Once again we could appear at a wedding without fearing a taunt or a question that evoked the shadow of Uncle Sohail's "other" wife.

So it was in the middle of that wedding season after the general's death that I attended a henna party with my grandmother. I usually enjoyed outings in which it was just she and I. When we arrived, Surrayya settled in the old-lady section of the room, where she wouldn't budge for the rest of the evening, assuming an immobility that allowed me at eleven years old to be a kid, rekindling friendships with whichever gaggle of distant second or third cousins happened to be in attendance. My grandmother did not care if I ran about with this random gang, all of us gorging on lukewarm Cokes and stealing samosas from trays forgotten by waiters sneaking a smoke outside the wedding tent. If I tired of this, I could choose to be a young lady and sit dutifully at my grandmother's side, absorbing details of grown-up conversations.

This party seemed to have been hurriedly arranged; there were too many people and too little room. Dinner was late and the wedding party had already dispersed. More important, very few of my cousins and friends had turned up. A scared seven-year-old and an uppity twelve-year-old and I had attempted conversation and completed a roundup of the still empty buffet tables. There was no food to be found by smell or sight, so we made our way back to our grandmothers and aunts and mothers to wait out our sentence in silence.

It was at this moment that a woman, clad in bright coral and blue, plunked herself in the folding chair on the other side of my grandmother. She smelled strongly of mothballs and attar, the perfume oil worn by women who eschewed any fragrance that contained alcohol. Surrayya squirmed ever so slightly in her chair and stretched her mouth into a forced smile. She moved her balled-up handkerchief from one palm to the other and sighed. The woman was the mother of one of Aunt Amina's sisters-in-law. Like us, she was related by marriage to Uncle Sohail's family. Her daughter, however, had borne her husband not one or two but four healthy babies, three sons and one daughter. She and her daughter had both attended Uncle Sohail's second wedding. They had showered his new wife with rose petals and presented her with gifts while Aunt Amina lay weeping in our back room two Decembers ago. A satin-clad carrier pigeon, this woman had in the past been the emissary of the jabs and prods Aziza Apa directed our way. Her twittering never bore glad tidings.

The woman began with a practiced list of pleasantries. First she asked about my grandfather's health, then proceeded to inquire lightly about my father, moved on with feigned concern about my mother's absence, and finally to her own litany of ailments, her creaky knees and her elevated blood pressure. Her relaxed chattiness did little to comfort my grandmother. Ever since the rejection of Aunt Amina by her in-laws, she had been subjected to countless verbal whacks, and most came in the midst of mundane banter. The woman paused, looked at Surrayya's tense face and declared, "We told Aziza at first, when it was happening, that it does not look right." She paused again, moistening her lips with her tongue and quickly scanning our faces for a reaction before continuing.

"We told her two or three times . . . We *understand* that Sohail wants children, but the woman he is choosing is not right. She looks even older than him, so it makes no sense . . . If you want children, you must marry a young girl, you know." It was hard to gauge the intent of this statement, so my grandmother said nothing at all, waiting for what came next. The woman continued, "See, now it has been almost two years, and where is the baby? There is no baby. Again and again we look to see if there is a baby; month after month there is no baby." With these magic words, the frown lifted from Surrayya's taut face. "Sohail has made a terrible mistake," the woman continued. "All this and no baby . . . We all know if there was to be a baby, there would be one by now."

I looked up at my grandmother and saw that she was smiling.

NOVEMBER 16, 1988

It started with a young girl who wanted a college education. Bushra Zaidi and three of her young friends set out for college one sweltering April morning like they did any other day. The black numbers on the Casio watches so many of the college girls wore indicated it was 10:30 a.m., when the midmorning classes at Sir Syed Girls College in North Nazimabad were about to begin.

The sun was already high in the sky and the city streets choked with traffic. Like all girls colleges in Karachi, Sir Syed Girls College was a fortress of high walls and gates designed to enclose girls yearning to learn and to keep out the men yearning for them. Men lounged and loitered around the gates of the college, hawkers selling coal-hot corn or ice-cold drinks, men loafing, men waiting, men pretending they were waiting for sisters to collect and transport at the end of the day. Men were not allowed inside, but getting them away from the premises was an impossible task.

So crowded was the area around the college gate that the bus dropped the girls off across the street. It was a bare five hundred yards of heated asphalt and flying dust between the bus stop and the open gate to the college. The girls always crossed it together, in unison, a short line clad in white and blue, walking hand in hand, forming a fragile human chain against the surge of traffic. That morning the four girls clasped their hands and began to walk across the road, as they always did, their leather satchels bouncing against their sides as they made their way across. They inched forward, expertly and slowly, through a pause in the traffic, a small stop in the hum of speeding cars and rickshaws and buses. Before long, they were halfway, then two-thirds of the way, almost there.

They probably did not see the bus coming from the other side. Yellow and fast and festooned with gilt decorations that flashed in the sunlight, it was bound directly for them. The driver would later say he did not see the girls at all. In an instant, they were crumpled and flattened, their warm blood pooling in cracks and crevices of the road. One was dead and three were dying.

The name of the girl who died was Bushra Zaidi. Her family had also come to Karachi after Partition, and she was one student in a college of hundreds like her who had wrested from reluctant fathers and brothers permission for an education. Her family was of modest means, and while they had done better than those who still slogged away in the city's slums, theirs was a frugal existence, shadowed by the knowledge that there was barely enough to go around.

The man who had killed her was a Pashtun, a member of the ethnic tribes that straddled the border between Afghanistan and Pakistan. They had arrived in Karachi in droves, fleeing the war that seeped into their villages. In the city they found jobs as bus drivers, and then called their brothers and sons and cousins to join the same trade. All of them drove private buses and few of them were literate. Together they controlled Karachi's transport system, ferrying millions from one hapless corner of the city to the other, through the narrow lanes of the old markets to the smog-choked avenues of the new commercial areas, to the north and to the south and the east and the west.

With the abandon of wild horses galloping over the sparse steppes of Khyber they drove their buses over Karachi's potholed highways, unaware or oblivious to traffic rules. Their recklessness was abetted by the riders themselves, each of them eager to get where they were going faster, trying always to beat the cruel clock of passing opportunities. A few moments saved could yield great benefits: being the first in a queue of hundreds, reaching some government office before it closed for the day, getting to work before the boss, getting home before dark. This was Karachi, and there was too little of everything. One or two people died in the path of the buses every day, their deaths either forgotten or forgiven or both.

Bushra Zaidi's case should have not been any different. She had no important relatives who could cash in favors and urge arrests. Her humble family neither entertained military generals nor had accrued patronage from feudal lords; they could not even boast of a savior cousin or two in some middling government post who would speak up for the female victim. And the bus that crushed her was owned by a man whose uncle was a police officer, a fact that shifted the entire equation in favor of silence, anonymity, and no markings of bereavement at all, not even the scant minutes of mourning generally apportioned to traffic fatalities. Bystanders tried to flag a rickshaw to take the bleeding girls to a hospital, and passing strangers stopped their cars and heaved the girls' torn bodies into the backseats of passing cars. All indications were that this event would be quickly forgotten.

At least an hour after the accident the incident was revealed to be different. A new generation of girls had been brought up behind the walls of that educational facility, unprivileged girls raised just like Bushra Zaidi inside the tight limits of airless rooms and insecure respectability, Karachi girls who had believed in college and education, and stared down and dodged the very buses that had killed their classmate. When these girls heard that no police report had been filed and no charges lodged against the driver for killing Bushra Zaidi, they grew agitated. Wet with tears and reddened with anger, they congregated in clusters around the cheap, painted desks, holding textbooks of anatomy and geography and Urdu literature, sweating and crying under the slow-moving fans. Their anguish and frustration swelled when their teachers tried to force them to sit down and fix their gaze once again at the blackboards covered with equations. They refused. When they were pushed out of the classrooms, they collected in the corridors; when they were pushed out of the corridors, they came outside.

Hours after Bushra Zaidi died on the street outside Sir Syed Girls College, the girls came out into the heat, into the hordes of men that still waited at the gates, into the blood puddles that marked the spot where their friends were hit. The police who had surrounded the college after the incident, the police who were refusing to register a report against the driver, now panicked. They had never before seen girls emerge into a street, young girls, college girls shouting slogans. The crowd of girls grew as more and more emerged from the buildings. A few hours after Bushra Zaidi's death, in the scorching late afternoon heat of a Karachi April, the street was full of angry, young girls. Slowly, the demonstration inched toward a police van parked outside the gate, their every step forward marked with their collective chant for justice for the dead Bushra.

The policemen in the van were outnumbered. Rather than standing by, allowing the wispy, unarmed girls their protest, they charged at them with the police van. It was mayhem. One girl at the front of the line folded to the ground in the first frontal assault of the van. Then the policemen in their black and khaki uniforms stormed the crowd of chanting girls and began to beat them with batons. These were untouched girls who never spoke to strange men, girls who were permitted to leave their homes only to get an education, girls who asked shopkeepers to place objects on counters to avoid even the barest brush of a male hand, girls who had never protested.

The policemen didn't care. They grabbed and groped the girls, their breasts, faces, and hair, intent on teaching them a lesson. They were being taught not to leave the boundaries of their campus, not to ask for something the men did not want to give them; they were being taught the consequences for speaking up. Other police vans arrived, with more men and more batons and more guns and more anger. Crumpled by their numbers and their guns, the weeping, beaten girls retreated inside the college walls and the terrified college administration shut the gates to hold back the swarm of armed police. But the military assault on the girls continued. Shells were lobbed over the college walls, streaming tear gas through the open windows of the buildings and leaving hundreds of girls crouched on the ground, coughing, sputtering, and crying.

After the killing of Bushra Zaidi, Karachi erupted. The story of the dead girl and the man who murdered her were whittled down to their ethnicities. She was Muhajir and he was Pashtun; she was dead and he was free. It was as if every festering suspicion, every slight between every Muhajir and every Pashtun had to be avenged. Angry Muhajir mobs set fire to Pashtun buses, their burned-out carcasses left charred and sulking at every intersection. Orangi Town, the slum that housed the children and grandchildren of the refugees, became the center of conflict, with Muhajirs fighting Pashtuns and gangs of Pashtuns striking back.

It was the beginning of an ethnic war that would outlive them all. In the days that followed, hundreds died, and from their blood a fifth ethnicity emerged in Pakistan. There were no longer Sindhis, Punjabis, Balochis, and Pashtuns, each neatly attached to a province in a country that then had four of them. This new ethnicity was called "Muhajir," or "refugee," an umbrella name for all those whose families migrated to Pakistan post-1947, all those who now lived in a Karachi straining at its seams.

Justice for Bushra Zaidi's death did not come until almost two years later, and it was a justice erected on the shoulders of ethnicity, of who belonged where. On November 16, 1988, national elections were held all over Pakistan. It was the first time Pakistanis had voted since 1971 and they were electing a prime minister after more than a decade of military rule.

On the eve of the election Karachi vacillated between two powerful women. On one end, at her tree-lined mansion by the sea, was the newlywed Benazir Bhutto, whose party won a national majority of seats. As the sun set that day, she knew her party was the only one with a majority and that for the first time in history a woman would serve as prime minister of a Muslim country. But on the inner edges of the city, in the slums of Orangi, in the squat houses of Nazimabad, in the teeming flats of Gulshan-e-Iqbal and Gulistan-e-Jauhar, another celebration reigned. Benazir had won the country, but she had lost Karachi. The city and nearly every electoral seat in it had been swept by the Muhajir Qaumi Movement (a political movement to obtain equal rights for Muhajirs, migrants from India). Their victory was a victory for another woman, the dead but not forgotten Bushra Zaidi.

NOVEMBER 1988

Uncle Sohail wanted to add a new floor to his house. The plot on which the house stood was small, a half plot really, as my grandmother had once smirked. It didn't have a garden or even a straggly backyard onto which the house could be expanded, so he decided to build up. It was not a novel trajectory; many in our neighborhood and throughout the city were doing the same. We could see stubby two-stories sprouting stately third ones all over the place, with balconies staring smugly over the roofs beneath them. Others squashed new bedrooms with attached bathrooms and even sitting rooms into what were once courtyards. These new rooms could then be crammed with chintzy sofas and stereo sets carted back by brothers and sons in Dubai. There was no longer any room for gardens; they were now abandoned as homeowners came to accept the limits of what they could coax out of stingy Karachi soil. They needed room for the next generation or for new arrivals to Karachi: daughters-in-law, grandchildren, and sometimes even their children. The bigger the brood, the taller the edifice. The bigness of a house, the numbers of grandchildren scurrying about, these dutiful homages also suggested a victory against that other burden of migration—the loss of the brood. It was a victory that the people of Karachi liked to publicize: the reassembled brood, all housed in one humungous space, was a testament to an immigrant family's success. Riches and relatives, the best of both worlds brought together.

The fervor to keep the clan together was further fueled by Karachi's economies of scale. In newly swollen Karachi, a good job at a bank or managing a small shop now meant a life of eternal cohabitation where all your roommates would be relatives.

Naturally, these additions never matched the original houses. Either the people had changed and realized their dreams did not fit the city, or the city had changed, had become bigger and fuller with new migrants atop old ones. Its new size required new dreams, and the distance between the two was sometimes reflected in the mismatch of the architecture. If the ground floor had been square and angular, built in the modest aspirations of first migrants, then the next one would be curvy and ornate, with flourishes of plaster flowers stuck on every surface. The second and third floors were the tastes of a new generation, raised on different visions, interested in aping other sensibilities. Sometimes this generational rebellion was subtle and reflected only in the choice of color and paint; one addition painted lime green and pink, and stuck to its unwilling beige parental wing in an act of unwilling compromise.

Uncle Sohail's case was different. The additions to his house reflected the desires not of a second generation but a second bride, and one who had moved in hoping for a child. Now, three years later, there was still no baby. So, during an ordinary afternoon visit, when Aunt Amina told us of his plans to build again, we gasped. This bit about constructing another level to the house immediately put meat and gristle on the bones of our suspicions. A man who could marry twice could certainly marry a third time; why else would he need a new addition?

We couldn't tell what Aunt Amina thought of the development. In the three years since the arrival of the second wife, her face had hardened into an impenetrable cast, broken only by outbursts that had become predictable to us. But we all focused on Aunt Amina as we considered the possibility that Aziza Apa was on the hunt for a third wife for Uncle Sohail. She had never really been able to choose the second wife, and perhaps now with proof that Sohail had not chosen the right woman to beget babies, she could get him a younger one. Maybe it would be third daughter of some poor family, too desperate not to relegate their daughter to being a third choice or to subject her to a gynecological exam to make sure that this time there would be no room for error.

As our speculations brewed, Aunt Amina remained solidly on my grandmother's bed, quiet, her face stuck in the sort of immobility she had perfected in the two years since her betrayal. When she did speak, it was only briefly, offering minimal details. There wasn't a third wife, she said. It was the second wife who wished to build the extra story from her own money earned at the bank. Sohail, however, had said that the newest part of the house would belong to Amina, as she was the first. The lowest floor would be rented out, he had triumphantly told her as the cement trucks and the contractor started to pull up. "Just think, Amina, an extra five thousand rupees every month for no work at all" was how he rationalized it. The new wife could not make him a father, but she had made him a landlord.

NOVEMBER 22, 1988

The chill had settled in stubbornly, and the women of the Bangash tribe in Parachinar, in Pakistan's North-West Frontier province shivered underneath their quilts as they put out the kerosene lanterns. It had been a busy day for them; seven goats had been slaughtered. Little boys, still permitted to roam among women, brought them into their courtyards to be cleaned, trimmed, and deboned.

The best meat was always cooked on the day of the slaughter, in large metal cauldrons dragged out for the occasion and emptied of their stores of lentils, scraps of cloth, even a bottle or two of perfume oil someone's husband had brought back from the city. The little boys helped drag them out, their surfaces like smooth coins that had passed many hands. In these cauldrons, set on the stones of hot coal fires, the fresh meat would be braised in clarified butter that had been made from the fat of slaughters past.

The tribe was celebrating the return of fighters, men who had gone off as youths to aid in the battle against the Soviets. They told stories of the sulky retreat of Soviet soldiers, their tanks casting sad lines of defeat on the snow of the Salang Pass. The men laughed as they recounted this, slapping each other on the back, their guns having been slung against the pillar at the entrance. The older men spoke of earlier wars, the oldest told of the British who also had come and drawn a line in the mountains that rose up beyond their horizon between Afghanistan and Pakistan. The white men had failed again, the toothless elder chortled in a voice that was barely a creak among the booming laughter of the young men.

The white men would fail again, the soldiers had told themselves as they hungered for fresh bread, as they watched gangrene creeping up the limbs of injured comrades on a rain-soaked night they were certain would be their last. But they did not think of those nights now as the smoke from the cooking fires rose. The day passed in triumphant stories, and the boys who had ferried the plates of meat into the courtyard hours earlier were sent to exhort the women to hurry.

The food was ready before dusk—rice, meat, bread, and huge dishes of yogurt. The eating began and the talking continued and their spirits rose to even greater heights. Outside as the night grew darker, their voices, lulled by food, faded into a slow contentment. The air chilled, and the embers flickered with red, the smell of wood smoke mixing with the smell of bones picked clean. The men drifted off to sleep, satiated and content to be in the company of their comrades rather than the women who had waited for them.

The women too were asleep, save one or two nursing mothers fumbling in the darkness to feed their babies. The young mothers curled up in the folds of their worn velvet quilts and stared up at the clear, star-sprinkled sky, dreaming of the future, perhaps with one of the men who had returned.

It was from the sky that the horror descended that night, when the high sparkles that looked like stars suddenly began to fall. Those who were still awake would have seen the hurtling plane and the encroaching shadow of a second, smaller plane; and finally they would have heard the scream of the missile. Everyone else would remember only the explosions.

Men, awaking with a violent jolt, reached for their guns and ran toward the flaming debris that littered the square where they had convened so joyously just hours earlier. Pieces of burning cloth and flesh fell from the sky and scattered through Parachinar, one of the Pakistani towns closest to the Afghanistan border. The women wailed and screamed, their voices rising over the flames and black clouds of burning fuel.

The first bodies that the men found were women, recognizable by the remnants of their long hair, somehow untouched by the flames. The men covered them with the cloths they had wrapped around their necks, leaving other women to care for their bodies. Whether dead or alive, women could only be taken care of by other women. Later, the women of Parachinar bathed and dressed the dead women, and then a single man was permitted to enter and carry one shrouded body at a time, taking care not to touch it by chance even once. The burial prayers could be said only by the men, and they were done before dawn.

Just when the women from the sky had been covered by the earth, brown trucks with green and white flags arrived, full of soldiers in crisp khaki shouting commands in Urdu and Punjabi, which neither the men nor the women could understand. They corralled the men away from the still smoldering wreckage, their commander conferring with the elder in a terse conversation that reminded all of past promises that had been made between the tribe and the military. This was the Pakistani military's catastrophe to manage, and the tribe would be compensated. The men held back and watched, unsure but grounded in their places, as twenty-eight bodies were carried from the wreckage into the vans. They did not tell the military men about the two bodies they had buried; perhaps they were scared by what they might do.

For three months the military men would not say what happened in Parachinar. The people who witnessed the incident would not tell their story for years. The bodies from the Afghan transport plane carrying thirty passengers that was shot down by a Pakistani F-16 would not be returned until the military could come up with an explanation. The Pakistan Ministry of Defense issued a statement saying "that a plane had been shot down by ground fire near Parachinar and that everyone on board had died." A press report issued later quoted a spokesperson from the ministry as saying that the plane had been asked to identify itself, and when it did not, it was destroyed.

Three months later a Red Cross plane carried twenty-eight bodies over Parachinar and back to Afghanistan, finally taking them home to be buried. They took with them a message from Pakistan to Afghanistan. With the Soviets gone and Zia dead, a new Pakistani military was in charge. In this new arrangement, the border straddled by Parachinar was real when the Pakistanis said so, and the night when the Bangash celebrated the return of their victorious fighters was the night when Pakistan had deemed that a lost Afghan plane was an enemy Afghan plane.

DECEMBER 2, 1988

Dressed in a satiny green *shalwar kamiz*, her head demurely covered in a white headscarf, Benazir Bhutto, at thirty-five years of age, took the oath of office, the youngest and first female prime minister of Pakistan. The image of her standing next to President Ghulam Ishaq Khan, who had fewer than six months earlier announced the death of General Zia ul Haque, was splashed across newspapers all around the world. A woman, young and beautiful, recently married and not yet a mother, was about to lead an Islamic Republic that had for more than a decade been ruled by a military dictator who had executed her father.

In the front row of the Grand Reception Hall of the National Assembly Building, where the ceremony was held, sat her mother, Nusrat Bhutto; her sister, Sanam Bhutto; and Asif Ali Zardari, the husband she had married a year earlier. It began, as official ceremonies always do, with a recitation from the Holy Quran. The man who recited the verses looked down at the Quran and never once looked up at the woman who would lead him.

It all seemed unbelievable in its speed and cruel serendipity. Just before Zia had died, the most prominent religious clerics had slapped their palms together and smoothed their beards in triumph as General Zia ul Haque had promulgated the Shariat Ordinance of 1988, saturating the bureaucracy of Pakistan with religious clerics. A new court had been created to enforce this law. The Federal Shariat Court's sole function was to police every jurisdiction in the country for any departure from the word of the Holy Quran and the Sunnah. This June decree was a victory for the mullahs, as they declared that Pakistan had finally been reclaimed for Islam. And now in December they were confronted with a catastrophe worse than they could have foreseen. A woman, who under the dictates of Shariat law could not be allowed to lead prayer and whose testimony in court would be counted as only half of a man's, was now taking the oath of office to lead the Islamic Republic of Pakistan.

While the mullahs squirmed and wept, her political opponents, also defeated men, wondered at the path of compromises that had got Benazir Bhutto to that podium. The oath itself had to begin with a series of assurances that, while she may be a woman, she was still a good Muslim and believed that the Holy Quran was supreme. The headscarf she wore that day, and every day in office that would follow, was yet another assurance. Everyone knew that Benazir Bhutto had not covered her hair until she became a contender for her father's political legacy, the leadership of the Pakistan People's Party, and now Pakistan itself.

The headscarf, like the husband, could have been a compromise meant to make Benazir, an icon of female power, a little more familiar and feminine. Asif Zardari, the scion of a feudal family and who seemed to have little of her ideological fervor or her affinity for the people, grinned widely from under his curly moustache as his wife took the oath of office. Perhaps it didn't matter to him whether it was money or marriage that made him powerful; all that mattered was the smug comfort that he indeed was.

DECEMBER 1988

In the dark inner rooms of the women's wing of Karachi's Central Jail, twenty-six-year-old Shahida Parveen could not see the new prime minister take the oath of office. The new prime minister had herself spent some time in the jail, between the episodes of house arrest and exile that had filled her life after her father's execution and before she left the country. But on that day, Benazir Bhutto was far from the grim realities of the life of a woman prisoner like Shahida.

Inside prison walls, this day passed like any other, with Shahida and the other women taking care of the children they had been allowed to bring with them. Mothers nursed their babies and played with the toddlers dressed in donated hand-me-downs. The prison remained suspended in the endless monotony and degradations of punished life—time spent waiting for relatives who never came, and always at the mercy of the abusive male guards who did as they pleased with the women, especially those imprisoned for sex-related crimes.

Shahida Parveen was on death row, awaiting execution by stoning. A year earlier, she and her husband Mohammad Sarwar had been found guilty of adultery and sentenced by a trial court under the Zina and Hudood Ordinance that had been promulgated by General Zia ul Haque in 1979 to Islamize Pakistan. Their crime was the failure to register Shahida's divorce from her first husband, which in the opinion of the trial court made her relations with her new husband automatically adulterous. The old marriage law, which was still on the books as part of Pakistan's civil code, clashed with the general's Islamic additions; Shahida Parveen had not known that divorces had to be registered, and so for the crime of marrying again, she had been declared an adulteress. The fact that she was pregnant counted as evidence of the act.

Shahida Parveen had not known about any of these laws, the old ones or the new ones. When her first husband attacked her in a fit of rage in his father's house and yelled, "I divorce you," once, twice, and then three times, and dragged her by the hair to the door, she had taken him at his word. So had everyone else—his parents, her parents, all their relatives and prying neighbors; everyone thought these words sufficient for a divorce. It was what they knew, what the imams in the neighborhood mosques told them: saying "I divorce you" three times was sufficient to get rid of a wife. But the Federal Shariat Court expressed a different opinion. The absence of a registered divorce meant that Shahida had been married when she took up with another man, and this errant wife must be disciplined.

In prison Shahida recalled a time when she believed her luck had changed, when a new marriage proposal had arrived a year after she had been forsaken by her husband. The suitor, Mohammad Sarwar, had been a simple man, and perhaps she would not have considered him back when she was young and whole and a virgin. But as a woman abandoned by her husband she was just grateful that her fate had not been sealed. How ironic it was, she thought as she lingered in prison, that by accepting this new opportunity for marriage she would be walking into an even more dire predicament.

But her new-found happiness was too much to bear for her first husband, Khushi Mohammad. As soon as he learned that she had married again, he raged and bellowed at anyone who would listen. A woman once his was always his, he declared. One of the men listening to his rants suggested he visit a lawyer. Khushi Mohammad found one who enlightened him about the laws, these weapons he could use to insure that the misery he had mandated could not be undone. With his lawyer's help he now told a new story. He had never divorced Shahida, he now insisted; he had never registered the divorce, or even said the words three times. The woman was still his.

Shahida's statement in own her defense ended up indicting her, because she could not provide documentary proof of her divorce from Khushi Mohammad. Under the Zina and Hudood Ordinance, her testimony amounted to a confession of adultery, because it did not deny her relationship with Mohammad Sarwar. Once she and Mohammad Sarwar, the man who had chosen to take a divorced woman as his wife, had admitted that they believed they were married, the case was closed, because no further proof that they were having intercourse was required. They were adulterers, and the punishment, they now knew, was death by stoning.

But suddenly, just a few days after Benazir Bhutto took office, Shahida Parveen and the women in Karachi Central Jail received news that an amnesty for all women prisoners had been granted by the new prime minister. All women except those imprisoned on charges of murder were to be released. It was a momentous announcement and the women who read it in the paper, the women who knew the laws and cared about rights, could almost hear the cheers going up in prisons, the droves of jubilant women cheering the young woman prime minister who had set them free.

At Shahida Parveen's prison, however, there was only confusion. The released women sat on the steps, waiting and wailing. They had nowhere to go, as the families they had left behind did not wish to take them back. In their eyes these women were "dirty," and no one knew what to do with them. "Think of your sisters," one mother said over the telephone in the warden's office. "Who will marry them if you return and remind everyone of your sins?" So the freed women sat on the steps, and some of them begged the wardens to take them back. Shahida was one of the women who had nowhere to go. If she went back to her neighborhood, Khushi Mohammad stood waiting, ready to exact the bloody revenge the new prime minister had forestalled. The women would be freed, but the law responsible for their imprisonment remained defiantly on the books of the Islamic Republic of Pakistan.

SEPTEMBER 1990

Three mosques stood to the west, north, and southeast of our house. The mosque to the west was called the Mosque of the Truthful, or the Masjid-e-Siddiqia, and it was the one whose calls to prayer pierced the air outside our windows. When we heard the muezzin clearing his throat by the microphone, my mother or grandmother and I, the women who prayed at home, would scramble to finish what we were doing—the final stirs to a curry, a hurried end to a phone conversation, some gobbled last lines of a juicy novel—as the sound was broadcast throughout the neighborhood. We would rush to our ablutions, take the special long scarves free of the stains and wear of daily life, lay out the prayer mats, and begin to pray.

I had never been to any of the mosques and I never wondered why. I didn't know a single woman who had ever been to a mosque or had any interest in going. The idea of staying home was sold as a reprieve unavailable to men. Men, by command of the Holy Quran and the Hadith, the sayings of the Holy Prophet, were required to pray in congregation, making the trek from their homes to whichever mosque was closest, stand shoulder to shoulder with other men, rich with poor, friends with strangers, all united in the fellowship of the Muslim community. How lucky women were not to have to troop outside at dawn or in the afternoon heat, many women would say. Besides, having the men leave for a while provided a respite of its own, from making cups of tea or conversation or whatever else their presence required.

But there were things we did not know. Since only the men went to the mosques, they were the only ones to hear the Friday sermons, which during the winter of 1990 kept stubbornly coming back to the subject of women. To the purely male congregation the imam of Masjid-e-Siddiqia and other mosques named for blessings and righteousness and Mecca and Medina, the men preached about the horror of having a woman lead the country. They poised their sermons on the backs of a single hadith from Bukhari: "Those who entrust their affairs to women will never know prosperity."

If we had really strained our ears at home, pressed our ears to the windows and shut out all the sounds of televisions or radios, we may have been able to hear a bit of what was said. We did not do so, and it was not certain that we would have cared if we did. When we laid our prayer mats, we didn't think about the country's leadership and we didn't pray as a community. My grandmother prayed downstairs by herself in her room, joined sometimes by Aunt Amina when she visited. My mother prayed upstairs in her own room, with me sidling up by her mat if I arrived just in time.

In the mosque, with its lines of men arranged behind a single man, the issue of who led whom must have seemed far more immediate. The idea of all of them congregated behind a woman was too blasphemous to imagine. It was that nightmare perhaps that whetted the consciences of the righteous all around the country, and it had now been realized. And in every mosque the man at the pulpit could describe in lurid detail the consequences of this nasty deviation.

The insistent fecundity of Benazir Bhutto stirred the lusty imaginations of the men in the mosques, amplifying their visions of the ruin that could be wrought by a wily female at the reins of the nation. Exactly nine months after her wedding, as Benazir Bhutto was campaigning for the first democratic elections in a decade, she had given birth to a baby boy, Bilawal Bhutto Zardari. Now, as prime minister she was pregnant again, expanding her brood and her cabinet, flaunting a swollen belly behind podiums at state functions. There she was on every evening newscast, her scarf slipping from her head often enough to be fit for a caricature on comedy shows, and failing to find the right Urdu word for the English thought she wished to express.

One man was particularly perturbed, and when Benazir Bhutto was seven months pregnant with her second child, he decided that he would make his move. Exactly one year after the elections that brought her to power Benazir Bhutto faced a no-confidence motion from Parliament that had elected her as their leader. The move was led by a man she had known well, her uncle Ghulam Mustafa Jatoi, whose hundreds of acres of land lay not far from her own fiefdom and who, along with her father, was one of the founders of the Pakistan People's Party. Even in this battle, the charge against one Bhutto was led by another Bhutto who held opposing views, who felt perhaps that a male Bhutto deserved the legacy a female had usurped.

On the chilly morning of November 2, 1989, hundreds of Pakistan's elected leaders trooped into Parliament House in their starched tunics and trousers. Many had been sequestered for days in an unidentified location at the foothills of the mountains near the capital. Benazir's party was fighting to keep her in power, and the opposition wished to oust her.

The opposition's arguments pivoted on the assertion that Islamic tradition did not allow a woman to be a head of state. The country had gone through such pains to begin the path of Islamization, the speakers attested, and the Constitution clearly stated that the Holy Quran and the Sunnah took precedence over all else. The Sunnah exhorted against entrusting any affairs at all to women, let alone the affairs of state. With a woman at the helm, the country of the pure would never be a country of the prosperous.

Amid the din of angry men booing and pounding their desks, Benazir Bhutto stood up to address Parliament that morning. She defended herself and her husband against the baseless charges of corruption that her detractors had leveled against her, reminding everyone of the tremendous price she had paid for power, the exile, the jail terms, the threats that she and her father, a martyr for democracy, had made for the nation.

When the votes were counted for the no-confidence motion, the opposition had won only 107 of the 119 votes it needed to succeed. The votes of only twelve men had prevented the ouster of the woman at the helm. Her speech had worked, at least this time. Just eight weeks later, Prime Minister Benazir Bhutto gave birth again, this time to a baby girl she named Bakhtawar.

NOVEMBER 1989

Aunt Amina was moving upstairs again. The third floor, so new that it still smelled of paint and plaster and had the tools of workmen littered in some corners, was not, after all, for a new wife. No one had expected it, but the judgments of those previously betrayed are never quite sound. So it was quite likely that Surrayya, her brow furrowing into a million crinkles at even the mention of Uncle Sohail's construction project, did not exhale until Aunt Amina mentioned that her move upstairs would be accompanied by the arrival of renters downstairs, and provided some details as to their identity.

With the dust from the carpenter making cabinets for her new kitchen mixing with the dust that rose in funnels from the cricket ground across the street, Aunt Amina moved a level above. The edges of her mouth, turned like the petals of a wilting flower, did not change their course. Nor did the catalogue of complaints that recorded the time and temperature of every one of Uncle Sohail's injustices become any less exact in its appraisals. Aunt Amina, with the entitlement of a queen who never questions the justice of the tithes that fill her coffers, moved upstairs to the floor built from the proceeds of her tormentor's employment.

Perhaps the initial arrangement had been unpalatable to all the women involved if not the man at the center. If Aunt Amina could not stop herself from listening in, from imputing meanings to groans and sighs and creaks and squeaks, it could just as well be that the second wife could not rid herself of the ghost of the deposed woman that lived upstairs.

The unseen does not disappear, but heavy curtains and solidly built subterfuges can make denial a possibility. Such was the case with Aunt Amina's move to the third floor, the first occasion since the tragedy that religious duty or compulsory custom had not mandated and that she had decided was worthy of celebration. At the dinner she held for us a few weeks after the move, she allowed an excited Uncle Sohail, constantly smoothing his moustache into the twirled ends befitting a man with two wives and a three-story house, to show us every nook and cranny of the new addition to his empire. From Aunt Amina, there were just a few sidelong smirks and eye-rolling grimaces behind his sweaty, house-proud back, the most pronounced when he showed us around the waist-high roof terrace where he had chosen to lay flooring in case they built yet another floor.

A day or two after that dinner we had to pay an unannounced visit to Aunt Amina in her new house, with its custom kitchen cabinets and bathrooms with showers instead of cups and buckets. Our visit was because of a simple act of forgetfulness, the sort of mindless misplacement that happens all the time. On her last visit to our house, Aunt Amina had forgotten to take with her the latest volume of *Pakeezah Digest*.

Pakeezah, or "pure woman," was a digest containing serialized stories to which my grandmother and Aunt Amina shared a subscription. It was a densely packed volume, its miniscule print cramming thousands of Urdu words onto its pages like all the angry wives of the city suddenly letting go. There were no pictures inside, but the cover always caught my attention and held it. It was invariably a painted portrait of a beautiful woman with a distressed expression.

And so it was that at half past five on an April afternoon, when Karachi's crows lined up on electric wires waiting for dusk and Karachi's wealthy were rising from their afternoon naps, that we pulled up before Uncle Sohail's enlarged house for the delivery of the digest. I was sent upstairs by myself with it, the fumes of whitewash a sharp, heady noseful in the landings between each level. The gradient of the stairs became a bit less steep as you climbed up, as if the faith of the builder in the height of his creation had improved as he got farther and farther away from the ground.

And at the top, Aunt Amina was waiting, in the long housedress she wore on weekdays when Uncle Sohail was not expected. Her hair hung along her back in a loose braid, her face was devoid of adornment, her whole being a picture of the carelessness of one not expecting anyone. She had been expecting the digest though, and she grabbed it from my hand. Her evening's entertainment had arrived, and I received a hug and a kiss and a prayer for the delivery.

It was on the landing between the second and first floor, where the stairs changed and became uncertain that I saw the other wife. It was the suddenness that stung and stunned at the same time. She stood at the doorway of the second landing, the spot where I had stopped hundreds of times on visits over scores of years, for until a few bare months before it had been the threshold to my aunt's house.

There she was, real and large and not at all the woman I had conjured up over the five years she lived in the shadow of our lives. Her face was ordinary, a sweat-beaded face indistinguishable from a million other faces on a hot, humid day in Karachi. It wasn't ominous or striking; it was round, like a tired beige moon long relieved of the expectations of illumination. The temples and the nose were dotted with the scars of previous pimples, and a thin layer of smoothed hair suggested a small bun behind the fleshy neck that connected face to body.

She disappointed, not because she was pretty or even ugly or interesting or boring or tall or short or intelligent looking or bearing on her forehead the telling mark of the simpleminded. She was a shock because she was so unremarkable, so lacking in anything special that as a result, she became an affront to the provocative idea we had constructed in her place. Uncle Sohail's second wife was like the lady you might meet at a visit to the next-door neighbors', or like the woman you could join with in accusing the tomato seller of being an extortionist, or like someone you might greet respectfully as the mother of some girl who was a friend of a friend. In her bland regularity she was an accusation as vexing and confusing as the betrayal she represented.

I said nothing to her that day, no greeting, no smirk, no angry glance, no truthful remonstrance, not a single word. An exchange would have bound us in too intimate a connection. I rushed downstairs slipping on the crumbling edges of the steps and said nothing at all to anyone.

CHAPTER 7

The Graveyards of Karachi

JANUARY 1990

It was not enough to be born in Karachi to be from Karachi. It was not enough to live in Karachi to be from Karachi. It was also not enough to be born in Karachi *and* to live in Karachi to be from Karachi. To be from Karachi, you had to prove that your father, and preferably his father before him, had been born in Karachi and lived in Karachi, and therefore were from Karachi. If you were from Karachi by these markers, you could claim to be from Sindh, the province in which Karachi was located. If you could claim to be from Sindh, you could claim a lot more—a larger quota for government jobs, a larger quota for seats in government colleges, a larger quota on belonging and so a greater chance of making your life in Karachi as comfortable as possible.

These facts of ancestry were captured in a document known as a domicile certificate. My brother, the first son born in Karachi after Pakistan became Pakistan, was the first to need one. The document was a registration requirement for the annual board examinations for the ninth grade administered by the Board of Education of Sindh province, the first of a series of exams and tests and forms and certificates that would be required as he tried to make his way to the coveted goal of medical school. The "domicile," as it was called, was recorded along with the roll number my brother was to be assigned. In the vast machinery of government quotas and allotments, where opportunity and ethnic identity were so closely intertwined, this number would identify him to the examiners and appear with the marks he received for that examination and each one afterward. You could not take exams without having the number, and you could not receive the number without the domicile.

The domicile noted your ethnicity and hence also whether you belonged to one of Pakistan's four major ethnic groups: Balochi, Pashtun, Punjabi, or Sindhi. If, like the millions of Muhajirs, you could not prove ancestry in Pakistan, you were left to compete for the tiny number of "merit" seats available in Pakistan's public universities. In effect it meant that millions of students from Karachi, the children of Muhajirs, competed for a few thousand seats in the city's government universities, while the rest were taken up by students who could claim Balochi, Pashtun, Punjabi, or Sindhi ethnicity based on their ancestors having been born, before Partition, in one of the four provinces of what would become Pakistan. Everyone else was a migrant, and so were their children and grandchildren.

That's where we ran into trouble. My grandfather Said did not have a domicile because he had been born in India before Pakistan was created. My father, Abdullah, also did not have a domicile because he had also been born in India, a month before Pakistan came into existence. My brother, studying hard for his ninth grade examinations, in which he would be tested in physics, chemistry, biology, mathematics, Urdu, Sindhi, English, and Pakistan studies, also did not have a domicile. None of them could prove that they lived in Pakistan, had lived in Pakistan, or were from Karachi. A birth certificate was not enough, the tired clerk at the window of the General Inquiries Office of the Karachi Municipal Corporation told Said at four in the afternoon, just when he was about to clamp the shutter down. A birth certificate was not enough, the clerk repeated with the lazy ease and confidence of a well-worn incantation, thrusting instead a pink piece of paper at Said's confused chest.

Said brought the paper home and laid it on the desk that had been moved to his room when he retired. Pushing back his reading glasses and wiping the sweat from the bridge of his nose, he read it again and again, his forehead furrowing as he tried to understand the instructions. When he was done, realizing that reading and rereading failed to give the clarity he sought, he copied out what it said on a separate piece of paper in neat blue ballpoint so that he could read it a few more times. He kept the original pink sheet neatly filed, where it would not be lost or torn and where its proclamations could be checked against the copy he had made. After these efforts, the requirements and procedure of obtaining a domicile in Karachi, of proving that you really lived there, began to become apparent to him. He needed to produce six photographs and certificates of every qualification held by the father and the grandfather of the applicant. A photocopy of the father's—Abdullah's—national identity card and copies of the neighbors' identity cards had to accompany the application as well, to insure that those who claimed to live in a place actually did inhabit it.

Said set out to fulfill the requirements that had been laid before him. He paid special attention to number five. It instructed unequivocally that if the applicant was under twenty-two years of age, the father's domicile had to be appended to the application along with the minor's affidavit. If the father had no domicile, it was necessary, of course, to make the father's domicile first. There were seven other steps to the domicile process, but Said's copied list stopped abruptly at this point. Before his grandson Zaid could claim he was a resident of Karachi, let alone a Pakistani identity, let alone a portion of a quota, his son, Abdullah, who had lived in Karachi since he was fourteen, had to prove that he indeed did so. The task of proving that his son lived in Karachi so that his grandson could take his exams and claim his share of a quota fell to my retired grandfather.

Perhaps he had not been in Pakistan long enough to know that the instructions, their convolutions and redundancies, their

labyrinthine details and parenthetical prescriptions were so confusing because no one was expected to follow them. No one, that
is, who could produce the sly envelopes of cash that would be slid
under files or the tips offered as gifts or the favors called in by
relatives in high positions. He did not know, or perhaps he did
not want to know, and so he decided to follow the instructions,
bit by bit and line by line. He began where it had all started. At
the photography shop in Saddar where they had taken their first
pictures in Pakistan, days after their nerve-wracking arrival. Those
had been the pictures they had used on the school forms for the
children, black and white square pictures affixed carefully with
glue on the marked-out square at the top left-hand corner. The
store had made copies of the children's birth certificates, as they
had to be attached to the forms. They had done it once for school
and again for college, and once or twice for something else in the
days when Partition was too recent and dictates about domiciles
did not exist.

The three men went to get their pictures taken at the same little
studio in Saddar and returned with the satisfaction of having happily concluded the first step. In their hands they clutched greasy
paper bags filled with meat and lentil kebabs and potato-pea samosas from Saddar that evoked with their aroma memories of the
family's first days. The photographs were picked up a week later,
"Khan Photo Studio" stamped in purple letters on the brown paper sleeves of each one. Said added them to the file in which every
step in the quest to obtain an official domicile was being safely
tucked away. The receipt for the photographs was filed, along with
the pink slip with the list of instructions, the first laminated and
the rest in triplicate. With these papers and pictures in place Said
determined that he had made an adequate map.

For the next four working days, Said awoke early, as he had done
when he had an office to go to, before retirement had partitioned
his days into blocks devoted to reading the newspaper or sipping a
second cup of tea until it was time to take his mid-morning doses

of heart and blood pressure medications. He bathed and shaved and dressed in the half-sleeved shirts that his tailor in Saddar had made for him in the last year of his working life, simple shirts made of cotton that Surrayya starched just a bit to prevent creases. He put on his watch and gathered his files, the original and the duplicate; he affixed his pens on the edges of his shirt pocket. Then he set out for the bus stop, carefully shutting behind him the black gate of the house he had built, sweating like everyone always did long before they got anywhere in Karachi.

The Karachi City Courts stood across the street from the Sindh High Court, a magnificent building of pink stone so fanciful in its grandeur that it suggested then and now some secret princess must be hidden within. There was none of course, only an assemblage of grim judges who never held court for matters as trifling as those troubling my grandfather. The docket for the Sindh High Court judges was laden with matters of far greater import: the complicated legal technicalities of tariffs on goods that arrived at the port, or the delicacies of tax policy. Feudal landowners who held more than one thousand acres could file for exemptions, of course; the law applied only to those who could not make their way around it.

So it was from the safe distance and within the freshly mown, dew-laden lawn that the Sindh High Court looked at the crowded arena of the ordinary, where a sweaty Said arrived a little before nine in the morning with his files defensively stuck in his armpit. The minutes before nine o'clock were important ones for the file-clutching multitude, who until that moment had to wait outside the gates. At nine o'clock they could rush in and clamor for the first or the fiftieth or the four hundredth spot in the line that would allow them access to the doors of officialdom.

By the end of the day, Said had learned the peculiarities of the domicile application line and even written down the names of the three clerks who rotated duty at the window. There was the laid-back one who smiled at mistakes and caressed his oil-slicked hair with his fingers; the other two, stern and stolid, sneered at them. It was because of the loquaciousness of the first that he had gathered information that was curiously absent from the form, and absolutely necessary if one was to avoid the disastrous consequence of denial of domicile. Other details came from the veterans of the line, experts armed with their own piles of files, some of them paid men who took on the drudgery of the line for a secret fee.

On the first day, Said managed only ten minutes in the line before discovering that a permission slip was required, which itself entailed navigating another line and obtaining a piece of paper that proclaimed official permission to stand and wait in this one. This took all day. He returned on the second day and managed to get about halfway, from the scorched courtyard to the stairs under the awning that cast the slightest shade over the waiting men. He had almost stepped inside the corridor when surprise struck again. A top official was visiting, and the higher-ups of the high-ups had decided the corridors were too crammed for making a good impression. "Clear them of people," they told their peons, who in turn cursed the crowd and cast them away. The domicile window was shut early that day.

On the third day, he reached the clerk. It was the chatty one, exuding fumes of coconut hair oil. Slick but nevertheless amiable, he was a man whose position at the window was still new enough to accommodate consideration for the supplicants that appeared before him. It was he who had pointed out a gross deficiency in the domicile application Said wished to file: all the documents were official but not "attested." Attestation required a further official stamp without which they meant nothing. "Get them attested," he told Said. "It can be done with the payment of a few hundred rupees to any one of the men sitting under the trees outside." Said had long wondered what these men with the stamps at the makeshift tables were there to do, and he was about to find out.

It was the fourth day now, and after all the gathering of attestations and permissions and the diversions to other lines and waits under dusty-leafed trees, he expected that day to submit the papers to obtain a domicile for his son, which would become the basis of domicile for his grandson. One of the stern clerks awaited him at the window this time, a nine-year veteran of the line, comfortable in his official omniscience and sporting a Faustian disdain for the masses he was forced to face every day.

The government-issue clock sitting on top of the picture of the founder, Mohammad Ali Jinnah, and behind the clerk struck 11:45 just as Said took his place before the domicile application window. This particular quarter hour was a delicate one, suspended between the clerks' tea break and the coming lunch break, but Said did not know its significance. He also might not have been able to tell if the clerk who stood before him was particularly susceptible to the smells of the dal fry and the steaming chicken *qorma* special already being delivered by the restaurant boy on heaped trays. Behind the clerk the clack of domicile-producing typewriters had already ceased.

The clerk said nothing as he looked over the forms, starting as he always did at the back of the packet of papers. His silence seemed a sign of fulfillment. He flipped one page and then another, moistening his perusing finger each time on the tip of his tongue, page after page after page undergoing his scrutiny. It began to seem that the form, after this fourth attempt in the line, this fourth trip to the domicile office, on top of all the trips and photo takings and file makings, all the other lines that had already been braved, would finally be filed that day. In the clerk's pause-laden perusal, Said even took some liberties, began to consider what he would do after this was over, perhaps before taking the bus home a stop at Bohri Bazaar to visit to an old friend who still kept a watch shop there. It was, after all, still only noon.

Then the clerk stopped on the first page. Turning his ballpoint pen around to the blunt end, he tapped underneath a line that said "Country of Birth." It followed right after the line that said "Date of Birth" and that stood next to the numbers 14 July 1947.

Next to "Country of Birth" in blue ballpoint pen, Said had carefully written "Pakistan/India." The clerk looked up and said, "It is Pakistan or it is India. You have to write one country in this line." Said had been prepared for this. It had been a matter of much discussion in the line itself, the question of whether you put Pakistan or India as the place of birth for children born before Pakistan was born. "You see, son," he answered, "there was no Pakistan or India when my son was born." And so he continued speaking into the whirr of the fans behind the clerk, "What was then India was also all of Pakistan."

The clerk did not agree. With the red pen he kept tucked behind his ear for just this sort of corrective opportunity, he did what omniscient clerks in government offices could do. He drew a straight red line across the clean blue letters in Said's handwriting that spelled out "Pakistan." It was only after he had eliminated them that he drew his tongue over his lips and looked up at Said. "It is 'India,'" he said. "Your son was born in Bombay. It is in India." He stamped the first page of the application with large red letters that read "SUBMITTED" and, handing Said a yellow slip with a date, slammed the wooden window shut and went off to lunch.

The line behind my grandfather remained, waiting for the window to open again, after the clerks had their lunch and their nap and read the paper and discussed its contents and called their wives. My grandfather turned toward home with a generation less to claim it than he had believed was the case. The domicile for my father was picked up and the application for my brother submitted. With my grandfather and father both labeled Indian in origin, my brother's claim to Karachi was brand new, only as old as his fourteen years.

JANUARY 20, 1990
Rubaiya Sayeed was only twenty-one years old when her father, the neatly bearded and white-capped mufti Mohammad Sayeed, became home minister of the Democratic Republic of India, a

prestigious position for the first Kashmiri Muslim man in the history of that country. For the five days he had held the office, the mufti had wielded more power than any Kashmiri; now responsible for internal security not just for the disputed slice that was his home but also for the entire smoldering swath of difference that was India. It was the home minister who could order curfews and cordons and strategize which antigovernment protests must be stanched immediately and which were allowed to fizzle to their own slow deaths.

Distracted by these important matters, the mufti was caught unprepared for what happened on his fifth day in office. It concerned his daughter, the youngest and most cherished of all his children. They had named her Rubaiya, after the couplets of poetry that the mufti liked to recite. A *rubaiya* was one verse, a single sliver of poetic perfection that held the whole universe, and that is the name the mufti chose for his last and most loved baby girl.

That Rubaiya could be plucked so flagrantly from the street where she had grown was simply unthinkable. It happened at a bus stop, just as sunset was settling on a December day in the valley over which Pakistan and India had battled ever since they were countries, its Muslim population and Hindu prince leaving it forever torn between the two. Rubaiya Sayeed, the child of a Muslim cleric who had chosen to side with the Indian government over Muslim freedom fighters, was a child of the disputed valley.

That evening she was returning from Lal Ded Women's Memorial Hospital where she worked as an intern. Her day had been spent amid the cries of birthing women and screaming children. The winter was hard on the hospitals in Indian Kashmir; the short, cold day, the proximity of birth, disease, and decline jolting in its intensity. Rubaiya was glad to be part of the action, a small girl but fierce in her determination to help others. At the hospital, she felt like she was part of the shootings and deaths, the distorted normality of life in the valley. She did not want to be a girl who watched from the sidelines.

They came from nowhere and swept her up, four masked men bearing weapons. In an instant, the slight young woman who had just stepped out of the dust cloud of a public bus was suddenly not there at all. After several long minutes the one or two people who had been close enough to see the men and the car in which they disappeared began to murmur, and then as five and then ten minutes passed, everyone knew.

She had been taken by one of her own, by Muslim men in a Kashmir where everything depended on whether one was Muslim or Hindu. The guerillas of the Jammu and Kashmir Liberation Front, a separatist group that had been fighting the Indian state for independence from Kashmir, would soon proclaim that the gesture was revenge for their own women, the distraught mothers and abandoned brides and widowed sisters whose men had been taken by the Indian government, by the Home Ministry led by the father of the kidnapped woman.

The forty-four days of Rubaiya's captivity were marked by terrifying searches and seizures. Each night Indian soldiers went door to door, bursting through, sending women scurrying into corners, their children wailing. Men would listen for the soldiers at their doorsteps and scurry out their back doors into the darkness of frosty fields, emerging hours later from their rocky hideouts. Those who didn't know of the hiding places or those still innocent enough to believe their innocence mattered were simply taken away by the soldiers, leaving a trail of weeping women behind them.

Halfway through Rubaiya's captivity, night raids that took the women began. After all, it was a woman, the daughter of a man who represented the unity of the Indian state who had been taken in the first place. Everyone knew that what happened to Rubaiya as she spent her days in captivity, what *could* happen to her, must happen to all the other women of Kashmir. If the kidnapped Rubaiya's purity could no longer be presumed, neither would theirs. The officials in Delhi debated whether or not they should accede to the kidnappers' demands and release the imprisoned Kashmiris. Would this humiliation create a precedent?

While the men talked in the capital, the women of Kashmir were left to endure the abuse of the soldiers. The women were taken into dark corners of their own homes while their men were handcuffed and gagged. The order had come from Delhi; a new chief minister appointed to the embattled provinces of Jammu and Kashmir had decided to teach the Kashmiris a lesson for harboring separatists.

On the night of January 19, 1990, the weight of their wrath fell on two neighborhoods. Chota Bazaar and Guru Bazaar were small settlements of modest homes, where women stayed inside and did not see strangers. For as long as they could remember, their lives had been defined by war. The first had come in the throes of Partition, when the boundaries of India drawn up by the British included Kashmir and the boundaries of Pakistan did not. It was Kashmir that kept the militaries of Pakistan and India on high alert ever since, stretched all along their borders from the mountains of the north all the way down to the deserts of Rajasthan.

There had been wars ever since for this piece of land, once beautiful and now bloodied. Through the years, the war that had been fought in the streets made its way into the women's homes. That night in January stood out as particularly brutal. The women who had not yet been raped and taken away wept and wailed for those who had, and the men who remained burned with anger at their own powerlessness. Amid the tears and the fury, a helpless uncertainty reigned in the little houses. The women stayed inside, but the men, whetted by their anger, streamed out into the soldier-filled streets.

Old men wrinkled and wrapped in shawls, boys who studied hard and never protested, boys who believed in peace and in a future as Kashmiri Indians—all of them poured into the streets. Angry and unafraid, they marched through the winding lanes and alleys, past shuttered shops holding meager provisions, past burned-down houses, past rows and rows of windows from where the women looked on.

The crowd gathered at the Gawa Kadal Bridge, swelling with the anger of those who were defying state orders, some for the first time. Those new to the uprising had no curfew passes and no weapons. They did not know Rubaiya Sayeed, they did not know the men who had taken her, and they did not know the boys whose freedom was being demanded. They only knew of the violations of their own homes and their own women.

The Indian soldiers saw the crowd on the bridge grow, defiantly taunting their curfew. Their bullets began to pierce the bodies that had just been chanting for freedom, protesting against the nightly invasions of their hearths and hearts.

Some fled behind walls and under the smallest spaces of store shutters wedged open by unseen hands, behind any shrub or shelter that would put something between them and the bullets. Those bullets were everywhere that day, a metal monsoon of carnage. The little market, the street, the bridge was covered with bodies. Afterward, when it was too dark and too quiet, only the bodies and their smell remained, three hundred lying in the streets, desolate and empty. Later it would be reckoned that ten men had been killed for every man that had been freed to obtain the release of Rubaiya Sayeed.

MARCH 1990

The street in front of our house was never completely quiet. If you woke from some confused dream, you would hear a sound reserved for that still portion of the night. First, the trill of a whistle, followed by a man's low and melodic moan. It was the night watchman, a man hired by the neighborhood collective. His task, paid by fee from every household, was to ride his bicycle in the hours between the darkest night and earliest light of dawn. One after the other the sounds would follow. They were meant to reassure the city dwellers who took silence to be a sign of something sinister, reminding everyone that while the neighborhood slept, someone was vigilant and all was well.

When the intruders did come, they came in the middle of the day. There were four men, two armed with Kalashnikovs and two with pistols. They barged into the house across the street just after the family who lived there had finished their lunch. It was a Friday. The family owned an electronics shop in Karachi's teeming downtown, and the men were all at home, drowsy after a big, spicy meal. No one remembers what pretext the robbers used to enter the house, whether the servant who answered the doorbell saw their weapons and unlatched the gate in a panic, or if someone had naïvely left the gate open, or if, as the more paranoid neighbors would insist, a servant had been paid to let them in.

It did not matter. Once the men were inside they went room to room and marched the family down the halls and into the dining room. Two of the men stayed with them while the other two swept the house, taking every wallet, purse, watch, and jewel, every piece of electronic equipment. When they were finished, they packed their loot into the family's two cars and sped away.

It was dark when the family broke out of their paralysis, and when they saw the house, they wished they hadn't found the strength to move at all. Everywhere they looked broken latches and scattered papers covered the surfaces, every piece of clothing turned over and torn in the robbers' search for anything valuable. They could touch nothing, the father of the family said, for the police had to be called and the First Information Report registered. The telephone at the police station rang and rang, so the men of the family went there themselves.

It was nearly one in the morning, and the whistle and the moan of the night watchman had just begun when the station house officer could be bribed and cajoled into visiting the scene of the crime. He was tall and thin with a sharp jaw and a black sliver of a moustache. He went through the house, nodding ruefully, and made a list of all the things that had been taken. He said little until he was finished, when he offered the solemn observation, "You had a lot of nice things." The family knew at once the robbers would never be caught.

My bedroom window, the one that had belonged to Aunt Amina, looked directly into their narrow front garden in front of their dining room. They had a lot of time to stare at our house, to wonder why no neighbor could feel their terror. When they related the incident to my mother a few days later, one of them told her that they were sure they had seen the curtain in my bedroom move, and that they had seen someone at the window. All of them had hoped that whoever it was would call for help and come to their aid, but no one had come. When my mother returned home, she told me to always keep the curtains in the bedroom window drawn, and never to look out that window again.

MAY 1990

Hyderabad, Pakistan, had served as the capital of Sindh for centuries, back when the now bustling Karachi was little more than a nameless fishing village. In 1843, when the British annexed Sindh to create another trade route to India, they focused their expansive energy on Hyderabad. It was in this humid city, a few hundred miles inland, where Amir Talpur fought the invading British forces. Rich and river-flanked, Hyderabad had been much beloved by the Talpurs. Descended from Mir Tala Khan, they had arrived in the region with the conquering Nader Shah. Their leader, Mir Fateh Ali Khan, had been declared Nawab of Sindh and hence the ruler of the mud fort that sat in the city's center. They would come to rule the region for at least a hundred years.

But a one-hundred-year pause was a sliver in the history of the land that surrounds Hyderabad. An hour or so outside the city one can find evidence of a story that began long before most regions of the earth were known to have been inhabited. In these dry and sandy expanses, it requires an imagination to picture the verdant towns that existed when the Indus meandered through following a route different from the one it takes today. Archaeological digs reveal that the Amri civilization, dating from 4000 to 6000 BC, once flourished here. A little farther away is the town of Kot Diji, whose ancient inhabitants created plaques inscribed with a picture language thousands of years old that have yet to be deciphered. The towns were destroyed by fire, flood, and conquest, leaving behind only fragments of the civilization's accomplishments, foretelling perhaps the destiny of the towns that would rise in their place.

Hyderabad now lies on the banks of the River Indus. The birthplace of the Sindhi language, it was the city coveted by the many conquerors of Sindh. It beckoned not only warriors; poets and writers came from all over the Indian subcontinent to be near the city's Sufi shrines, which lit up just like they did in Bombay and Bahawalpur. The descendants of the Sufi dervish Jalaluddin Surkh Posh Bukhari settled near the town, bringing with them their own followers. They searched for the divine on the heat-hardened plains, where they built humble mud houses with triangular towers on the roofs to try and lure the winds to the rooms within.

The mud fort Pacco Qillo, or "Strong Fort," stood deep inside the city, built by the Sindhi ruler Mian Ghulam Shah Kalhoro, who ruled the area in the late eighteenth century when British ships had only just begun hauling India's resources to England. Thick and formidable with a commanding central tower, it was one of the strongest military garrisons in the region, housing hundreds of soldiers and casting a shadow on all the enemies glancing greedily at the riverbank city. Traders from all over southern Punjab and throughout Sindh province set up shops around the fort, its many inhabitants providing a market for their carpets, sugar, spices, and silk. Many languages were spoken and many deals made: it was not the God of the Muslims or the Hindus that ruled here but the deity of the exchange.

When the British came, they bought guns with them, so thick walls and strong forts were no longer needed. Pacco Qillo, and the whole city of Hyderabad, languished after the British annexation of Sindh. To ship what they had plucked from the land, the British needed a port. This inland river town did not fit into their plans, so Hyderabad was forgotten, and the attention of the British shifted to Karachi.

Hyderabad's neglect lingered after Partition, another grand mapping feat by the departing British. Millions of Hindus moved away from Sindh just as millions of Muslims were arriving in Karachi with their dreams of life in a truly Muslim land. Some of the arrivals did what so many searching for gold often do: they staked out a spot far enough from the others where opportunities were yet to be found. They chose to travel farther inland, to Hyderabad, and the unoccupied nooks and alleys around the abandoned fort became their destination and soon their home.

For decades after their arrival in 1947, the Muhajirs, the migrants who had come to Pakistan from India, lived in and around the Pacco Qillo, its bricks and bones now echoing with the sounds of Urdu rather than the Sindhi poetry of centuries past. As they did in Karachi, the Muhajirs took over the businesses abandoned by the departing Hindus and established new ones of their own. The city of Hyderabad became the place where the old Sindhi civilization met the diverse dreams of a new country, where those who had lived on the land for centuries brushed up against newcomers who wanted to be a part of the Islamic Republic of Pakistan.

And for a while at least it seemed the two could coexist. The Muhajirs built mosques and businesses, piling the new on the old and bringing liveliness to the city. Sweetshops sold delicacies from faraway places in India, and minarets blared the call to prayer five times a day, drawing men into mosques that filled and emptied with the rhythms of the day. Cultural and religious differences kept the Sindhis apart from the newer arrivals. The Sindhis were still deeply set in the feudal ways of patronage and of favors based on relationships that stretched over generations. The Muhajirs in turn frowned secretly or not so secretly on the Hindu rituals of the Sindhis, their customs of touching feet and breaking coconuts reminiscent of temple rituals they had learned to keep out of their own Muslim devotions. They knew, after all, how to be Muslim in a non-Muslim land.

On the afternoon of May 27, 1991, less than a year after Benazir Bhutto, a Sindhi, had taken office, unexpected visitors took the residents of Pacco Qillo by surprise. Amid the usual sounds of the afternoon came the roar of police vans. In minutes the armed officers spread through the winding streets and alleys of the old fort. Because it was the middle of the day, many of the men were at work; the frightened women and children left behind promptly retreated inside their houses where they remained scared and confused. The police cordoned the area and began bellowing through megaphones, "Come out of your homes" and "Surrender your weapons."

The women wept and wailed at the siege suddenly confronting them. They had no weapons, and they did not know what the police wanted from them. From their windows they could see the policemen clad in khaki and black and the guns pointed at them. Hours passed and families used to having only what they needed for the next meal began to run out of food. The temperature inside their homes was over a hundred degrees. Men expected to return home at the end of the day never came, having been held back by the police. With the children's hunger and their own captivity and the commands that came from the megaphones, the women gradually grew frantic.

At dusk, when they could no longer take the avalanche of sounds and the absence of their men, they took their children and began to leave their homes. They had nothing to protect them, so they carried their copies of the Holy Quran on their heads. Old women and young women clutching crying children, all holding books over their heads and streaming out in a sad, thin line into the streets. The books would protect them, they had told themselves and their children; the Qurans would show the policemen that they were innocent women forced from the sanctuary of their homes, where they were honorable, and out into the unprotected streets, where good women never ventured without their men.

The police had waited all day under the fly-filled riverbank sun. Now, as they saw the procession coming toward them, they cocked their guns and began to fire, showering bullets into the procession. Screams of women and cries of children echoed through the walls of the old fort, but the carnage continued. When the police were done, bodies of women and children lay in the streets and alleys, their blood pooling into rubbish heaps and trickling under fruit carts.

According to some counts, more than eighty people died that day, most of them women and children. The residents of the ill-fated Pacco Qillo said there had been many more, bodies carried off by the police to unmarked mass graves when they realized they had killed those who never could have fought them. Years later, the Sindh policemen who had been carrying out the orders would also tell their versions, each one insisting that they had been told that a group of terrorists with a cache of illegal weapons had been hiding inside Pacco Qillo. They had believed that snipers were hiding behind the women and children, so they had fired and fired and fired again. The Sindhis and Muhajirs had long had differences of custom and language, but until the incident at Pacco Qillo, few would have imagined the fault line between the two becoming so bloody.

JULY 1990

They gathered because of a betrayal. The men and boys met at the Kokan community center located near Uncle Sohail's three-story house to discuss a neighborhood matter of great urgency. The community center still retained the smell of the chicken *biryani* that had been served at the wedding ceremony hosted there that very morning. At the wedding banquet they had feasted, and although they had washed their faces and combed their hair, and some had put on a fresh kurta or sprayed a wisp of cologne, they all had the disheveled look of wedding guests encountered after the revelry.

For as long as they could remember, the lane on which the community center stood was mostly inhabited by people they knew, who had congregated in the area more than a decade ago when the Housing Society sold them the land plots. Across the street from the houses of the Kokan Housing Society was a large and empty tract of land. Here, the more daring Kokani boys, the grandsons of the migrants from India and sometimes their friends, improvised games of cricket on nights when there was little else to do. It was a convenient depository for them, less than a stone's throw from the houses at the edge of the lane. When arranging games or a rendezvous, the boys referred to it simply as "the ground." They felt it belonged, if not by design then by default and entitlement, to them.

The Kokani owner of the ground had moved away from the neighborhood a long time ago, his investments bearing greater fruit than the middling and sometimes failing deals of those left behind on the lane. Piece by piece he had bought up choice sections of Karachi. The land in front of the lane he had simply let be, even after he and his family moved to an ornate and commodious bungalow near the ocean to be surrounded by the rich. At first he would return to the lane a few times a week, exchanging slaps on the back and guffaws and sharing childhood memories, a cigarette or two, and snips of gossip. Then he had started showing up at the Kokan mosque only for Friday prayer: the society was, after all, far away from his seaside bungalow, and managing his many properties took time. His sons grew and the eldest married, and somewhere around this time he stopped coming around altogether, presumably focusing on his new life in a new neighborhood.

It was this eldest son's idea to convert the ground into a commercial venue for weddings, and eventually he had managed to convince his reluctant father. The idea smacked deliciously of profits. People kept coming to the swelling city, requiring them to squeeze into smaller and smaller spaces. This made gatherings a problem. How was one supposed to entertain the entire family and all the future in-laws with appropriate aplomb in a tiny apartment crammed with too many people and the residues of their comings and goings? The answer—for those who had wandered too far from ancestral villages or who had made momentous migrations—was the wedding hall.

At the time, wedding halls were cropping up everywhere in Karachi, sometimes a whole line of them stretching out on a single road leading to some faraway suburb. They were pink and white or red and yellow, like miniature copies of fantasy palaces, bearing names like Paradise Dream, Royal Garden, and Sea Breeze Castle. At these venues, festivities could be bought in packages and guests feted in hefty numbers, increasing the debts of aging fathers and requiring loans against the future paychecks of graduating brothers. Each building had a booking office on the premises, where a nice man offered colorful brochures featuring dream weddings, installment plan options, and salon packages and honeymoon suites that accompanied a booking at their venue.

The news that the ground was slated to be a wedding hall came neither through the owner nor his son; it was the reasonable deduction of those who witnessed the sudden clearing of the lot. A week before this meeting, the lane dwellers of Kokan Housing Society woke up to the roar of two majestic bulldozers clearing the thorny babul bushes that grew on the fringes of the ground. Adherents of the urban creed are fast to interpret construction as a positive omen, not considering its potential for destruction. So at first the residents and boy cricketers were not all that concerned. Perhaps the ground was being transformed into a park, they told themselves, an act of benevolence by an old boy made good who wished for the neighborhood children to have a safer place to play.

But the clarification came fast, and when it did there was no denying it. The bulldozer was followed by crews that raised the stage where future brides and grooms would be presented to family and friends under lights bright enough to assure good photographs.

And after the arrival of the billboard the horror was complete. "Destiny Gardens" was spelled out in the unlit neon tubes tucked on the truck bed. The total transformation had taken a little less than a week: the clearing began on Sunday and the billboard arrived on Wednesday.

On Saturday the men gathered at the Kokan community center to discuss what could be done about the new development. Their defeat, however, was evident in their resigned poses. All that was left to decide were the precise terms of a respectful surrender. Uncle Sohail, affecting all the mannerisms of the recently wronged, sat at the center of the gathering. It was his house, after all, that was one of those closest to the end of the lane, closest to the monstrosity of commercialized nuptials that had now arrived at their doorstep. "We cannot allow this to happen," he began, having decided to take on the role of the most wronged victim. "If this happens, our lane will be changed forever," he continued, undeterred by the silence around him.

"We cannot stop him," a grizzled, wrinkled old man said solemnly. His words freed others to speak of the realities of the situation, for many of them had come to offer reasons for the rout than to gather resources for a battle. They cited the lateness of their response and the already-cleared land. One after another, the obstacles were enumerated, interspersed with the objections of one or two others who, like Uncle Sohail, stood to suffer most from the increased traffic. This troubled minority told stories of the changes to come, of the noise and the guests, strangers from all parts of the city pouring into the street and onto their doorsteps.

It was the fear of these vast hordes of wedding guests that finally prompted some action. Two gates would be erected, one at each end of the lane, sealing it from either side. These gates would separate the lane from the larger street where the wedding hall would be. Every night, the gates would be locked after nine o'clock and opened only by residents, who would be given a key to the padlock. They could not stop the wedding hall by filing the requests for injunctions and stay orders and zoning objections that better-heeled neighbors with closer connections in the judiciary could have mustered. But they were not so poor as to do nothing and were still protective of their respectability, and so the gates were approved by a near consensus. Uncle Sohail, still disgruntled that no greater action would be taken, refused to vote.

He had his reasons, stated and unstated. The Destiny Gardens sign that hung over the newly established wedding banquet hall would confront Aunt Amina on a daily basis, whether she was alone or with Uncle Sohail. Weddings would take place every day in a bonanza of unceasing celebration. The words "Destiny Gardens," bright pink and blue against the Karachi night, and the fairy lights would cast their manic nuptial mirth on Aunt Amina's room and on the roof terrace Uncle Sohail had built for some peace and solitude.

MAY 16, 1991

It was easy to eliminate a woman but not so easy to erase her memory. A single television appearance by the same man who had sworn Benazir Bhutto in was all it took to strike her down. The now wide-hipped, headscarved Benazir, with toddler and baby and husband in tow, was dismissed on charges of corruption. She had promised too much and delivered too little, and her husband, everyone insisted, had stolen too audaciously.

The disappointed, sun-darkened boys sitting by the tanneries on the Lyari River in Karachi, the sharecroppers gathering grain and sugarcane for their feudal overlords in Punjab, the shoemakers sewing soles beside the railway station in Lahore all turned on her suddenly. Promised change had not come and it had to be the woman's fault. The woman had not filled their growling stomachs, she had not deposed the local despots who wreaked havoc on their precarious existence, and she had not given the bread or the garment or the house promised in the melodic slogans heard at every election rally. Their short stores of patience were exhausted by gibes of other men who said their votes had cursed the country by handing a woman the affairs of state, men who scolded them daily, or at least weekly, from the pulpits of their mosques.

The soiled country had to be sanctified again, and the ceremony took place on May 16, 1991. A new prime minister, clean and pure as only a man could be, had introduced a bill that would allow the country to expiate for the sin of electing a woman. This ultimate act of the country's repentance would be a return to the truth, to the destiny from which Pakistan had drifted.

Prime Minister Nawaz Sharif, elected with a two-thirds majority in the National Assembly with his coalition of the Islami Jamhoori Ittehad (Islamic Democratic Alliance), quickly introduced the Enforcement of Shariat Act of 1991. Unfurled before a Parliament of men clad in pristine white tunics and vests tailored to hug rotund bellies, the Enforcement of Shariat Act declared itself the supreme law of Pakistan. The act next declared that all Muslim citizens were required to follow Shariat, and that the state, under auspices of the act, would insure that Shariat was taught in schools, practiced in law courts, and dominant in matters of state, economics, and exchange. Swooning with repentance, no one seemed to notice that the act neglected to say what Shariat was or which version of Shariat among the many existing schools and subschools of Islamic thought and countless splinter groups would determine these important questions.

It was a well-enacted and properly executed rite done with the effortlessness of the most practiced rituals from royal wedding to holy acts of purification. And, as is the case with all well-enacted rituals, the obedient population would not balk at the details. That the Constitution had already declared the Quran and Sunnah to be supreme; that the injunctions of a previous purification, allowing for the stoning of women and the policing of errant sexual liaisons, had never been taken off the books by Benazir; and that all the new vows of loyalty to Islam had been sworn before and enacted in law were minutia that interested no one.

No one remembered that laws supposedly enacted in the name of Islam and Shariat, which made the woman, even if she was in a position of supremacy, still only equal to half a man had never been removed from the country's statute books. Those laws—the legacy of General Zia ul Haque, who had tried to Islamize the country by passing laws that regulated the sexuality of women and subjected them to floggings and stonings—had all remained on the books during Benazir's tenure; she had not even attempted to remove them. But like the previous dalliances of a finally wedded king, the mistaken first choices of an awkwardly democratic Pakistan needed to be forgotten. New vows of return to purity and male supremacy would accomplish that, piled as they would be atop old ones, already existing ones.

The Enforcement of Shariat Act of 1991 blazed through the Parliament of Pakistan, then through the Senate, and onto the shiny, polished desk of the president, who, flanked by a picture of Mohammad Ali Jinnah, the founder, on one side and the green and white flag on the other, happily signed it into law. The best way to protect against making the wrong choice was, as the provisions of the act read, to limit the number of choices an unreliable population could make. With the government banning all that was wrong, that could be thought wrong, that could accidentally be wrong, nothing in this newly purified country could be wrong.

JUNE 1992

At dusk the tanks rolled into Liaqatabad, a scrappy neighborhood in Karachi's central district. It was summer and the dusk had come late, near eight o'clock, amid the cozy atmosphere of family dinners and the theme songs of the daily soaps blaring from blinking television sets. Along the three- or four-story apartment buildings that lined most of the roads, little boys were completing last-minute runs to corner stores and men were speeding home from work on their motorbikes. They were the ones to hear the news on the streets and bring it home to the women.

While people peered down at them through windows, behind gates, and between alleys, the same beige-brown Al Khalid tanks everyone had seen marching in the convoys on Independence Day and Defense Day and Pakistan Day crept through the streets like the sandy crabs on the beaches at the edge of the city. Shopkeepers selling meat to last-minute customers or haggling over a kilo of onions with a harried housewife felt uncertain enough to draw down their shutters just a bit, and then a little more. They counted the tanks with increasing unease and then watched as the frightening scene unfolded.

The tanks were followed by khaki-topped trucks driven by soldiers. Most people had never seen the Pakistan Army at such close quarters, and now they could make out the olive, khaki, and brown amoebic shapes of their camouflage. From beneath their olive helmets, the soldiers looked out at the streets of Karachi, at the plastic bags and rotting fruit peels and other rubbish heaped high on street corners. In every truck, one or two soldiers stood erect, weapons pointed up at the windows above or the flat rooftops of smaller homes, their fingers dangling on the triggers.

It was the beginning of a different kind of sunset ritual in the city, that of curfews and searches and gun battles and shoot-on-sight orders. The soldiers had come at the behest of the generals in green-hilled Rawalpindi, where men sitting with flags and medals hanging heavy from their shirts had pored over maps of Karachi and devised a plan to clean it up. The city was contaminated, the soldiers had been told, full of people who did not belong, people who hoarded guns in their homes and bullets in their pockets and loyalty in their heart for the homeland of their forebears, for India. The people of Karachi had to be taught a lesson and the soldiers were there to do so.

This lesson would be a long one—nearly two years long. The next morning the subdued residents of Azizabad, Liaqatabad, Orangi, North Nazimabad, and Qasba Colony would wake up to a besieged city. Sandbags were piled in heaps next to traffic lights, and behind them crouched soldiers in camouflage, their gun barrels peeping out at schoolchildren too young to know to avert their gazes. There were thousands of these soldiers. Their presence assured that the cleansing of Karachi would render it truly Pakistani and devotedly faithful.

Over the next few months the residents of Karachi would become familiar with other weapons in the soldiers' arsenal: the long lists of men they believed were involved in activities against the Pakistani state. One by one, the supporters of the Muhajir Qaumi Movement, which had rallied the city and brought it into the assemblies and the Parliament of Pakistan, were cornered. The Muhajir Qaumi Movement (MQM), which had first won elections in 1988, now controlled most of the electoral districts of Karachi. They represented the "Muhajirs," the migrants from India who had settled in Karachi, politicizing their presence in the country and constructing it as a fifth ethnicity. The other four predominant ethnicities in Pakistan all had their own provinces, the Punjabis with the biggest and the Balochis, the Sindhis, and the Pashtun each with their own. The Muhajirs, the MQM had proclaimed, could thus lay claim to Karachi. In a world defined by ethnicity, those who had aimed at being just "Pakistani" had lost out—they were now eternally "muhajir," or "refugees."

The army came to Karachi to capture them, round up the political activists of this new party who were claiming Karachi and other urban areas of Sindh as theirs. They were not hard to find. Some were captured in those fervid first days, taken from beds and street corners and shops to undisclosed locations, where they were hung up and beaten so that they would give up the names of others, who would be beaten in turn.

On the worst days the curfew lasted nearly all day, the enforced quiet breaking only between 6:00 and 9:00 a.m. and between 5:00 and 8:00 p.m. At six on the dot the streets would erupt with people, everyone rushing to do whatever needed to be done. Mothers rushed to doctors' offices with children who had taken ill the evening before; young men rushed to work in the rich parts of the city not under curfew; and the day laborers and hawkers rushed to sell in three hours what they used to peddle in a whole day. Curfew or not, they would tell anyone who would listen that their children needed to eat.

From the beginning of the military operation in Karachi to its official end more than a year later, the city was suspended in the artificial rhythms of the military. It determined when people could move and when they must be perfectly still. Those who did not live in areas dominated by the Muhajir Qaumi Movement read day after day about the killings and disappearances and arrests. Under those reports, the newspapers published more pragmatic details, the hours of curfew that day and the alternate routes others must take to get around the areas of the city being punished by the military in order to cure it.

Within a year, a great many people would lose their lives or disappear without a trace, and the rest would learn how to navigate the new Karachi of curfews and missing persons. Children learned not to talk about politics and never to say where their fathers were born, and especially not if they had been born in what was now India or Bangladesh. The soldiers could stop anyone on the street at will, and they did, making examples of them and asserting time and again that those purged were diseased tumors that had made Karachi so sick. They were ruthless in their acts of excision. Bodies were dumped under bridges and girders and in ditches and alleys. Those alive at the time of abduction in one corner of the city were found dead months later in another. The total number killed, with some of the missing never reported and others never counted, is still uncertain, though it is estimated to be at least two thousand.

The military did not fight with guns alone. Another battle was waged on the pages of newspapers, with information, the lack of it, or deliberate deceit numbing the rest of the country into confusion and uncertainties. For every MQM worker whose body was found in some ditch or empty lot, the army released pictures of "torture chambers" run by the MQM, justifying their crackdown on the party. These pictures of dank inner rooms with exposed electrical wires hanging from ceilings appeared in national newspapers and magazines, lulling into silence those who wondered about the army's intentions in Karachi. Barbarity breeds barbarity, readers may have thought, as they mulled over the news in Lahore or Peshawar or Islamabad over another cup of tea. But in Karachi the searches and the disappearances, the killings and the discoveries of bodies went on and on. The military, it seemed, was not at all in a hurry.

On February 16, 1994, in the midst of Operation Clean Up, the dark-skinned, clean-shaven Altaf Hussain addressed a crowded rally in Karachi. In just twelve years he had organized a minority that had not until then had a name. As a student leader he had rallied the children of migrants to organize against the politics of feudalism, patronage, and military domination. Now in his thirties, he could not speak to the gathering in person. As the leader of the MQM, he had been forced to flee the city after a record three thousand criminal cases were registered against him. But even by telephone he was a firebrand. "We sacrificed two million people to achieve Pakistan, not to see our children killed and elders humiliated by the law-enforcing agencies," he railed to the cheers of the remainder of his supporters, who seemed unconcerned about his physical absence.

But if Altaf Hussain was too far away to be caught, most others were not. Ten months after the February speech Altaf Hussain's elder brother and young nephew were picked up by the military for interrogation near the headquarters of the MQM in the constantly curfewed suburb of Azizabad. Their bodies were discovered in a ditch in the industrial town of Gadap four days later. The marks on them indicated that they had been tortured.

JUNE 1994
Sacrifice was a matter reserved for the men. Eid ul Adha was the second biggest festival on the Muslim calendar, commemorating

the sacrifice that Abraham had made many millennia ago, when divine mercy had replaced his son Ismail with a lamb. And so the slaughter of an animal marked every Eid. My grandfather, father, and brother were in charge of fulfilling the duty for our family, but because my father worked during the weekdays, my retired grandfather took the lead.

The selection of the sacrificial "lamb" at the livestock market was taken very seriously. The lamb need not and most often was not a lamb at all but a goat or a cow or even a camel; it could be any of the animals that Muslims were permitted to eat. Its selection factored in a complicated set of variables, including age and price and size and constitution. The men had to open the mouths and slap the flanks of hundreds of goats and cows to determine which one was healthy and which one would be worthy of selection for our family this year. When the lucky animal was found, a goat whose skin was taut and healthy, whose eyes shone with promising clarity, whose limbs did not wilt due to dehydration or exhaustion or simply age (disguised by the pulling of a few telltale teeth), the haggling would begin.

I, like all the other women of my family, was not privy to this process, but between my brother's hurried telling and my grandfather's detailed one a clear picture of it emerged in my mind. The task of settling on a price alone could stretch into an hour, for the men who sold the animals were in no hurry. They would start by citing a price that exceeded what the animal was actually worth by two or three times. These tricks of haggling I knew well, having seen them practiced with relish or resignation every time my mother or grandmother bought a kilo of tomatoes or a bolt of cloth. An animal was far more costly though, often close to three or four paychecks, with hefty cows costing as much as a small wedding. This made the sacrifice an even heftier responsibility, and I understood that this bargaining was of real import, its additions and subtractions equal to thousands instead of tens or hundreds of rupees.

The women did not see the animal until it arrived at the door, and the black gate was opened. In rolled the Suzuki minitruck revealing the sacrificial cargo tied up on the truck bed with an array of ropes and wires. Said and Zaid would accompany the animal's delivery in a rickshaw, which was Said's preferred mode of transportation for the purchase of livestock, something he, a city man for generations, did only once a year. The goat would then be tied in the back garden, between the coconut trees where its bleats and baas would punctuate the sounds of the house.

The goat would remain the men's responsibility until the day of Eid. This meant shopping for its sheaves of hay or bags of grain, feeding it, and making sure it was as comfortable as possible until its last day on earth. If the goat was particularly boast-worthy in appearance or demeanor or size, it would be paraded up and down the neighborhood and introduced to other animals procured and reared for a similar purpose. Only after the sacrifice was done, after Said or Abdullah or Zaid had taken the sharp cleaver the professional butcher handed them while he held the animal down by the neck, after the blood had been drained from its throat, its hide skinned, and the large pieces of flank and shin and chest quartered into pieces was the animal handed off to the women.

But then it would be truly ours. The goat was brought into the kitchen on large steel trays reserved for this very purpose. We'd get to know it well, carefully cutting the slabs into smaller pieces, washing, drying, and sectioning them into tens of separate plastic bags whose tops would be tied with rubber bands. The division itself was mandated in the Holy Quran. Separate portions of sacrificed meat were for the poor, for our neighbors, for relatives, and for ourselves. But the rules were, as always, broad and general, and it fell to my mother, my grandmother, and me to determine which sections of the animal would be given to which relatives as gifts. A whole leg, which could be roasted to feed a large family, signified special affection, while stew meat was a cursory gesture for an acquaintance or second or third cousins. By the time the daylong sectioning of the sacrificed goat was concluded, many relationships would have undergone this yearly reappraisal. All this conducted under the pressure of sacrificed meat arriving in an avalanche from the homes of others; this was inevitably followed by the not-so-small matter of readjustments, as the received meat revealed the truth about our standing with others.

In 1994 Eid ul Adha fell in the middle of the second summer of curfews and cordons, when getting around the city was hampered by sudden gun battles, shops shutting down in the middle of the day, and roadblocks. Often you had no choice but to abandon your car and walk the miles to your house, only to return to no car or a car stripped of seats and steering and stereo. In that summer of continuing tumult, when the heat was familiar but the uncertainty still new, Said and Zaid were determined to make their annual pilgrimage to the livestock market and select the animal that would be our family's offering.

That Saturday arrived with the heavy humidity of a summer morning in Karachi. Saturday was only a half holiday, and the men had calculated that this would mean a less crowded market, an easier time getting there, better deals and greater discounts, and ultimately a sturdier animal. But with the morning came unwelcome news. According to the newspaper, an army raid the night before in a congested downtown neighborhood had left behind a slew of bodies.

The newspaper delivered another deflating piece of news: the MQM, to honor its slain activists, was calling for a day of mourning. Shops and markets must be shut down, they demanded, to register their protest against the ongoing bloodbath in Karachi. We knew their demands would be met, as all shopkeepers, scared of their shops being burned down by angry MQM workers, would acquiesce. There would be no livestock market that day.

Said and Zaid each spent the day in a sulk, though for different reasons. To Said the sacrifice represented, even decades after his arrival in Pakistan, a new freedom of expression. Unable in

Bombay to complete the sacrifice in the crowded lanes around the mosque, that he could do so in his own backyard, in the house he had built, in the country he had chosen was a confirmation that his decision to leave was the just and prudent one, some salve on the painful memories for which even wealth could not compensate. For him the sacrifice was a renewal of vows: a remembering to be grateful that he lived in a Muslim country and could complete with freedom the rites of Muslim sacrifice.

My brother, Zaid, was upset for less noble reasons. There he was, thwarted once again by a city that seemed to have no mercy on the plans and hopes of its young. The trip, only postponed my grandfather assured him, lingered as an idea in his head, mingling with the fresh memories of all the cancellations and disappointments of the past year. There was the outing to the beach disrupted by the kidnapping of a friend's father; the concert that concluded a half hour after it began because of a bomb threat; the exams carefully prepared for again and again and again only to be put off due to curfews and killings and strikes and sit-ins. As he sulked about the house, picking up this book or digging through that drawer, he moped with all his teenage ire at the injustice of being born in a city so unpredictable, so determined to snap whatever hope it dangled in front of him.

In the retelling, that first surprise of the day would be nearly forgotten. The one better remembered occurred after dinner, after we had gone upstairs to our beds and the nightly episode of *The A-Team* had concluded, and the house was dark and the black gate locked and the night watchman employed on his rounds that my grandfather's chest pains began.

By the time my grandmother called for us, he was gasping for breath; by the time he could be loaded in the car, he was barely clinging to life. By the time he arrived at a hospital emergency room, clearly overwhelmed by the double whammy of a citywide strike and suspended ambulance service, Said had already drawn his last breath. When they called Surrayya from the hospital, she did not need them to say the words to know that her husband was dead.

——— ———

The funeral was held between noon and midafternoon prayers the next day, as the Muslim tradition of burying the dead with as much alacrity as possible dictated. In the fetid heat of Karachi, it was one religious injunction that served the city's dead well, insuring a dignity of which they would otherwise have been deprived. Burial too was a matter for the men, who could insure the proper purification of the body, the correct measures of cloth that would become the shroud, and the proper transportation of the body from home to the graveyard and finally to the grave.

The women remained inside and apart and behind. In the hours after my grandfather's death, we receded into the bedrooms, groups of cousins and neighbors and aunts gathering around my newly widowed grandmother. They waited at the sidelines to hand things to the men when they came to ask, looking for scissors or clean vessels or buckets or extra copies of the Quran.

When all the rites were completed, the deceased made ready for his last journey. The room in which he lay was cleared of all men to allow the female relatives one final good-bye. Then the women receded into the house as funeral procession composed of men chanting verses from the Holy Quran lifted my grandfather and left. Not a single woman, not my grandmother or mother or aunt Amina, was permitted to go to the final funeral prayers at the mosque and the cemetery where my grandfather would be interred. These were the rules. Women could bring impurity to the fulfillment of last rites, and purity was crucial to insuring the departed an entry to paradise. The moment of Said's death also began Surrayya's *iddah*, a period of three months and ten days or three menstrual periods during which it was mandated that the widowed woman remain sequestered from unrelated men—from anyone other than brothers or sons or men she could not marry.

The task of the women was keeping the memory of the departed. In the days after his death, as they counted out prayer beads, recited special verses for the dead, and flipped through the pages of Qurans worn with reading, the story of my grandfather Said was told again and again, sometimes recounting his sudden end but more often recalling only his kindness, his mirth at the birth of his grandchildren, his generosity at the weddings of his daughters. Every day for the first three days and then every Sabbath evening until forty days had passed after his death, the women came and comforted, dried Surrayya's tears, and calmed her fears. As the shock of the first days passed, she began to speak a few words, to add to the stories. With the passage of time, she began to add stories of her own, her stories and the stories of all the women coming together to keep alive the memory of the man who was no more.

CHAPTER 8

Loving and Leaving

DECEMBER 2001

In the fallow month of Ramzan, when weddings were on hold, the purveyors of Destiny Gardens had concocted a cleverly pious scheme for the use of their premises. During Ramzan the five daily prayers were increased to six, with the last held right before the dawn preceding the next day of fasting. Most of the mosques in Karachi still did not permit women, and even if they had, the awkwardness of entering with men and scurrying to a shielded corner to escape the male gaze almost guaranteed their decision to stay away.

The middle-class women, who bore their formidable mantle of responsibility with bravery and pride, could not, after all, toss propriety aside to fulfill a religious calling. For generations they had imbibed the idea that the women who turned up at the doors of mosques were the downtrodden, forsaken by fate and family, who came with their palms outstretched and faces covered in shame. The Holy Prophet had never turned away a supplicant from a mosque or a female who turned up at its door. To be at a mosque could be interpreted as being in need, and no middle-class woman wished to risk such a terrible misconception.

Thus there was money to be made by providing a venue for women who wanted to gather at Ramzan without judgment, and in lieu of weddings, a setting where women could catch up on gossip. That Ramzan of 2001, when the fasts were short like the days, Destiny Gardens filled the vacuum by putting up a sign advertising "Lady's Taraweeh Prayer at 10:00 P.M. Nightly." The red and white cloth sign was sedate, designed to flutter in the breeze to catch the eyes of women in the back seats of cars.

On the first night a handful of women scurried past the gates and into the hall, their faces painted with smiles. Most of them were related to the wives of Destiny Garden's owners and were therefore required by this relationship to attend every such outing. Such was the price and reward of having wealthy relatives.

On the second and third nights, the women dragged more of their curious friends along, women in black burkas adorned with rhinestones or lace or ribbon, just like the wives of the sheikhs in Arabia. After the first week the gathering ballooned to a few hundred; by the middle of Ramzan the owner of Destiny Gardens knew he had hit the jackpot. Soon the wealthier ladies were sponsoring evenings, offering catered snacks and sweets to their gathered friends and paying the fee for Saudi Arabian clerics to lecture the women (from behind a partition, of course) on the ways of fulfilling all the requirements of being a good Muslim woman, wife, mother, sister, and daughter. There was so much to learn, the gathered women nodded to each other after each sermon, tightening their headscarves before they went outside. They were coming here to pray, to do the work of the divine, and it would surely be approved by an exacting husband or whining son or disapproving father. After all, who could keep a good Muslim woman from prayer and knowledge of her faith?

Aunt Amina never set foot inside these gatherings. These were the same women who reminded her that it was her duty, as a Muslim woman, to bear a second and even a third and fourth wife if her husband so chose. She watched them in their adorned burkas trooping in to the brightly lit wedding hall, its sound system blaring verses of the Quran at the same volume as it blared Bollywood numbers in other months. She laughed. Whatever the spectacle, everyone would come to the circus, she thought, eager to assess the fresh, new girls being delivered to the marital market.

It was just such an evening at the end of Ramzan that Aunt Amina was contemplating her half-married life. She had undertaken various rituals to close her days. In the early days of the second marriage she had tried out the state of nothingness for size, choosing not to cook or eat all day during those weeks when Sohail would be gone, feigning death almost, in the misguided hope that her visibly wasting form would provoke some concern or hesitation before tasting the morsels and mouthfuls he consumed in her company. Ramzan would soon arrive, and she cried at the tragedy of opening the fast alone, something she had never done before and something she imagined no one, except the most destitute and forsaken, had ever been subjected to doing. But after the third Ramzan alone, she decided to move on, her own pathos worn out with overuse.

Some five or so years into the new arrangement, after some particularly dark days, the reality that the new divided order was there to stay finally dawned on her. In this moment of self-awareness she had made a pact, vowing that even on the days he did not come she would live life just as fully, eat and drink and laugh and smile with just as much fervor as she did when he was there. This schedule was outlined and posted: a proper meal cooked and ready and heated at dusk, consumed at the table and not on a sofa right before bed. She had to wake early and not sleep until ten, clean and pick up the rooms before evening, and shower and change into new clothes before 5:00 p.m. She would be visible and alive and existing with or without his presence to validate it.

She followed the list closely for an entire week, joyfully dressing and preening and preparing her favorite dishes with relish, hoping secretly that the smells and sounds of her now fully lived life would waft downstairs and provoke speculation. This new plan brought her strength and even pleasure as she assiduously reviewed the list, praising herself for sticking to it.

When he left the following Friday, she did not lift the curtains or wake at the early hour or change her clothes or take a shower. But she did not cry or weep or lament either; and in place of the fervent emotions came an indolence that was if not soothing then at least less exacting than the dictates of her plan. She began slowly to do as she wished, without sadness or considering how it would be perceived. She began to grow accustomed to listening only to her own thoughts and finding resolve within.

Thus she was not prepared for the knock on her door one dimly lit evening in the holiest last days of Ramzan before the Eid moon was sighted. It was not her week with Sohail, and in the manner of the many such weeks she had spent alone, she had broken the fast by herself, with a single date and a cold glass of milk flavored with her favorite rose syrup. Sated, she said her prayers against the soothing hum of the television, its blue lights flickering over her prayer rug as the darkness settled outside.

Then the knock came again, the low insistent rap, rap. It could not be Sohail, as he had a key and was no doubt bound for some family gathering at the home of one of his relatives. The realization that Sohail was not even in the building made her a bit afraid, and she wondered for a second if she should pretend to be asleep. But then, because she couldn't decide, she went to the door.

Through the peephole she saw her, a smiling woman, her head small and black and round in a headscarf, her body covered and buttoned in swathes of thick polyester. It was the other wife. "Please open the door," she said, noting immediately the presence behind the peephole. In earlier years, perhaps Aunt Amina would have just receded, let the knocks continue and be met with a silence. Perhaps she would have asked the other wife why had she done it? What was it like to steal another woman's husband?

Yet that evening Aunt Amina was drawn by the desire to see her up close: to see the gray at the temples, the wrinkles on the brow, the face so much plainer, so much more worn by worry than her own. It was a long moment of looking, stretched by the largeness of an encounter too big to fit into it. The other wife opened her mouth and her words fell fast and incoherently in a pile on the doorstep. She was dressed to go to Taraweeh prayers, she said, and had come to ask Aunt Amina if she would go with her. It was only across the street, and she saw it every day from her window and had always wanted to go. She did not want to go alone. The words came out in a clutter, raspy and garbled and hurried and scared, as the unmoving Aunt Amina listened.

When she remembered this encounter, Aunt Amina could not recall if she had uttered a polite "Sorry, I cannot come," or offered a terse "I cannot come," but she was certain that her response was a refusal. Whatever the words may have been, the door shut on the woman who, after a decade of living downstairs, had suddenly come calling. Aunt Amina couldn't recall if she had actually seen the face of the other woman, that broad unremarkable face, crumble from hesitant hopefulness into anguished disappointment.

MAY 16, 2002

The cemetery of the white, or the "gora," has sat in the center of the city ever since there was a city. Its name, Gora Qabristan, remained long after the British had left, and long after the "white" people who settled in the area made arrangements to be buried elsewhere. The people buried there now were brown and poor and unable even to imagine the white people who had laid claim to its first graves. Their spare, meager graves competed for space with the older plots marked with marble and stone, their curved Madonnas rising up from the sodden ground. The new ones stood just apart from the rest, as if embarrassed.

The arch over the door at the entrance announced the date as 1845, marking when Gora Qabristan was consecrated as the Karachi Christian Cemetery by the chief collector of the city. His own wife would be buried there, the regal Lady Phyllis Lawrence, who had followed her husband to the city after his appointment. Lady Phyllis loved racing horses on the newly inaugurated Karachi

Racecourse that the British officers had built. But on June 30 she fell from her steed and was battered in a mad crush of horse hooves and hard earth. Lady Phyllis was buried in Karachi, and her husband erected for her an elegant portico, arched and delicate and shady, a final resting place for a wife who fell far from home.

The shaded mausoleum still stands today at the edge of the cemetery, its once gorgeous vista marred by stubby buildings skirting its sides. But other graves around Lady Phyllis's have fallen on even harder times. The saltwater never sits too far from the surface in cities like Karachi, built as they are on land reclaimed from the sea. That, along with human excretions from the nearby slum buildings, has flooded some areas of Gora Qabristan today, taking over with every passing year more and then even more of the graves within it.

The dark hours are the most trying for Gora Qabristan, when prowling dogs, unsated from the trash heaps already picked over by slum children, wander amid the shadows of the crosses and addicts lie deadened amid the graves. On a dark night sometime in the middle of May 2002, a white body was dumped amid the graves. When it would be found, the severed head and limbs and other pieces of it, no one would know, or in any case tell, who had left it there. It was the body of Daniel Pearl, a reporter for the *Wall Street Journal* who had come to Karachi in search of a story about Al-Qaeda and its operatives working in the city. He had been kidnapped months earlier in January, and ever since then, American and Pakistani investigators had been searching for him under a glaring media spotlight. Their search ended at Gora Qabristan, the Cemetery of the White, which sits beside Sharea-Faisal, the city's main road that leads to the sea to the west and to the international airport to the east, both places where Karachi can be left behind.

AUGUST 2002

The *iddah*, or period of waiting, lasted three months and ten days—three menstrual periods—and applied to both widows and divorced women. It was unclear what the women would be waiting for. Its intention was the pragmatic regard for concerns of paternity, of insuring that children born after a husband departs by way of death or divorce could be properly pinned to the correct paternal line for the purposes of inheritance and familial obligations. So the women, young or old, disappeared into this period of seclusion that promised, at least theoretically, the possibility of emerging again eligible to be married or restored to social life, reassigned to another man.

I never saw any woman surface again. My grandmother, an old widow, was no different. Like all the other widows, women who faced the task of justifying a lone existence in a strictly paired world, my grandmother's sudden submersion into seclusion brought on by her husband's death became the first step in a transformation from the living into something less. Slowly in the days and weeks after, she began to change from a woman invested in the living and the longings of the world around her to one focused only on the world that existed beyond life, where she would once again become part of a pair.

She had always been pious, had always prayed all five of the obligatory prayers, and had always been the one to read the Quran cover to cover every Ramzan. But if prayer had been the activity for the time between meals and tending to Said and sitting with Aunt Amina, now it had become her primary activity, with small breaks for all the rest. An ordinary piety would not do for a widow. Perhaps she knew from the examples of widows and menless women who had passed before that her transformation had to be so complete that she almost became a spirit living in this world, a shadow in prayer waiting to be lifted to the next one.

She slept alone downstairs, insisting on keeping her windows flung open to the front garden so she could enjoy the night breeze. Her day began in the dark before Fajr prayer, when the jasmine planted just outside her windows gave off the headiest scent. She still performed her morning ablutions, her brown skin loose on her bones, in the marble-tiled bathroom that she and Said had gazed at with such disbelief when they first built the house.

After Fajr prayers she added several more of her own, reading special verses of the Quran that she deemed particularly power-ful in the luminescent first moments of the day, when only the most faithful rose and prayed to their maker. Sometimes after Fajr prayers, when the household was beginning to burst into activity, she would rest until her breakfast of a single cup of tea and, only sometimes, a half slice of bread. On many days she fasted, and far more than what was prescribed, each fast expiat-ing, cleansing, shoring and storing for the life beyond death, her own and her husband's.

By midmorning she returned to the Quran, three or four of the thirty burgundy-bound volumes she and Said had bought for that first Quran reading Khwani when the house was being built. She set herself the goal of finishing eight to ten a day, the entire Quran read every three days for so long that she barely had to look at the pages. She read in the name of her husband so that he should be spared the travails of the grave, and in her own name so that they could both be forgiven their sins and reunited before their single maker on the Day of Judgment and ultimately in paradise. Sitting by the window of the unused formal dining room at the margins of our house, she kept reading, glasses perched on her nose, until the call to Zuhr prayer filtered in from the mosque to draw her to another form of worship.

She permitted herself only one or two worldly indulgences. One of these was insuring that her son and grandson were prop-erly cared for, with the meals they liked cooked with the greatest of care. Even in her transformed state, aligned toward preparation for the next world, she made sure to sniff under the lid of every pot on the burners, ready always to start a curry or boil lentils her-self to insure that the standards that she had set for the household were upheld even as her own reign over it drew to a close.

The other duty was the phone calls she made to Aunt Amina. For years, according the established routine, these came in the mornings one week and in the evenings the next when Uncle Sohail was with his other wife. The phone calls in the evening were longer, beginning just after she had drawn her hands over her face to complete the last supplication of the Asr prayer. They continued softly until the sky dimmed and the call to the Maghrib prayer sounded from the mosque.

The two women, one who had spoken only to herself and the other only to God throughout the rest of the day, talked about things that may have seemed strange to others. Aunt Amina focused on the still pressing catalogue of slights from an absent husband whose betrayal still stung even as it failed to rattle. Surrayya responded with her stories of a man now gone, what his thoughts would have been on the weather that day, on the rudeness of a servant, or a film they had seen together thirty years ago in Bombay. At the call of Maghrib prayers, their discourse concluded and they set off again for the worlds beyond their reach and to the men who lived in them, one woman returning to prayer and another to the habits she had perfected for alternate weeks of her life.

SEPTEMBER 2002

The first white people, the British, in the region had come for trade, seeing in the sandy desolation of Karachi a nascent port from which to lug the sugar and spices and silk of the subcontinent back to the shores of England. The clock tower they had built still stood guard at Keamari Port even though the time was incorrect. No one cared much about this small detail; the tower remained because it was, like the smell of fish and the wetness of the gangplanks, part of how things had always been. So the tower that had kept the British on time continued looking out on waters no longer blue but a sludgy, sulking black, with traces of oil spills and the complex effusions of chemicals. The ships came still, merchant navy ships with Pakistani captains, hardworking boys carrying hefty cargoes of oil for the Arab sheikhs who employed them.

Now there were also American ships with cargoes meant for the American boys fighting over the border in Afghanistan. If the ships of the British had carried goods away after gathering them from far corners of Lahore and Jodhpur, the shipping containers of the Americans arrived bursting with them. They promised not to include guns, just food, uniforms, flak jackets, helmets, and fuel for the thousands of American soldiers waiting in Helmand and Kunduz and Kabul and Mazar-e-Sharif.

The cranes unloading the American ships stood out against the dwarfish buildings around the port and the worn rags fluttering on the fishing boats. One by one, they unloaded the metal boxes full of materials for war. As was customary, an illicit trade soon began among the crane operators and the customs officials, and soon the American military gear could be bought at one of the many markets that stretched on the road between the port and the city. If the officers of the Pakistan Navy knew about this, they did not say anything. After all, everybody had to make a living.

But the Americans did not come just to Karachi's port. They also came looking for terrorists, the men they believed were hiding in the nooks and crannies of Karachi, the men who had killed Daniel Pearl and had planned the attacks of September 11, 2001. These men bearing secrets and potential carnage could be sheltered by the late-arriving Pashtuns or the mafias in the madrassas of Binoria Town or deep inside the slums of Korangi, Landhi, and Orangi. There were so many layers of humanity and places to hide that anyone who didn't want to be found could breathe and burgeon with a peace unimaginable in other places.

Karachi was a city made for hiding. Everyone was running from something in Karachi: the migrant from the Afghan border hiding from money lenders, the secretly married couple hiding from the condemnations of their village's tribal council, the children of the Muhajirs hiding from the military, the drug-addicted

factory workers hiding from the bosses from whom they had stolen. With so many seeking escape in Karachi, a complex mechanics of hiding developed. There was always a way of getting where
you needed to go under an assumed name, always someone who
could be paid or bribed for their services.

This is what the agents from the Federal Bureau of Investigation, their binders and hard drives bursting with the names and
pencil-drawn profiles of terrorists, were told when, in late 2002,
they met their Pakistani counterparts to lay out their plans. The
men they were looking for were not all Pakistani, many were actually Arab, just like the men who had blown up the Twin Towers and the Pentagon. But the trails they had followed all led to
Karachi, to a cobweb of safe houses that had to be emptied out
if the men were to be caught and their plans aborted. The Pakistanis from Inter-Services Intelligence nodded, their faces blank
as they sipped their cups of tea. They told the Americans that if
they wished to catch terrorists, they must grow beards and wear
Pakistani clothes and try their best not to look white.

SEPTEMBER 2002

The bottom floor of Aunt Amina's house was being vacated by
the renters. They were a large family with six adults and four children who had lived crammed into its four rooms for more than
ten years, ten hot summers and ten mild winters jammed between
doors that would not give and walls that would not stretch to accommodate their expanding lives.

One afternoon in September, three large pickup trucks took
the renters to their new lodgings in the Gulshan-e-Iqbal neighborhood, their broken tables and rolled rugs and television sets all
packed together and covered with shabby sheets for the journey
across Karachi's streets. Aunt Amina entered the apartment for the
first time in a decade. Standing in the doorway, looking through
the portico under which Uncle Sohail ushered her into a married
life, she wept.

Before her was complete destruction. The tile floor of the courtyard was hacked and wounded in so many places that the gray
concrete underneath stood jagged and exposed. Inside the emptied
rooms the walls still bore the resentful weight of lives stacked into
impossible proximity: a child's multiplication table stuck to a poster
of a Bollywood starlet's almost-exposed breasts; bathroom supplies
in the kitchen; a hotplate in the living room. In the kitchen, the
walls were darkened with the grease of a million meager meals.
They had not bothered to clean up, and the droppings of their cre-
ations now lay thick and heavy and black and stinking behind the
stove, under the sink, and in every crack and corner.

And it smelled of the sweat of hundreds of unwashed nights,
of the newborns' urine, of the sickness the deceased grandmother
had suffered. Children's paint had spilled in one corner and in another a woman's henna-stained fingers had accidently touched the
wall. Each room bore its own store of ghosts who refused to leave
through the now-opened doors and windows.

How had it become this way? Aunt Amina asked herself as
she walked from room to room. The images of two decades before came back suddenly against the squalid reality before her:
this was the room where she had sat dressed as a bride; that was
the room where she and Sohail had eaten their first meal alone;
that the room where she had waited for the sound of the vegetable
seller. Not since the day Sohail had married his second wife had
these memories been so alive. Once a repository of images from
the days when her marriage was whole, the rooms had become
squalid squares that housed the resentment of others.

She had never met them, these people who had arrived armed
with the recommendations of Aziza Apa, people whose background was known to no one, but whom Sohail had eagerly
deemed appropriate. She had not wished to argue then; she was
so focused on what was going on in the other half of the marriage that she couldn't stop to consider what was happening in the
lower half of the house. She had stayed upstairs, on her new floor,

without any memories of happier times or sadder times, wanting only to be freed from looking down into the courtyard. She had been too high up to notice the squalor accumulating below, too annoyed by the sounds of so many children to notice the fate of the rooms that had once been her own.

Wandering with Uncle Sohail, Aunt Amina made him promise that it was she who would select the next tenants and supervise the renovation of the ground floor. Future tenants would not be those forced on them by Aziza Apa or anyone else; there would be no one who would wreck the house that they had built, a house that was hers and his together. "No more," she said amid the tears that soaked into the handkerchief she held on her nose. She decided, amid the wreckage, that she would reclaim some part of what had once been her own, of what she remembered as good.

SEPTEMBER 2002

Most of the houses in Gulshan-e-Iqbal had been built in the 1980s, with the money husbands and sons sent back from their toil in the Persian Gulf, on oil rigs and construction sites and in cabs and factories. The men came back once or twice a year with sweaty wads of dirhams and riyals rolled in pockets sewn inside their pants and swathed their wives and mothers and sisters in black burkas covered with rhinestones. To house the women and the children they sired as regularly as their visits, the men built mansions of glittering resplendence, which they hoped would excuse the fact that they did not live with their wives for most of the year. The Gulf boom had long ended by 2002, but these faded beauties still stood. Next to them sprouted apartment complexes and the smaller "villas" and windowless, gardenless "garden homes" that the postboom generation could afford.

It was a chauffeur working in one of these houses who snitched first. Goaded gradually by the agents of the Inter-Services Intelligence (ISI) who had been lurking about the neighborhood market for weeks, noting the comings and goings in the area while drinking tea at the roadside café, the chauffeur coughed up just the leads the Americans had hoped for. The snitch's boss was a rotund man of few words named Mohammad Ahmad Rabbani, whose movements seemed far too furtive and restless for the usual husband returning from Kuwait. Even more interesting to the ISI were the people the snitch's boss entertained. The men going in and out of the house were not posturing Pakistanis but Arabs, stumbling to give the snitch even a few words of instruction in Urdu.

The ISI found the boss and questioned him in his own house. It was a cordial interview run by the Pakistanis in Urdu while the Americans watched from the fringes. His properties were "guesthouses," Mohammad Rabbani insisted, where he played host to various visitors from the Gulf who wished to visit Karachi to oversee the charities to which they donated. The men weren't terrorists, they were philanthropists or their agents who wished to check in on the orphanages, religious schools, and mosques they funded. That, Rabbani repeated again and again, was all he knew. Before they let him go, the ISI made Rabbani write down the addresses of all the "guesthouses" he owned in the city, matching them against their list.

Ten minutes from the Housing Societies, Tariq Road had been the ritzy shopping hub of the eighties, when the first malls, aspirationally named "Shalimar Center" and "Glamour One," opened to attract shoppers away from the crowded alleys of Saddar and Bohri Bazaar. Like Gulshan-e-Iqbal, Tariq Road's glory had waned under the assault of time. The air conditioning in the modern "shopping centers" worked for just a few months. When it sputtered and finally gave way, the hundreds of shops became dank, airless cells reeking of sweat and packing materials. Pedestal fans, loud and whirring, arrived, and skipping over their wires as one navigated a winding course became a modern version of skipping the sewers and puddles in the open-air markets of old. Despite these realities of commerce in Karachi, Tariq Road remained the dream palace for hopeful brides and hopeless housewives, maybe not the prettiest or the richest, but those most determined to replicate the patterns popularized in the Sunday newspapers. Neon-lit shops lining each side of the street peddled everything from cotton brassieres to bejeweled bridal dresses in every hue and shade.

The second house the ISI raided stood behind such a row of shops. The neighbors had long been chased away by rising property values, not to mention the supply trucks unloading all night and the robbers who targeted the shops. The boarded-up houses that remained awaited the speculators who would purchase them to cash in when prices rose. This, the Americans believed, was home to Al-Qaeda.

Inside they found a gaggle of people, men and women and children, pretend pieces of a family that did not seem to fit together. When the investigators from the ISI, with the FBI watching as always, had sequestered them in one room, they went through the whole house, room by room and drawer by drawer. In one room, they found twelve SEGA game consoles whose unscrewed backs revealed they had been rewired to detonate. In another, twenty well-sealed plastic packages were discovered to contain carefully wrapped passports, which were later determined to be intended for the members of Osama Bin Laden's family. The children in the house, two boys, were the sons of Khalid Sheikh Mohammad, the man who coordinated the 9/11 attacks.

The final raid of the summer took place one day after the raid on Tariq Road. Building 63C on Fifteenth Commercial Street was much like those surrounding it in the sparsely inhabited block, close enough to the ocean to absorb a whiff of salt and rotting fish, and nondescript enough that it was seldom singled out for inquiries. The men from the ISI and the FBI kept vigil over it through the night, watching the dim lights in the apartment going on and off. With the creeping dawn and the call to prayer, four men emerged from the apartment and walked toward the mosque a few hundred yards away. When they returned they were met by the Pakistani paramilitary, dubbed the Rangers, who would take the lead in storming the apartment. On the stairwell of the darkened building, they grabbed two of the men. As they did so, the others who had already run up into the stairwell began to shower them with grenades and machine-gun fire. The siege of Building 63C had begun.

The military cordon around the building thickened as vans of Pakistan's news stations arrived to scoop the story before a hot, relentless day dawned. At around 10:00 a.m., a barefoot woman clad head to toe in a black burka emerged from the building, holding by the hand a small girl dressed in red. No one knew who she was or what she had been doing in the building. At noon, when speculation about the building's inhabitants had reached a fever pitch, a group of heavily armed Rangers were finally able to fire several tear-gas shells into the apartment window. Chants of "Allaho-Akbar," "God is great," rose from within the building.

Within ten minutes several Rangers stormed the apartment. The hunted men were holed up in the kitchen and showered the Rangers with cutlery when they entered. "Bastards!" the men yelled at the Rangers in English. "You will go to hell!" One of the men held a knife to his neck, threatening to kill himself if he was captured. The man was Ramzi Bin Al Shibh, the man who had coordinated the activities of all the 9/11 hijackers. The date was September 11, 2002, and by the time Al-Shibh was led to one of the ISI's secret sites in darkening Karachi, the sun was just rising on the East Coast of the United States on the first anniversary of the attacks.

JANUARY 2003

Aunt Amina decided to supervise the cleaning of the first floor herself. She was convinced that it could be restored to its former glory, unsullied by renters and betrayals. It would take more than just will, of course, and so large quantities of cleaning materials—ten packs of a bleach of high potency, twelve packs of orange phenyl, a whole row of the green and white bottles of disinfecting

Dettol—had been lined up in the courtyard ready for action. With them came brushes, three plastic buckets, and four reed brooms, as well as one with thicker bristles for wet floors. Ten boxes covered with brown paper, with a large red cross printed on their square-bellied fronts, also stood at attention; they held the poison to be laid down for rodents and any other creatures that the droppings of the renters had attracted.

These boxes were opened first, under the scrutiny of Aunt Amina. The woman Ghafoora and the old man Hameed, a couple who had been hired by Uncle Sohail to assist Aunt Amina in her project, carefully cut the seals on the top. They had been hired cheaply, paid by the day, because they were old and thus in the twilight of their ability. With Aunt Amina huddling behind them that first day of the job, they spread the rat poison in all sixteen corners of the four rooms on the first floor. When that was done they laid the poison along the walls of the courtyard and in the cracks of the broken tiles that had become stained by mud and rain and wear. In the very old bathroom, with its chipped green tiles and the squat green toilet, they laid some extra poison.

This was all they had time to do the first day, because the deliveries had not arrived until late and Hameed and Ghafoora had insisted, as the one condition of their employment, that they were to be let go before the Maghrib prayer every day. They had to take three buses and walk a mile before they reached their house near the airport, and at Hameed's age he was less able to push and jostle the wiry bodies of younger men or clamber lithely to the top of the bus for a seat on the roof. Being an old woman, Ghafoora fared a bit better, but what good was it if she got on a bus without her husband? So it had been decided that whoever hired them had to allow them to leave just before dusk, when it was still cool, so that they would fare better on the journey home.

The rat poison laid, Aunt Amina drew the bolt on the door with a clang and turned the key in the padlock. Upstairs and alone that week, Aunt Amina huddled by the window of her third floor apartment. She watched the hunched Hameed and the chador-bundled Ghafoora hobble under the blue, pink, and green lights of Destiny Gardens. And then she once again tuned her ears to the sounds and silences below. She listened as she ate her dinner, a kebab in two slices of white bread, annoyed that the sounds of her own chewing made it harder to hear the scurrying below. She imagined the rats dropping dead one by one as they ingested what was laid out for them.

When morning came, she watched the clock for the arrival of Ghafoora and Hameed, for their huddled figures in the stairwell and their hesitant knocks on the door. Once the three of them were together again, they went below, ready to begin the work of recla-mation. Not much death had happened there. The sun streamed through the courtyard, revealing only the lineup of cleaning supplies, the quiet boxes of whitewash and untouched bottles of bleach. The piles of rat carcasses she had imagined, whose corpses felt like a crucial first step in the cleansing she had planned, were not to be found in any of the places where the poison had been scattered in lethal amounts. Its fumes had killed some smaller things, spiders and roaches and piles and piles of fire ants.

The rats must have fled, they thought, like the renters, fazed perhaps by the fumes of the poison and the prospect of change. Aunt Amina with her staff of two proceeded with the plan for the day, sweeping out and mopping up every surface, carrying out the junk left in corners where the backs of cupboards or the under-sides of beds had offered the impression of eternal hiding places. The old couple made trip after trip, carrying it all outside and dumping it onto a large pile in front of the house, until the pile stood taller than either Hameed or Ghafoora.

The four-burner stove on which she had cooked her first meal for Sohail had to be dismantled. She watched the old man as he took the wrench and pulled the pipes from where they met the gas connection. The stove was wedged away from the wall and pushed toward the door. Its absence left a clear, dark imprint on the wall, a square of whiteness unblemished by the grime of the interven-ing decades, an accidental remnant of the newness of her mar-riage when everything was a clean slate. It brought some comfort to Aunt Amina. At the end of the second cleaning day, the white square was all she needed to remind her of what she was attempt-ing to restore.

It took another day to clear the house, to remove the two aging fans from the cobwebbed ceiling and to replace the leaking faucets in the kitchen. On the fourth day the bottles and boxes of chemi-cals were brought out to bleach away the past. Ghafoora and Ha-meed scraped and mopped and wiped with their faces covered, his with an old rag, hers with a scarf wrapped tightly across her face. Aunt Amina watched as the walls, stripped now of pictures and posters and nails, were splashed white with the wash that Hameed mixed in the courtyard.

One week into the cleansing of the first floor all traces of the renters had all been eradicated, their forgotten treasures heaped on the mound of trash out front and carried away by a Suzuki van to the unknown place where all such things in Karachi went. After measuring out the final days' payments in a neat pile for Ghafoora and Hameed, Aunt Amina drew the padlock over the door of the first floor and bid them good-bye.

AUGUST 2003

Benazir Bhutto was not present in the courtroom on the day that the Swiss court in Geneva convicted her and her husband Asif Ali Zardari of money laundering. "There is no doubt in my mind," wrote Daniel Devaud, the magistrate assigned to the case, "that her behavior is criminally reprehensible in Pakistan." She was not in Pa-kistan either, as she had been banished into exile nearly four years earlier when her second government was dismissed like the first, on charges of corruption. With her three children and her aging mother, she had in the wake of that cataclysm gone to Dubai, shut-tling between the desert emirate and their other home in London.

Everyone knew where her husband was. Asif Zardari, the turbaned man Benazir had wed years ago, sat in jail in Karachi. His was not an ordinary prison, not the dank sweat-and-blood-soaked dark rooms reserved for lesser criminals. He was a VIP, and prisoners of this ilk got two of their own rooms, with air conditioning and two attendants. Food was brought every day for Mr. Zardari from 70 Clifton, the headquarters of the Bhutto clan from whence his father-in-law had ruled. He was allowed as many guests as he wished and he entertained them with aplomb. Many stayed for hours, listening to stories and exchanging guffaws in the prison salon.

A diamond necklace had supposedly given the couple away to the Swiss after it was found lying in a vault in Geneva, placed there perhaps on some quick jaunt the two were accustomed to in their days as rulers. The story of the necklace, rumored to have cost 120,000 pounds and studded with many glittering, sparkling diamonds, was a murky one, beginning at a jeweler in London's Knightsbridge where it had been paid for. She would insist later that it was he who had bought it, with the gains that would later be traced to a company in the British Virgin Islands, where he stashed kickbacks for government contracts given to private companies operating in Pakistan. She would later be quoted as saying she had refused it when he had presented it to her. No one, of course, knew exactly what the story of the necklace, or for that matter Benazir and Asif, really was.

On the day they issued the judgment, the Swiss were not much concerned about whether the necklace was a present from a beloved husband or a long-imprisoned one or both. They had connected the dots between the foreign companies Cotecna and SGS, which had been given a contract for the inspection of goods arriving inside Pakistan, and the 6 percent of their earnings that were transmitted to bank accounts registered to two front companies in the British Virgin Islands. A Swiss lawyer, long known to the Bhutto family, had set them up with Citibank accounts.

The first was under the name of Asif Ali Zardari himself and the second in the name of Nasir Khan, Benazir's brother-in-law. It had all come together when the money for the diamond necklace bought in Knightsbridge, by Bhutto or for Bhutto, was, according to a *New York Times* report, paid for in part from one of those accounts.

In this way Benazir Bhutto and Asif Ali Zardari bore the news of their coupled crime separately, she in Dubai raising a family in exile and tending to an aging mother and he in prison amid the swirl of lackeys and well-wishers who came to rack up the favors they hoped he would be able to pay back tenfold when he managed to climb back up the slippery rungs of power. They had separate lives in that apolitical interval. She tried to keep her reputation: she made jaunts to New York for lectures and attended dinner parties at the homes of those who had feted her when she was in power, reminding everyone now that even though in exile, she still existed.

It would be a whole year until the husband and wife were together again, as Asif Zardari was mysteriously freed and then arrested again and then freed again in November 2004. After the November release, he was finally allowed to fly to Dubai and into the arms of his wife. This was an older wife and behind her were the children, growing too fast. After their years apart, there was perhaps little time to consider the consequences of sins past, of diamond necklaces and secret companies. There was instead a future to consider together, and for Benazir and Asif that also meant a return to power.

MARCH 20, 2004
It was early spring, when the heat could still be handled by fans and breezes. These few and precious pleasant weeks would soon be gone, to be replaced by the infernal months of April, May, and June when the heat would rage. Uncle Sohail's second wife had stopped working a few years earlier; the news of her early

retirement only coming to Aunt Amina after she witnessed one, two, and then three weeks in which she did not descend into the car with her husband and drive away with him.

With the departure of the renters and the cessation of their constant comings and goings, their cries and curses, only the sounds of the two women were left to punctuate the days. These came regularly enough to be soon memorized by Aunt Amina: the door shutting when Uncle Sohail left for work in the morning, the door opening downstairs to let in the maid, the clang of teapots, the blender starting and stopping on whichever floor Uncle Sohail was expected for dinner that evening.

In those days of almost silence, the women upstairs and downstairs were two lone dwellers separated by a single floor. Their sounds coursed more closely in the new emptiness that surrounded them, the choice of the television show upstairs informing the one downstairs, the smells of frying garlic and onions whetting the appetite of the solitary reader upstairs. If the women had once listened for each other deliberately in the early days of a divided husband, of newly constrained lives carved into weeks of lingering and longing, now their sounds were subtler, less perceptible, and the persistent passions that had once suffused the house had become softer, eroded by time.

Aunt Amina hated by habit, but even this hate she had nurtured for so long had become familiar, cozy in its constant presence. She still told the latest story, now two years old, about that spurned overture of friendship when the other wife had arrived at her door, bedecked in the burka of the modest believer, wishing to make a trip to the prayer sessions at Destiny Gardens. What a spectacle they would have been for the neighbors, she still mused, the two warring wives of Sohail, finally reconciled and trotting together like good, obedient women who acknowledged the right of their husband to marry again and again and again. That gripe she would carry to her grave, she still said, although she had fewer occasions to recall it.

She would never forget that she had never assented to his second marriage. She had opposed it and she did oppose it and she would oppose it and she would not let him forget it. So she made him remember in countless ways, in the lines of her forehead if he accidentally mentioned *her* by name while he was upstairs, in the flat silence of her turned back when he arrived later than he was supposed to on the morning when her week began, in her terse nos when he tried to make an excuse and shuffle a day from one wife's share to another's. Those were the nonnegotiables, the battles whose early carnage had established the course they would take when they recurred, with the same formations of troops, the same lining of defenses for the three people bound together in one marriage.

When she was by herself, though, the sounds downstairs infused her day with the solace an isolated prisoner takes from the shufflings and heavings of another. During the long stretches when the electricity came and went and came again, they suffered together as the loud drone of the power generators rattled glassware and china in the identical glass cabinets Sohail had given his wives. They wondered why the owner of the newly built house next door had had each and every window tinted into an impenetrable blackness. They heard the cries of the madman, who in the past year had taken to walking up and down the street, hurling abuses not at people but at the piles of trash.

It was on one of these ordinary mornings of separated togetherness that Aunt Amina noticed some omission in the regular sounds that rose up from the floor below. It was her week and a Tuesday. She and Sohail had woken at seven in the morning when the electricity shut down, the ceiling fan stopped, and warm air settled down on them.

Sohail had slunk to the bathroom and she had put the pot on for tea, splashing her face with water at the kitchen sink, hot and groggy from a night of only intermittent electricity. The tea would be good, she thought, as she went through the motions: measuring out tea leaves that she kept in the empty tin of powdered milk; the waiting; the spreading veins of brown when the tea hit the boiling water. She waited for the first boil, then the second, and added the milk and waited for a third boil, the rituals cemented into the movements of her limbs. She strained the tea and filled the thermos; the power came back on and the neighbor's generator stopped its droning as she remembered that she still needed to iron a shirt for Sohail to wear that day.

He left as he always did, after he ate breakfast and read the front page of the newspaper with his second cup of tea. It was an old habit, as was his loquaciousness, always so exacting in the morning, his quips and observations and pronouncements on the price of this or the result of that, in contrast to her preference for a slow, silent start to the day. She saw him to the door, to insure as she always did that his descent was singular and uninterrupted by a pause at the door of the woman downstairs, to whom the morning and the week and the husband did not belong.

She fell asleep again that morning, lulled by the calm that always settled over the neighborhood between ten and noon, after the men had left for work and the older children for school, fewer people around doing the asking and the demanding that went on during all the other hours of the day. Off she drifted, amid the low sounds of a woman haggling with a vegetable seller and the window shutter straining against the breeze.

When she awoke she was disoriented, in that odd limbo that follows a stolen sleep. It took a few confused moments and a fumbling grasp for the little clock on the bedside to remember that this was her second waking, that breakfast had already been accomplished, and Sohail had already departed to work. It was only then, after she had remembered all the duties already performed and assured herself that no one had witnessed her nap, that she realized that she could not hear anything downstairs. Not the television that marked the other wife's waking and her sleep, or the telephone conversations with mothers, sisters, and friends that happened in the interim. Perhaps she had gone to the bazaar, she decided, but it was still early. Other than the butcher or the grocer, none of the stores opened before eleven. But she would not be there, for with no husband to welcome, what woman would cook?

She forgot to wonder as she started the curry and then turned on the television, chopping the onions and shelling the peas for the rice and curry she had planned for their evening meal. A show about the old buildings of Karachi awakened her memories of the buildings of her youth, the crumbling structures now splayed on the screen. There was the Café Grand that was no longer grand, the now squalid insides of Empress Market where she and her mother had amassed such stores of delicacies without the barest scent of refuse. She had not been to Saddar in more than a decade, she realized, and now perhaps there was no Saddar left to go to.

It was midafternoon, after her lunch of rice and yogurt, and after she finally emerged from her mournful reverie, that she remembered again the silence downstairs. She began to listen more intently now, but she could hear nothing. She began to wonder if she had missed a departure, a quick slip out to the stores while she had been busy making dinner, but she knew it could not be. The woman's departures were usually loud, preceded by the squeaky turn of the metal armoire where she must keep her money and the clang of the metal keys she turned in its lock. The sounds would tell Aunt Amina that her companion wife was on her way out, and it would always be confirmed by the bang of the inner and then the outer door.

But Amina had heard none of this. Her foreboding grew until concern turned into paranoid imaginings. Had she and Sohail slipped away, gone together and forever, tired of sharing their marriage with a vestige like her? Had the woman abandoned the husband after she found that he was not the man she had dreamed he would be? Had she left him once her tripart marriage, cobbled together by dint of religious prescription, was old and creaking with disappointment? The possibilities came so fast that she could not order them or even taste the individual flavors of each against the more familiar tastes of her own hopes.

The mechanics of a surreal day are often lost. Aunt Amina managed to get into the other wife's apartment, the home that had once been her own, but the details of just how she did so are now forgotten. Perhaps with a key from the old days, spirited in some corner of a drawer. She might have quietly opened the door with the key, or she could have asked one of the little boys from across the street to climb through the courtyard window and scurry to the front door to let her in.

It was Asr when she entered, and the mosques were making the call for midafternoon prayer. The children were home from school, playing laughing games of cricket and begging their mothers for money to buy candy. She remembered, as she stepped into the sounds curling from the open widows, that they were so much clearer and more immediate on the second floor.

The shock was not the sounds but the alterations. The walls were now painted in purples and pinks, so unlike her own apartment's whites and beiges. He had lied, she immediately realized, when he had told her that he preferred them. Here it was, her husband's other life, lived downstairs and on alternate weeks but for years and so different, so purple. Revolted, she would have turned back if not for the heavy silence. *She* could not be there, Aunt Amina determined; if she had been, she would have come out to defend her territory, to keep her from seeing in all its lurid colors the second life lived below.

But she was there. She was in the kitchen, on the floor by the fridge that Aunt Amina hadn't seen since she moved upstairs years ago. The kitchen was the place she least wanted to see, and she came to it after having walked through the length of the apartment. The other wife lay on the floor on her stomach, face down, the door of the fridge still ajar. It must have been open for some time, as water had pooled on the floor by the body. She did not want to touch her or turn her over or shake her to see; she knew at once. She wanted to scream, but the scream did not come. Several hours later, Uncle Sohail returned home and, seeing the door of the second-floor apartment ajar, risked angering Aunt Amina by stopping in. There he found them, his two wives; one dead and one alive, in the same room for the first time.

CHAPTER 9

A Return to the Original

MARCH 2004

The funeral was held the next morning. The night before was a long one, distorted by the havoc over the arrangements and the details of informing everyone and getting the announcement of the death read over the mosque loudspeakers. Some of her relatives came, two or three women with pinched brown faces clutching wadded tissues, their noses red with rubbing and crying. At the door, they gazed confusedly at Uncle Sohail, waiting for instructions, some clues over protocol before scurrying into the bedroom where the dead woman had been laid on her bed.

The question of space was crucial; the house was big but each floor was small, and separate spaces had to be provided for the men and women who came in droves to mourn the death. The middle floor could not accommodate them all, and Uncle Sohail, along with two or three other men from the Kokan community, the men who always showed up at such times of crisis, had to make some decisions about options. The ground floor, cleaned and empty and shorn of furniture, everyone agreed, was the logical place to receive the men.

Dawn broke and the men began to gather in greater numbers. As the tea came to a boil in the kitchens all around the neighborhood, a *maulvi saheb*, a religious cleric, arrived from the mosque and began reciting verses from the Quran. His voice, smooth and milky and melodious, rose in long, languorous chants from the courtyard in the middle of the house, filling all three of the floors. The men huddled and greeted each other, speaking in low tones, and then made their way to the bereaved husband. With head bent, Uncle Sohail stood at the entrance in the crisp, starched white *shalwar kamiz* he normally wore on Eid or for weddings. One by one the men clasped his hands, nodded and embraced, and murmured some words.

After the dead woman was found, Aunt Amina's first instinct was to retreat upstairs. In those first confused moments when she was stunned and unsure, she believed she could still hide in her upper floor sanctuary. But the matter of a deceased woman was a delicate one; the woman's own mother was dead and the peculiar dimensions of their family, the absence of daughters and mothers-in-law and son's wives, left unfilled a crucial position in the operations of mourning. The role of mourner in chief among the women could not be assumed by just anyone; it had to be a woman of authority, a woman who knew the women who would be coming and could greet them, who could take from them the condolences they had come to offer, to be returned in kind when they suffered a similar loss.

The women awarded this honor to Aunt Amina, the first wife of the man who had just lost his second wife. Up they climbed to the third floor and knocked on her door. After the first group came, another followed, and soon there was no point to locking the door. The pile of shoes outside it, the slides and the heels and the flip-flops, was an indication to new arrivals that the women's gathering was inside. There was no choice. Aunt Amina had to hurriedly bathe and change, dress in white, and sit in her living room, where one of the women had covered the floor in white cloth.

The women sat around her in a circle on the white cloth. One of them had lit some incense, and another had brought the Qurans and placed them on a table in the center of the room. The relatives of the first wife, the plain-faced cousins, the one widowed and the other a spinster, who had come the night before, stayed at first on the middle floor, unsure of their place in the pecking order. There they busied themselves with the things that had to be done: preparing the shroud, bathing the body, and making it ready for the men who would take it for burial. When this was done, they sat awhile, their hands folded in their laps, until they too ascended the stairs and sat at the edge of the room where Aunt Amina officiated over the gathering of mourning women. She pretended she did not see them.

A messenger came from the men to say that it was time for the bier to be carried away. Led by obedience and practice the women filed out and down, for it was a ritual to see for the last time the deceased woman who would never be seen again in the flesh. So Aunt Amina returned to the room with the purple walls to look again at the face of the woman who had passed. On each side of her stood women who watched, searching for the subtext they knew made this funeral, this last good-bye, different from the others. "She looks peaceful," one of them said, as she knew was supposed to say in the presence of someone who has passed from this world into the next.

AUGUST 2005

It was supposed to be a new beginning for the city. Smart and slick and goateed Mustafa Kamal was a mayor with a plan for a city without a plan. Kamal was a child of Karachi, of its schools, of its eternal questions of belonging, of its hopes and disappointments and realities. His parents had migrated from India and come to the city with their burdens of dreams. He was born in the city and raised among people trying to reconcile those dreams with the realities they had landed on. Like all the hopeful, aspiring children of the Muhajirs, Mustafa was not rich and not poor, and he was averse to the lordly politics of the feudals and their children, their SUVs full of armed guards and their entitled romps all over Karachi.

Coming of age when the MQM first took over the hearts and minds of migrants and their children, Mustafa Kamal had got his political start working as a telephone operator at the party's office in Azizabad. Speaking the curious mix of Urdu and English so specific to Karachi's middle-class kids, he looked and talked unlike the politicians of old. Each gesture, each volley of words, like *infrastructure, global, megacity, revitalization,* rained on the ears of hopeful Karachiites who saw Kamal wresting them from the past of lost dreams and into the future of new ones. With Kamal at the helm, the reclamation of Karachi could finally begin.

Mustafa Kamal endeared himself even more because he had a plan for the city. To get people's attention, he first announced that Karachi was a city of nearly sixteen million people with bustling industries and shops and houses, cars and motorcycles and rickshaws crammed into circumscribed space, all jostling against each other, apparently without a plan.

Not only was there no plan, Mustafa Kamal and his similarly eager cohorts told the newspapermen and the television channels, there was not even an accurate map. The city had grown and expanded chaotically, with a road built here and a bridge built there, hundreds pouring in from one village and thousands pouring in from another, some sticking together in one portion of a slum and others setting up a shantytown. There were places police didn't go, buildings built by sly developers who paid off local thugs who extorted money from shopkeepers and protected the whole operation. The city was wild, and to tame it a map and a plan were required.

The master plan for the city of Karachi that Mustafa Kamal, elected mayor of the city, set out to have prepared in 2005, fifty-eight years after Partition and in the wreckage of other uncompleted plans, would attempt to tame Karachi's growth. The plan makers—among them not only political functionaries and businessmen but also engineers, town planners, statisticians, and urban historians—asserted that the key to this was to control development, to provide boundaries for the unbounded and incentives for the apathetic.

One of these boundaries involved the idea of a "sunset clause." Ranging from five years to perpetuity, the sunset clauses would rein in the builders who bought land and used a single building license to build several stories on lots permitting only one. The administration of Mustafa Kamal enforced a long-forgotten building control ordinance and added additional regulations, including a new permissions process for builders. Any new building plan would be submitted to special development authorities who would review and provide preliminary approval of any development project. After this, the plans would be submitted to the Committee for the Development and Growth of Karachi, which would remain the final arbiter on development decisions.

Kamal's Strategic Development Plan 2020 read like a manifesto for Karachi's future. It promised to make it a "world class city" with "investment friendly infrastructure." Its choices reflected the creation of a city more for the aspiring middle class instead of the barely surviving poor. "High rise" apartments would obviate the need for upgrading settlements, "flyovers and expressways" would eliminate traffic snarls. There would be "malls instead of markets" and "global capital investment" instead of old-fashioned begging and courting Islamabad bosses for money. To make this Karachi possible, the poor would be shipped from the center of the city to the periphery, less seen and better ignored.

The waterfront would be reclaimed and transformed too, into an expansive twenty-six kilometer stretch of world-class hotels lining a promenade cooled by the Arabian Sea breezes. Forty thousand acres of beachfront development projects required bulldozing parks to make room for mansions, pavilions, and entertainment complexes. With this plan, Karachi could do it all and have it all. But among those who sat on the committees that discussed and implemented the plan were some who had worked on past plans, in 1985, 1994, and 2000. Others even remembered the plans of 1978 or earlier. Nobody spoke of the old plans now, having decided that it was time to let go of the past and believe that this plan for Karachi, the Strategic Development Plan 2020, would be the plan that would defy the obstacles that killed the previous plans, allowing new rulers to realize new ideas.

OCTOBER 8, 2005

Nestled in the foothills of the Himalayas and the Hindukush mountain ranges, Swat District was as idyllic and serene as Karachi was gritty and exacting. It was a place people escaped to, and the ruddy-faced, gray-eyed locals of Swat were happy to accommodate the Karachiites' desires for reprieve from the routines of too many cars, too little electricity, meddling mothers-in-law, and unstable jobs. Those who could come were moneyed, and their rupees stoked the tourist economy of Mingora. The bazaar in the main market of the Swat District's biggest town displayed stall after stall of embroideries and beautiful woodwork that the men in the market procured from craftsmen in the mountains, up in the recesses of Gilgit Balitistan in stone dwellings set on steep hills navigable only by those who lived there. The bazaar was also full of guides fluently wheedling Pakistanis in Urdu or tempting British or the American climbers in English. Just a short drive from the capital, Islamabad, Swat was appropriately remote and always hospitable. A chilled beer and a place to pray could be found within a few steps of each other. Tolerance, the people of Swat believed, was necessary for tourism, and tourism was their livelihood.

The bazaar in Mingora was just beginning to bustle in the minutes before nine o'clock. It was a late start, for it was the month of Ramzan and most had fallen asleep again after the dawn meal. Shopkeepers were just opening their stalls for the foreign tourists when the earth began to tremble. A few perhaps felt the first gentle shakes that made the windows rattle. Within seconds, though, the tremors began, and then the crumbling, the violent toppling. The people who had been in their homes rushed outside and some who were outside inexplicably rushed indoors. Rocks and glass and the wood from crumbling houses flew; cars crashed into those fleeing or lying on the ground injured. Cracks appeared in the earth, rending trees from the ground and swallowing people.

The epicenter of the earthquake of 2005 was twelve miles east of Muzaffarabad, in the strip of Kashmir that Pakistan had wrestled away from India. But Swat was close enough to be left bloodied, rubbled, confused. It was days and weeks before helicopter scans of the mountainous territory revealed entire villages flattened, entire populations eradicated. The nearly one hundred fifty aftershocks razed so many more of the hardscrabble villagers' dwellings. The official death toll was initially said to be 74,698 people, but the final count was dogged by disagreements between this or that government agency and was never publicly announced.

In the days after the earthquake, aid poured into northern Pakistan from all over the world. Even those believed to be enemies made efforts to rescue the hundreds of thousands of people left without shelter on the steppes and promontories of affected mountains. On October 28, 2005, then prime minister of Pakistan Shaukat Aziz called on those affected by the quake to come down from their mountain homes into the cities and valleys to obtain medical care and aid supplies. With snow already falling on the treacherous mountain passes and aftershocks continuing unabated, it was the only way to get to them.

But in Swat, where hundreds of homes and hotels had fallen, another group of people descended from the mountains. They came not from the east, where freedom fighters from Kashmir were waylaid or hiding, but from the west, the villages around Peshawar and near the border with Afghanistan. They had long hair and long beards, and everything about them was dark: they appeared at night with cloths wrapped around their faces and wearing mottled brown and blue *shalwar kamiz*. They came into the markets of Mingora, the newly quiet bazaar shorn of tourists. One evening they made their way through the small shops and at gunpoint took all the music CDs, DVDs, and posters of women that they could find from the terrified shopkeepers who had managed to survive the earthquake.

On that Ramzan evening, after the fast had been broken at dusk, the men who had come from the hills piled all the CDs and DVDs and pictures of women into a heap in the middle of the bazaar. Then their leader, a man named Maulana Fazlullah who led a group called Tehreek-e-Nifaz-e-Shariat-e-Mohammadi, gave a short sermon. The earthquake had been sent to punish the people of Pakistan for their abandonment of Islam, for their profligate ways of watching obscenity, listening to the tainted sounds of that which had been prohibited, allowing their women to go about uncovered in the streets, and straying from the correct path. The bodies, the fallen buildings, the cries of motherless infants, the maimed fathers and mothers left to suffer in the cold nights were bearing divine punishment for these sins. As the flames engulfed the pile, the orange light illuminated the wrapped faces of Maulana Fazlullah's followers.

NOVEMBER 2005

There was no stipulated mourning period for a widower, not like there was for women, who had the neatly prescribed three months and ten days or the length of three menstrual periods for the task of moving from a life of wifehood to widowhood. The task of mourning for a man was of different proportions. It could even be said that the normal amount of sympathy allotted to the man left without a wife to tend to him was reduced, in Uncle Sohail's case, to further nominal proportions given that he still had one wife left.

There was also the complication of reinstating a marriage that had been halved with such precision for nearly two decades. Should it simply return to what it had been? And could that even be, the revival of unthinking, unscheduled days and weeks and weekends belonging only to each other? Given the swiftness of the other wife's death, perhaps the transition should be delicately handled. And then there was the question of whether it should be done at all, whether either of them, now decades into their habit of longing and parting and waiting, could begin a new chapter in an old marriage.

The first few days were the easiest. The demands of performing for the audience of mourning guests, the seldom-seen relatives and curious neighbors, kept them both busy. The third day was the end of the period of mourning required for all except widows. On the traditional third day of mourning, Uncle Sohail, wearing his clean, starched *shalwar kamiz*, went to middle floor where he had spent alternate weeks for the past twenty years. He opened the windows, lit incense, and waited for the mourners, as was required of the day, the men staying with him and the women ascending the stairs up to Aunt Amina's floor, where she sat with them, prayed, and read the Quran for the departed soul.

After the third day fewer people came, and then even fewer until it was clear that, henceforth, it would be just Aunt Amina and Uncle Sohail left to each other. The question of the future hung between them with a doleful silence. The ground floor lay empty and now also the middle floor, an expanse of unused space in a city of people crushed together. After the first week, and for the second, third, fourth, and fifth, Uncle Sohail followed the erratic patterns of a man suspended between a living wife and a dead one. Within him waged the war of habits: the habit of one-week spurts with two different women, the habit of being cared for always by the one or by the other, the habit of leaving and good-byes.

But the longing for a freshly cooked meal or a bed with clean sheets or a hot cup of tea goaded him out of the most tender memories. Confronted by these needs, he told himself that he could not live in the past, wallow in its tragedy. At those times, he would turn off the television, turn off the lights, and go back upstairs to the clean house and sheets and the living wife, and he forgot for a week, or for a while, the burden of having to keep the memory of his dead wife alive all by himself.

JULY–AUGUST 2006

The skies darkened and the rains came to Karachi, gently cooling sunbaked foreheads. As they always did in the first hours of their fitful romance with the rain, people celebrated. They packed picnics and crammed into Suzuki vans to go to the beach and frolic in the choppy waves. The women fried fritters of flour made from chickpeas and served it up to the men with chutney made from green chilies and tamarind. Children squealed as they jumped in puddles, took outdoor showers under the gutters, and caught tadpoles and then freed them. Like the first moments of everything that came to Karachi, the first hug of the monsoon was always a joyous one.

But the rain didn't stop and things started breaking down. The power was first to go. At first people pretended not to notice; the women kept frying the fritters, the men hitched up their pant legs, and everyone pretended it was all still good fun. The children kept playing, not noticing that the puddles were becoming fetid, that the rainwater was mixed now with the water from the sewers.

They pretended until the electricity had been off for eight hours, then ten, and then a whole day. They started to worry a bit as the ice in their refrigerators began to melt and the food stored in its recesses, frozen meat from the Eid before, chicken pieces for curries, garlic peeled and cleaned and stored in bags, began to drip. Without electricity, there was no water to drink or for bathing or to wash dishes or clothes, no way to pump into overhead tanks what would come flowing out of people's taps. The water fell from the sky, the taps ran dry, and the people began to get upset.

The heart of the old city of Saddar, where the British had once lived, where the roads had been clean and orderly, and where my grandparents Said and Surrayya had arrived and lived in awe amid such spaciousness, was badly hit by the monsoon of 2006. Under the surface of streets that had become canals, water burst through drains designed for a city of four thousand but bearing the waste of four hundred thousand. This time it was too much for the choking sewers, and they sent rivers of waste into the streets.

In this dank heart of the city stood the Sobhraj Maternity Hospital, a sandstone building built in 1928 by a Hindu financier who had lost his wife in childbirth. The hospital, which had brought babies into Karachi, increasingly the babies of the poor and then the very poor, for decade after decade, braving monsoons and floods and wars and cataclysms, also gave up that year. Constructed decades earlier, the storm drain that ran under the hospital was lower than those of the adjoining areas. That year the avalanche of water that came through it from the shops of Urdu Bazaar and the eateries of Burns Road made the drain under the hospital give way. It strained and seethed and finally burst, unleashing water and sewage into the hospital and under the beds and stretchers on which women lay writhing in labor.

The beds were old and immovable. The stretchers were newer, but their wheels didn't work. The fathers-to-be, the new fathers, and the two or three doctors who had braved the rains to come to the hospital asked the orange sellers and banana sellers, who now sat on their empty carts without any produce to sell, if they might borrow the carts so that extremely pregnant women, women in the throes of childbirth, could be wheeled out of the hospital. Twenty carts were rounded up, and they became beds, delivery tables, and stretchers for the women and the babies born in Sobhraj Maternity Hospital in Karachi in August 2006.

Mustafa Kamal, the mayor who had been working so hard, so diligently to develop a master plan for the city spent day after day roaming through the neighborhoods of burst sewers and submerged homes. He hitched up his own pants and carried and set up a folding chair, forcing lazy work crews to unclog pipes, remove debris, re-string power lines. As he moved from place to place, from Azizabad to Liaqatabad, from Saddar to Tariq Road, from Gulshan-e-Iqbal to Clifton, he was asked many questions and heard many excuses. The Karachi Water and Sewerage Board would not work with the Karachi Development Authority, who insisted that the task of clearing the streets belonged not to them but to the Karachi Municipal Corporation. If there had been an organizational map, it would have revealed a city carved up into a million little turfs and territories and bureaucracies and pensions and payoffs. But there was of course no such map. Perhaps then, wading through the foul waters left by the monsoon of 2006, the maker of the master plan of 2020 realized that Karachi's problem was not the absence of a master plan but the presence of too many masters.

MARCH 2007

Two years seemed a long enough time to mourn the departed. For two years Aunt Amina had been the only wife doing the caring and yet only one of two wives being cared for. She had tolerated and even accommodated the rituals of mourning and the uncomfortable position of listening to the sometimes feeble and sometimes effusive praises that visiting mourners heaped by ritual or rote on her ears. "She was such a good cook," one neighbor woman, sweaty from her climb upstairs, had pronounced as she undid the heavy nylon burka she had put on to walk the ten steps between her own house and Aunt Amina's stairwell. "She always sent us the most delicious sweets every Ramzan," she had continued.

Aunt Amina smiled and nodded, never letting her guests get an inkling of the reality that neither woman had ever, never on Eid or during Ramzan, on their sickest days or their most joyous ones, ever eaten a morsel cooked in the other's kitchen. In the early days after the second marriage, if Uncle Sohail had made the mistake of bringing a plate of food from downstairs to upstairs, it had provoked such a storm of tears, followed by such a frigid coldness of mien that he had never dared to repeat his mistake again. The food from downstairs, the feelings from downstairs, and the existence of downstairs had stayed downstairs for as long as there was a second wife living there. The mourning women broke the rule on the day after the funeral, and it was perhaps the shock of the death, or the suddenness of it, that allowed Aunt Amina to concede, for the sake of appearances, to the story of wifely sisterhood that everyone wished to believe.

Those old enough to remember the initial misgivings fell into the story too. "Time heals everything," they would say awkwardly to each other, forgetting the stares they had poured on the house with the two wives and the giggles and snickers in their kitchens when they saw the newlywed couple drive off in the car on workday mornings. They had felt so thankful then to have their husbands, their fat or sweaty or bald husbands, all to themselves. They were unable to resurrect that thankfulness now in the quiet room upstairs where Aunt Amina received them. It was such a neat and clean room, free of the encroachments of a daughter-in-law who needed more space or the grown grandchildren who had nowhere else to sleep.

It was not these women who tormented Aunt Amina anymore. What bothered her now was Uncle Sohail's unwillingness to let go of the woman he had married against her will. At first, his departures into reverie seemed admissible, a natural expression of grief she resented but had to permit. So she sat quietly and tried to pretend that everything was as it had always been. When Uncle Sohail slumped downstairs after dinner and sat there for hours she said nothing.

On Fridays his vigils would last longer than usual. The Fridays after the death of the second wife he would go to prayers at the mosque as usual and come upstairs for his meal. Then he would announce with a rehearsed coldness that stung in its preemptive clarity that he was "going out." He would go downstairs, and she would hear him open the windows, open and shut a drawer or a cabinet, and then settle into silence. It was these long, noiseless Friday afternoons of nothing that frightened her, taunted her, assaulted her with the notion that even though she had outlived the second wife, she had failed to hold the primary spot in his heart.

On some Fridays she tried to console herself with what she had gained. No longer was her life divided, no longer did she dread the Sunday evenings when he would descend the stairs into the arms of another woman for another week. No longer did she lie in bed worrying about what would happen as she got old: the vulnerable alternate weeks when she would be uncared for and unheard from. The passion with which she had weighed his affections and counted on his guilt, measured against the divine command of the perfect justice she was due, had dissipated.

But with the passage of many Fridays and his unerring devotion to spending them downstairs with the ghost of what once was, Amina's sense of abandonment began to sting. What she had first allowed with the lenience of a benevolent victor permitting the vanquished some small moment of repose, she now began to consider a crucial lapse in judgment, a chink that would grow into a chasm that would wrench from her again what was finally hers. He did not *want* to get over her, she thought, getting angrier and angrier through the long Friday afternoons.

Soon the poison from Friday spread into the rest of the week, into breakfasts and lunches and bedtime embraces, into all conversations and trips to purchase groceries and each and every one of the familiarities of marriage that had so recently reentered her life as undivided wholes. Schooled well in the art of fighting a living opponent, she battled a dead one, a woman whose every failing had been erased by death and whose every endearment was embellished by an absolute absence. At the store together, if he reached for a jar of jam whose flavor she disliked, she decided immediately that *she* must have liked it. If he paused for too long in the middle of a conversation, she felt the presence of the dead woman's words. The assault of the second wife was constant.

They needed a new beginning, she concluded, a beginning in which the arrangements of the decades, the habits of the divided lives did not intrude. She had to take back not only his life but also his memory, and install in its place a new one, with other recollections, stories about her and about how they had been before. Stories of the day he had come to see her, stories of their short courtship and furtive first glances at each other on their wedding day, stories of their first days together when he had not doubted, nor thought of anyone else, not doubted their marriage and the solitary solidity of one husband and one wife. After two years Aunt Amina decided that she had to wrest back her marriage. She made a plan to conquer the memories of her husband.

SEPTEMBER 2006

In an instant, there was darkness. The lights on the streets outside the Aiwan-e-Sadr, where Pervez Musharraf, the army chief turned president lived, grew dark. The high-voltage bulbs that shot bolts of blue light outside the Supreme Court of Pakistan went out. The lone bulb in the shop that sold cigarettes just outside the diplomatic enclave also stopped shining. Suddenly, on the evening of September 24, 2006, in the middle of newscasts on television, while dinner was just beginning to be served to senior bureaucrats, and lesser bureaucrats were complaining to their wives about not being invited to meetings where dinners were served, and the clerks of the lesser bureaucrats were wondering why their wives had not yet served dinner, all Islamabad went dark.

It took a few minutes for the TV and radio stations with their own power generators to realize that this was no ordinary outage; that the lights had dimmed not simply over Karachi or Lahore, for that was not news, or Peshawar, for that was certainly not news, but over the whole country. This was news. They sent out their men, who had been dragged from their own half-eaten dinners into the news vans that would take them to the darkest possible spots of the cities, which they knew would attract people to the only lights available, their camera lights.

It was just a little while before the country began to wonder if this was a bigger and perhaps more meaningful darkness. It felt different from the routine power outages that interrupted their playtimes and prayer times. The news of the historic proportions of the darkness spread in the old-fashioned way, from one person to another.

Because the president had recently announced that parliamentary elections would be held soon, and the cauldrons of power, set to simmer since the most recent coup seven years ago, seemed suddenly to have reached a boiling point, everyone now suspected that the darkness portended something more threatening than simply a countrywide darkness. Everyone suddenly remembered that the president, who was also the chief of army staff, was not in the country, and this made them even more uneasy; perhaps it was another coup, a coup to replace the man who had taken power in a coup, under a darkness that was no ordinary darkness but a national one.

At 10:00 p.m. Tariq Hameed, the chairman of the National Power Administration Board, whose own house remained lit with a private generator, issued a statement saying that no sabotage was involved and the power outage was due to a technical problem. Then the officials of the Ministry of Information, who were accompanying President Musharraf on his trip to New York City, told other officials who had been left behind that the president was doing fine and that the information about his well-being should be shared with the rest of the nation. The officials assured the nation that even though this was an extraordinary sort of darkness, it did not mean that anything else was afoot, that some big change was underway.

Nobody listened, and as night fell and the lights flickered, people watched for tanks to come rolling into Islamabad, for ranks of soldiered men to appear on street corners to enforce curfews. Perhaps a new leader was behind the darkness, stealthily taking over before things became worse; someone from within the military, a younger leader, a rebel who did not like the general who had struck a deal with politicians convicted of corruption. Perhaps there was such a man, angry at President Musharraf for striking a deal with the Americans, permitting them to kill Pakistanis via remote control and to ship the weapons and fuel of warfare through Pakistan to the hungry white soldiers in Afghanistan. Sitting and sweating in the darkness, the people wondered whether there was such a man, a man who would stand up to America, who would keep out the corrupt politicians, a Pakistani man who would lead Pakistan out of the darkness. They wondered for hot, sticky hours over cups of tea or glasses of nothing until the lights finally, slowly came back on, and they realized then that it had all just been an ordinary darkness, interrupted finally by a mediocre light.

SEPTEMBER 2007
One year after that meaningless darkness, Karachi was festooned with flags again, the black, red, and green of the Pakistan People's Party. After nine long years in exile, Benazir Bhutto had managed to outwit all the men who would have kept her from returning to the country and managed to wrangle permission to return. The long odds that would have deterred so many had somehow evaporated in the short span of four months. There was the matter of the military general who had taken over the country after the last coup, when the government of her rival, Nawaz Sharif, had been dismissed. Then there were the corruption cases, enormous piles of them, the ones for which her husband Asif Ali Zardari had languished in prison for many years. The weight of accusations had been heavy, almost immoveable, and she had borne it for eight years.

Then it was gone. Some said a secret deal had been reached between General Musharraf, whose power was waning, and the banished Benazir. Now, the same unelected general had granted her an indemnity from prosecution. The National Reconciliation Ordinance, signed by General Pervez Musharraf in September 2007, made it painless for Benazir Bhutto to return to Pakistan. With his signature her exile ended and the daughter of the country, pure once again, was ready to return to rule.

The event was historic and the drama of her homecoming had to be perfected. The first act was the announcement by a top official of the Pakistan People Party's: "I want to give the good news to millions of Pakistanis," the mustached man declared triumphantly amid the cheers of party workers who already knew what he would say. "And I want to give you the date," he awkwardly continued into the din. "The date is 18 October and the place is Karachi . . . She will return to her home city of Karachi."

His words were lost in the storm of cheers; the crowd had known the date as well and was eager to start cheering, as they knew they were supposed to. In the days leading up to her return, there were even more cheers. There were the cheers of a forgetful people now fitfully waving flags into the sky, ready to welcome once again the woman who had brought democracy to Pakistan. The cheering banished easily the memories of the two times she had been dismissed for corruption, the millions she had been accused of stealing, and the hundred-thousand British-pound diamond necklace she had bought with the money of Pakistani taxpayers.

SEPTEMBER 30, 2007—MAKEEN, SOUTH WAZIRISTAN

Baitullah Mehsud was a small man in a world where size mattered. Like many small men who have much to prove, he had learned to overcome with charisma what he lacked in stature. Any remaining deficits had been made up by luck, and the blessed fortuity of being in the right place at the right time. Few who have seen them would consider the craggy gray-brown hills and valleys of Makeen in South Waziristan the right place for anything. Since the start of the war in Afghanistan it had become a particularly hardscrabble place; the apricots and apples that grew in the farmers' orchards around the scant settlements often rotted in the trees, their ripe promise interrupted by the security cordons that allowed nothing in and nothing out of Pakistan's tribal areas.

What may have been an unlucky time for fruit was a good time for ripening leaders. The gushing influx of men and money from Al-Qaeda nourished those locals who held the most promise as fighters for Islam. It was as if the owners of the largest chain of food stores in the world had descended on the tiniest corner store and announced suddenly that it would be their headquarters. Where militancy was concerned, Waziristan was becoming a boomtown, and Baitullah Mehsud, a child of Waziristan and a man of Waziristan, had a lot to peddle to the foreign financiers who looked to make his place their place as well.

He rose in their ranks, plowing through with aplomb and without his lowly peasant origins haunting him as they would elsewhere in Pakistan. Like all other boys bred in this stark landscape, his only schooling was the local madrassa, where he learned to memorize the Quran, rocking back and forth and avoiding as best he could the instructor's cane, which came down hard across the knuckles of any boy who missed a verse, a prayer, or a preaching. In the hours between helping at home and memorizing the Quran, he, like all the other boys of the region, learned to scramble up and down and about the hundreds of caves that dotted the hills that surrounded their home. One could evade elders and even cross borders without ever emerging from their depths.

Baitullah Mehsud's home base was Makeen, a rough-hewn town now sitting in the middle of the two militant volcanoes of North and South Waziristan. By the time he had become a fighter, Makeen was an ideal headquarters for recruiting and training followers and for planning operations. It was these Pakistani troops who would pave Baitullah's ascent. On August 30, 2007, thousands of men he had culled from the nameless hills and unheard of towns of Pakistan's northwest fought the Pakistani Army, which was armed by America and charged with flushing out militants from the northwest frontiers of their country. After a battle both bloody and loud, with gunfire and death and uncertainty echoing through the dry, gray horizon, Baitullah Mehsud's men vanquished their

opponents. Not only were they victorious but their army of for-
eigners and tribal boys also took not one or two but two hundred
forty Pakistani soldiers hostage.

The victory would change everything for Baitullah Mehsud; he
became a household name in a country whose multitudes of militants rendered most of them nameless. The vanquished men were
counted, recorded, and kept as hostages for two months. For the
entire time it was Baitullah Mehsud, short, unassuming, and polite,
who negotiated with the Pakistani military over what he wanted,
what they wanted, and what sort of agreement might be reached to
insure the release of the soldiers. During the entire time, his men
guarded the two-hundred-odd prisoners in the massive training
facility they and their foreign financiers had built for the purpose
of jihad.

At the end of September 2007 a deal was reached. Its stip-
ulations mandated that the two hundred forty captive soldiers
would be exchanged for twenty-five Taliban militants being held
by the Pakistani authorities. The exchange happened one afternoon at the end of September, and Baitullah Mehsud himself was
said to have welcomed back the freed captives. Each one of the
released men, as the Pakistani government would later acknowledge, was a trained suicide bomber. They would not stay in Waziristan for long, for Baitullah Mehsud had given them missions
all over Pakistan.

OCTOBER 2007

Asif would stay in New York City and Benazir would go to Karachi. The city where she was expected to arrive watched with trepidation as it was invaded by vast numbers of people desiring to
make history. Because history is erected on the bent backs of the
forgetful, large numbers were required. Since few in Karachi were
forgetful enough, they had to be imported in large numbers from
other parts of Pakistan. They brought with them a tremendous
din: men waving flags, men shouting slogans, men whooping with

delight, men making signs of victory; a sea of men elated at making up a little piece of a historic event.

Fed by the mass arrivals, the story of historic return grew fat. Eight years, eight such long years, the groggy newspaper readers thought as they unfolded the pages and saw pictures they remembered, read promises just like the ones made twenty-one years ago when Benazir had returned the first time, chin up and chest outstretched against the glare of another military dictator. In their heads, the symphony of return played, interrupted now and again with the odd chord that suggested something unknown, something ominous. Had the world, Karachi, and she changed in the meantime? Could they go back to what once was and pick up the story of democracy, of a woman-led country, where it had been interrupted? Was a more portly Benazir, padded by the weight of babies borne and worries overcome, win over a city swollen beyond its capacity with countless migrants?

They sat quietly with their questions as the Bhutto cavalcade in Dubai readied to board the plane that would bring Benazir and one hundred fifty of her closest supporters back home to Pakistan. Elbowing their way to proximity, these one hundred fifty were the chunky men and few women who most ardently hoped for positions in the future Bhutto government. A Bhutto government, everyone agreed, was nearly a certainty, for when had a Bhutto return not been followed by a Bhutto reclaiming of the torch? In all the forgetfulness of the moment, this fact had not been forgotten. As the convoy grew ready, they fretted about their distance from the woman that was its magnetic center, nervously eyed the men sitting closer, trying to read their lips as they whispered into the ear of Benazir Bhutto. In turn, the men who sat closer or closest worried that their hard-won positions would be usurped by others who wanted them just as desperately.

"Jeeay Bhutto!" or "Long live Bhutto!" was the cry that went up in the plane as it entered Pakistani airspace. No flight attendant could restrain the pandemonium within, the tremendous tumult of a returning heroine. Benazir Bhutto and her entourage landed at Karachi's Jinnah International Airport without any untoward event marring their arrival. The sky was clear and blue and hot; it was a typically dusty October afternoon. Benazir cried as she left the plane, and the avalanche of waiting flashes caught every dropped tear and showed them to all the country. And so in the sea of people, the shower of burgundy rose petals, the sweat and the pushing and jostling of reporters and party workers, of people who had been promised this or that, the first episode of the historic return was concluded.

It took two hours for the procession to exit the plane and arrive at the VIP lounge at the airport, and another two to exit the airport. The sun had begun its descent over the horizon. Time did not seem to matter to the woman at the center or to the hundreds of her closest supporters working hard to keep their positions close to her. It did not seem to matter either to the hundreds of thousands of Pakistan People's Party workers who waited all along the long road from the airport to Mohammad Ali Jinnah Road, where Benazir Bhutto would make her historic address to a rally of her party workers. The distance between the rally site and Jinnah International Airport in Karachi was approximately twenty kilometers, and two hundred officers of the Karachi Police had been assigned the task of guarding the entourage as it made its way from one end of the city to the other. With the size of the crowd, they had estimated it would take an hour for the motorcade to arrive.

The procession moved slowly, more slowly than even the slowest estimates. Four hours after it began at the airport it had traversed only about five kilometers. It was dark now and the lights of Karachi, always dim, flickered on and off on different parts of the route, shedding only intermittent light on the people leaving, joining in, cheering, and chanting. Bhutto herself stood with her white veiled head poking out from the sunroof of a truck. No longer delicate but stolid and middle-aged, she waved to her supporters hour after hour after hour, replenished from her long rest of eight years. She did not tire or complain or weary of the slow pace. She was not in a hurry, for she was already there, in Pakistan, and this was her moment.

It was luck that saved her. When the blast hit, abrupt and re-sounding, she had just ducked down into the safe shell of the truck. It was her first break after eight hours of being on her feet, and it happened to come at exactly the right time. But if the explosion was sudden, it was not a surprise. The hundreds of thousands of terror-weary Pakistanis watching on their televisions at home, the ones who had seen year after year after year of mounting terrorist attacks in the eight years that Bhutto had been gone, would only cluck their tongues. They could have told her so. The details were similar to other bombings she had missed in her absence. Two suicide bombers, one wearing a vest holding five kilos of explosives, wading through the crowd and sidling up to a motorcade of thousands until they were at its center. One hundred forty were killed in the bomb blast that ripped through Benazir Bhutto's return procession and several hundred others injured.

Benazir Bhutto managed to survive. In the aftermath, she was scuttled away at great speed, taken from a scene of carnage where cries still rose from mangled bodies and torn off limbs and blood soaked the flags of the Pakistan People's Party. She did not see the piles of bodies or pieces of arms and legs and torsos that were re-covered from the cars and buses in which they perished. She did not see the blazing pools of gasoline that had bled out of wrecked vehicles. They were the only lights on the darkened street where the blast had occurred; the streetlights were not working, so the fires illuminated the grisly task of taking away the bodies and saving the wounded.

Pallid but still alive, Benazir Bhutto retreated into the home she had built by the sea soon after her son Bilawal had been born, after she had won her first election and become the first Muslim woman to lead a Muslim country. When the teams of police investigators

sent by the inspector general of the Sindh Police arrived, she refused to let them inside. She was certain, she told her supporters
and advisors, that the next attack against her would be carried out
by men wearing police uniforms, and she would not let any of
them, not a single one, inside her home. Not knowing what to do,
the policemen, who had been sent by their bosses in the Sindh Police to ask questions and to start an investigation, shrugged, turned
around, and went home. Night descended on Bilawal House and
sea breezes blew onto its lawns. Benazir Bhutto was home again
for the first time in eight years. As she slept, the churning rumor
mills began to throw out bit by bit the names of possible culprits.
The Pakistanis who had stayed awake into the night after yet another bloody day listened to them before they went to bed.

NOVEMBER 1, 2007

The meal sat on the square dining table in the middle of the only
room of the house that was lit, on the top floor. It was Friday and
Amina had cooked the meal she cooked every Friday, the same one
that was cooked at her mother's house. It was fish curry, cooked
with roasted tomatoes and pungent garlic and a freshly squeezed
lemon, just as she had been taught in the kitchen of the apartment
where her family had lived when they first arrived from India.

She had cooked it so many times that she could do it in her
sleep. Now she looked at Sohail and realized that he could just
as well eat it in his sleep. There was a sluggish automation to his
motions, curry over rice, fish over curry, chewing and swallowing,
a stray belch coming forth every now and then. He kept his eyes
on his plate, the same plates they used every Friday. Fridays and
fish curry were special, and their special status was signified by the
nicer china that she always brought out for the occasion.

Friday of late was also the day of disappointments, when it had
only alternately been so in the Fridays past. This Friday, like all the
other Fridays since the other wife had passed, he had gone downstairs into the cavernous silence of the middle floor, where Amina

believed he had erected a shrine to his second wife. This posthumous monument, she had grown convinced, was far more formidable even than the real, mortal woman in whose memory it was created. Under its spell, the husband who returned was wrapped in an impenetrable membrane, stubborn and impervious to the curries and conversations of the living.

This Friday she had a plan. It was the plan she had been developing in the loneliness of many Fridays, as she strained to hear his movements downstairs, his steps and his sighs echoing in the silence. It was clear to her now that death alone could not make her marriage whole again. She now realized that a greater act of change was required, a return to what had been before, before an interloper arrived. Only she remembered those days well, the aimless mornings, the pure silences untainted by the thoughts of another, the security of knowing that each was possessed singly and equally and perfectly by the other.

They would move downstairs to the first floor, she concluded. The old first floor that had been scoured and painted and for which they had still not managed to find suitable renters. That blank slate would be the venue to return to, the new old beginning, to reclaim the marriage as it had once been. In the weeks since she first had this idea, it had percolated and become robust with detail. This new venue had emerged as a stage, with the same props from the first scenes of their marriage.

She had chosen this Friday to tell him about it. It would be done ever so delicately, between the fish curry and the rice pudding, the aperture between one part of a carefully prepared meal and the next. As he ate now, unthinkingly pushing morsel after morsel, she rehearsed the words of the request and the terms of the proposition. She had already preempted his objections that renovations were needed to the bathroom and kitchen. They would not be an obstacle, she would insist, she could handle it all, plus the rooms were airier and brighter, even if just a bit smaller. If that didn't convince him, she would set out her trump card, the aching knees and backs of their approaching old age. "The bottom floor would be so much more convenient," she would say, requiring no rupees to be shelled out to neighbor boys to carry up this or that, no heaving sighs when none were to be found and kilos of onions and potatoes had to be lugged by him up three flights of stairs.

She began as she put down the delicate dish of bone china in which she had set the rice pudding she served on Fridays. "I was thinking," she said as he lifted his head, "that we should move downstairs. Not downstairs just below I mean," she continued, registering immediately the silence, the confusion on his face, "but downstairs to the bottom floor, like before." He heard her, but he said nothing, his spoon clinking against the bottom of the dish of pudding as he ladled three spoonfuls into his bowl. The pudding was dotted with raisins; he loved them, and she had put in twice as many as usual.

Sitting down and ladling pudding into her own bowl, she continued with some slight assumption of victory. "I think it will be good for us, you know. . . . I have been going down, and it is so airy and light after I had it painted white. And then," she continued, eager to unload her best bit before any interruptions, "we are getting old, and climbing up and down the stairs every day and every time you buy groceries and milk is too much." She looked at him, peering through the membrane of memories that bound them together and kept them apart. She looked at his eyes, his moustache, his forehead and saw the man she wanted him to become once again, the man she had seen from the window of her bedroom, the man who had said he knew from the moment he saw her that she would be his perfect bride. She looked at him now and waited for an answer.

He did not look at her, and for a long while he did not say anything. Then he cleared his throat and with the softest of voices poured out in words venom more deathly than blows. "You know, Amina, twenty years ago when I married her, I learned for the first time what it was to be happy, to be with someone I truly understood and who truly understood me." He looked directly at her now, over the empty plates of curry and the almost full bowl of pudding. "I could have left you then, as so many men do. We did not have children and your father could have given you a home." He stared at Amina, her face flushed as if freshly slapped, and he kept on, his eyes glassy and his lips wet. "I did not leave you because I did not want you to be disgraced, to live like an abandoned woman, and so I . . . *we* put up with you, put up with you when we did not have to, when we did not need an interloper, someone watching and hearing and listening and blaming. Now she is gone and I am left here with you. . . . Leave me be. We will never move to the first floor, or to the second floor. They are sacred for me, for they are what I shared with her, and even if she is gone I will not let you take what was hers."

DECEMBER 15, 2007

It would turn out to be one of the most important days in the history of the Tehreek-e-Taliban Pakistan. In the middle of the dry winter, when men huddled around smoky stoves in the *hujras* (meeting rooms) dotted all over the tribal areas, a historic gathering was about to be achieved. Its architect was Baitullah Mehsud, the short man so many had underestimated and who now stood to take the helm of a movement whose resilience against armies with far greater resources baffled the world.

On December 15, 2007, Taliban commander Baitullah Mehsud called together a *shoora*, a meeting of commanders and allies from all over the tribal areas of Pakistan. The men came from the seven tribal agencies as well as from the "settled areas" of the province of Khyber Pakhtunkhwa in northwestern Pakistan. Sitting on the backs of Toyota trucks, their guns held up like staffs between their thighs, the men poured in, men who had fought disparate battles all over the region, had worked tirelessly to exhort local populations to give up their sinful ways, to keep their women indoors, not to listen to music, to stop straying from the path of Islam. They came from North and South Waziristan, from Khurram and Orakzai, from Mohmand and Bajaur. They came also from Kohistan and Buner and the Malakand Division. Maulana Fazlullah's men came from Swat, they were the men who had descended from the mountains after the earthquake and vowed to restore the rule of Islam to the little village.

In gathering these men, tribal elders and seasoned fighters, warriors who had fought all their lives in Afghanistan against the Russians and now against the Americans, the new arrivals who came from Uzbekistan or Yemen or Libya, Baitullah Mehsud was able to make the unprecedented happen. After hours of negotiation, all the members of the *shoora* agreed to unite under the leadership of the little man from Makeen who had brought them there. Under his leadership, they decided the consolidated organization would be called the Tehreek-e-Taliban Pakistan. With its formation, tribal enmities, ideological differences, quibbles about whether or not foreign fighters should or must be accommodated were put to rest. Under the banner of this single organization, the men agreed, they could wrest Pakistan back from the un-Islamic forces that had taken it over, fighting until the end and by whatever means necessary.

Before the men of the Tehreek-e-Taliban departed to make the journey back to their homes, Mullah Omar, the newly selected Tehreek spokesman, issued an ultimatum to the Pakistan Army. Reported the next day in newspapers and television channels all across Pakistan, the declaration gave the Pakistan Army "ten days to cease all operations in Swat, withdraw all troops from the region, and close all military checkpoints between North and South Waziristan." Mullah Omar wrote, "Our main aim is to target US allies in Afghanistan but the Government of Pakistan's ill strategy has forced us to launch a defensive jihad in Pakistan." If their words went unheeded, Baitullah Mehsud, the new leader of the Tehreek-e-Taliban Pakistan, said, "the Government of Pakistan will be paid back in the same coin." The ultimatum's ten days would be up on December 26, 2007.

The news reporters who wrote down the date, and the readers who read it in the paper, did not know then it would be a significant one. No one knew that the day after, December 27, 2007, would be the day Benazir Bhutto, the freest woman we knew, would be assassinated.

———— EPILOGUE ————

My grandmother Surrayya died on a Sunday while I was visiting my parents' home on my frequent trips to Karachi from America. She was eighty-four and had been ill a long time, her suffering a cause of anguish for us all.

As is our custom, we buried her before dusk. When the three days of traditional mourning were done, I visited Aunt Amina at her house. Night was just falling, and the bright lights of Destiny Gardens across the street were already on. Workmen were unloading chairs, and the tents blazed with lights. There was going to be a wedding that night.

But the lane itself, absent streetlights, was the dim gray hue that hangs over most of Karachi. Even so, I could see how it had changed. The original people, those first migrants from India who had harbored dreams of replicating the community they had left behind, are nearly all gone or in the process of going. The houses became too small after new floors could no longer be piled atop one another. No more rooms could be wedged into gardens and verandas and garages. The parents and grandparents had died, and homes had to be sold so the proceeds could be divided between siblings and smaller places bought in farther suburbs. Only the very wealthy or their children could afford to live independently in their own homes and away from family entanglements; in other structures, large families divided lives and rooms and resources as they always had.

Some, a few golden sons, had made it big and moved to mansions by the ocean. The sum of it had been an emptying out, a changing of hands to families who did not care to know their neighbors. Some of these newcomers painted their windows black so that no one could see inside. Others had posted armed guards outside. Straggly men with faces frozen in eternal suspicion, they walked up and down the short frontage belonging to their masters, their AK-47s slung over their shoulders. The straps of the guns were decorated in traditional patterns of Pakistani folk embroidery.

Aunt Amina's house remained unchanged. The stairwell leading up to the third floor, where she still lived, was dark. We climbed up the first flight and to the middle floor, which had not been inhabited since the death of the other wife. Its door stood darkened, solid, and unmoved. The stairs leading up to the third floor had crumbled a bit over the years. They had never received their final coats of cement, never been made permanent. I stumbled on my way up, afraid to fall in the darkness. No light filtered up from the ground where a lone bulb lit the entrance to the stairwell. Aunt Amina heard me, and she opened her door: the light from her rooms fell on the last few steps up.

She was not alone. The shadows of two small children clung to hers. When I hugged her, they shied away. They were the children of our cousin, I learned, who was now Aunt Amina's tenant. An even later migrant from India, the bottom floor had been rented to him. Now the children sidled behind her, sizing me up. Uncle Sohail, stooped and pale, shuffled into the room from the bedroom next door. He walked with a cane, the discomfort of the effort visible in every shuffling step, a diminished man whose illness in the years since the stroke had become a part of him. He had recently been admitted to the hospital with a sick heart, he told me after he sat down. He had refused a pacemaker, because, he said, life had already put him through enough.

The two children, the boy and girl, did not notice Uncle Sohail at all. They remained stuck to Aunt Amina, peering at me from their secure positions at her waist. They came every day, she told me, so that their mother, who recently had a third baby, could get her household chores done. Their books and toys were strewn on a table nearby. When the little girl decided to speak, a torrent of words fell from her mouth. She told me her name, her brothers' names, the name of the school she went to. Aunt Amina smiled. We sat and watched the kids, and Uncle Sohail talked a bit more about his recent health troubles and the weather. It had been so cold, he mumbled, but it was getting warmer now. We hung our heads remembering how hard and unforgiving Surrayya's last days had been. "Those who suffer in this life are spared punishment for their sins in the hereafter," Aunt Amina murmured.

When I rose to leave a while later, Aunt Amina followed me to the door. "Don't forget me," she said, her eyes wet behind her glasses. Her father and now her mother were both gone; there were fewer reasons for her to visit her brother's house, to remain connected to him, and through him to us. Words felt wooden and inadequate, as they do in such moments. "How can that be?" I told her, "I cannot ever forget you, I grew up with you." Back in the bedroom now, Uncle Sohail coughed loudly. As I started down the stairwell, the two children rushed in front of me, unafraid, navigating the darkness with expertise. They made the journey many times a day.

I could never forget her. The shadow of her marriage, her exclusion, her accommodation of a life she had never expected had cast its imprint on my own life. The memory of her misery weighed on me; the questions about her choices plagued me. How real had they been? How helpless had she been? These familiar thoughts twisted about my mind as my own marriage was arranged, as I became a bride and left Karachi for America. They were with me when I left the marriage that had been chosen for me, when I decided to rebel, when I returned to Pakistan and then returned to America, again and yet again. My story was built on hers.

A few days before my grandmother died, the newspapers announced that parts of Karachi were now officially under the control of the Tehreek-e-Taliban Pakistan (the Taliban Movement of Pakistan). The civil war that had been a possibility was now real in Karachi, and its casualties—policemen, doctors, students, journalists—appeared every day, their bloody or shrouded corpses splashed over the pages of newspapers and on television screens. These images are as menacing as a recently published map of Karachi that shows the city encircled by Taliban-controlled areas in the west, the north, and the east. The only side of the city not enclosed is the one that opens out into the sea.

When measured, the Taliban-occupied area measures 470 square miles: about one-third of Karachi. This in turn translates to nearly 2.5 million people, mostly the poor and Pashtun, whose lives are now directly under Taliban control. Sometimes the newspapers run stories of life in this alternate universe. One of these articles claims the Taliban have already appointed emirs to rule over these various bits and pieces of the city. In their jargon of emirs and emirates, one-third of Karachi is now part of the "Emirate of Pakistan." Mobile vans with Taliban judges and enforcers are said to roam the lanes doling out "justice" to thieves and drug addicts, who suffer amputations and floggings for their sins. It is more justice than the police have been able to provide or the actual city courts to promise. The people accept it. At least someone is interested in resolving our problems, they say.

The resistors are failing. Since September 2013, nearly thirteen thousand people have been swept up in an operation to "clean" the city of militants, gathered during more than ten thousand raids into the city's alleged militant strongholds. Army Rangers, who have now made Karachi their near-permanent home, carry out the raids. They are helped by the Karachi police, whose string of constantly changing chiefs reflects the uncertainty about who really controls the city. There have been five chiefs since 2013. One of them,

Chaudhry Aslam, was killed by a huge bomb planted on the ramp of a major Karachi highway. The explosion was forceful enough to catapult the multi-ton bulletproof SUV he was riding into the air. He was killed instantly and the Taliban took responsibility.

The rich or powerful or visible are not the only targets. A few days before the police chief was killed, a group of Taliban soldiers unleashed a different variety of mayhem. In the middle of a night in January 2014, they crept up a hillock on the edge of a poor Karachi slum. At the top was the shrine of Ayub Shah Bukhari, a poor man's saint, where tired men went to supplicate. They believed the saint was an intermediary with a better connection to the Almighty, and so they begged him for better jobs, easier lives. Like them, the shrine itself was meager, the pale green of the building fading against the sand-laden winds that blew over the dry hillock. Six of them were there, praying in the dark and cold of the night.

The Taliban assassins killed all of them. They bound them and lined them up in the shanty by the shrine and cut off their heads. They left behind the machete they used for their butchery, blood and tissue still visible on the blade when it was photographed and splayed on television screens. The Taliban did not believe in anyone interceding for the Almighty. Anyone who tries to pray at one of the hundreds of shrines dotted all across the country is, in their view, a heretic. To make sure there was no confusion on this point, they left a bloodied note by the bodies, claiming the killings as corrections, examples of what would be done to those who persisted in praying at shrines, to saints, to anyone but the God they prayed to.

The only place to escape the Taliban is in the suburbs by the sea. On the road that leads there, the face of Benazir Bhutto still stares out from a placard. Her image flanks that of her young son, Bilawal Bhutto Zardari. He is the new chairman of the Pakistan People's Party, and he has vowed to protect the culture and heritage of Pakistan from the Taliban. He announces his message again and again, usually via Twitter, sometimes at film festivals or concerts held in secured locations. The road to Bilawal House, the mansion Benazir built when she first became prime minister is now entirely blocked off with layers and layers of armed guards and security cordons. Bilawal Bhutto Zardari lives beyond them, in the house that bears his name.

——— ——

I was just a little girl when, through a haze of whispered conversations, I first learned about Aunt Amina's predicament. It was an odd thing then for a man to take a second wife, even if it was, under the way the men interpreted the Holy Quran, a technically permissible one. I did not know any other women who lived in such an arrangement. In the years since, as Pakistan has slipped farther and farther into an increasingly unquestioned conservatism, polygamy has come into the open and is even encouraged as the form of an ideal Muslim family, fitting the idea of Pakistan as a model Muslim state, an Islamic republic. Social activists argue that multiple marriages will solve the problem of destitute women and children who are without male guardians. Clerics remind everyone that promoting what is already permitted will end illicit affairs and prostitution.

If you notice an absence in these social prescriptions, it is the voices of women. Unraveling the emotional scars created by a life of competing for a man, the daily smites of being overlooked, ignored, or unloved, is not a wound Pakistani women wish to open to the world. In self-exposure lies further vulnerability, and the private has in our imaginations always been protected. But letting this realm remain private has rendered the effects of polygamy invisible. In such an arrangement is the assumption that the private and public are entirely separate realms, and that the indignities of one do not replicate in the other. And yet it is on the memories of marriages we know and see that our own are patterned.

ACKNOWLEDGMENTS

A tremendous thank-you to my family near and far who remain my strength and without whom neither I nor any of my writing would have been possible.

Thank you to Philip Gulley, whose encouragement was invaluable and the first step in making this book a reality.

Thank you to Julia Serebrinsky, who held my hand through every moment of writing this and after, and without whose wisdom, insight, support, and friendship I could not have written this. Thank you to Stephen Hanselman, whose optimism and spirit kept me going and who had faith in me as I began this journey.

Thank you to Amy Caldwell, whose skill, care, and support nurtured this book and gave me courage. Thank you also to Beacon Press and their commitment to giving voice to this story.

Thank you to Hedgebrook Writers Residency, where I wrote so much of this book. The warmth of Cedar Cottage and the lovely meals and fellowship of that unique place and the wonderful writers it brings together permeate this book.

Thank you to the editors at *DAWN* newspapers, some of the bravest people I know, for publishing my column every week. My exchanges with them and with my Pakistani readers are the backbone of this book.

Thank you to *Guernica* magazine and their amazing editorial staff. Thank you, Joel Whitney and Michael Archer, founding editors of *Guernica*, for having faith in me and all the new writers you publish in every issue. Thank you to Katherine Dykstra, who edited the essay that became the germ for this book.

Thank you to all my dearest friends, who listened to the stories, my anxieties, fears, and hopes for this book in the years it took to make it possible. Gratitude also to the strong women I am so lucky to have in my life.